THE LADY AND THE GENERALS

By the same author:

The Lady and the Peacock
Tokyo: the City at the End of the World

THE LADY AND THE GENERALS

AUNG SAN SUU KYI

and Burma's Struggle for Freedom

PETER POPHAM

LONDON · SYDNEY · AUCKLAND · JOHANNESBURG

1 3 5 7 9 10 8 6 4 2

Rider, an imprint of Ebury Publishing,
20 Vauxhall Bridge Road,
London SW1V 2SA

Rider is part of the Penguin Random House group of companies
whose addresses can be found at global.penguinrandomhouse.com

First published by Rider in 2016

www.penguin.co.uk

A CIP catalogue record for this book is available from the British Library

Hardback ISBN 9781846043710
Trade Paperback ISBN 9781846043727

Printed and bound in Great Britain by Clays Ltd, St Ives plc

Penguin Random House is committed to a sustainable future for our business, our readers
and our planet. This book is made from Forest Stewardship Council® certified paper.

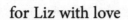

for Liz with love

CONTENTS

LIST OF ILLUSTRATIONS

BLACK AND WHITE PLATES
(All photographs taken by author except where stated)

1. Aung San and his wife Daw Khin Kyi with Suu as a baby: photo in Aung San Memorial Museum in Natmauk, upper Burma.
2. A young Suu with her diplomat mother in India: photo in Aung San Memorial Museum.
3. Aung San's birthplace in Natmauk, now a museum.
4. Survivors of Cyclone Nargis in Irrawaddy Delta, five years on.
5. Heat haze over parliament in Naypyidaw.
6. The large symbolic *patta* or alms bowl at the entrance to parliament.
7. The gleaming marble halls of Burma's parliament.
8. Politicians in uniform *gaung baungs* (turbans) in parliament.
9. President Thein Sein (centre) at a conference in Rangoon in 2014 (*Thwin Maung Maung*).
10. Suu's Naypyidaw home where she stays when parliament is sitting.
11. Ashin Wirathu: firebrand Buddhist leader in his monastery in Mandalay.

LIST OF NAMES

Note on Burmese names: Burmese do not have surnames, only given names that may number between one and four. Usually all given names are used when addressing someone, often preceded by an honorific, such as 'U' (for an older man) or 'Daw' (for an older woman).

Aung San Suu Kyi's family and entourage

ALEXANDER ARIS (Burmese name Myint San Aung): Suu and Michael's first son.

KIM ARIS (Burmese name Thein Lin): Suu and Michael's second son.

AUNG SAN: Suu's father, hero of Burmese independence struggle; often referred to as 'Bogyoke' (pronounced 'Bo-joke') – Burmese for 'General'.

AUNG SAN LIN: Suu's elder brother, who drowned at age nine.

AUNG SAN OO: Suu's eldest brother, emigrated to the United States; engineer.

DAW KHIN KYI: Suu's late mother, nurse-turned-diplomat.

MICHAEL ARIS: Suu's late husband.

DR SEIN WIN: cousin of Suu's; prime minister of National Coalition Government of the Union of Burma (NCGUB) in exile.

DR TIN MAR AUNG: Suu's personal assistant and companion.

ADRIAN AND LUCINDA PHILLIPS: Suu's British brother- and sister-in-law, Lucinda being her late husband's sister.

National League for Democracy (NLD)

MAUNG THAW KA: naval hero-turned-writer and poet, a Burmese Muslim, adviser to Suu; died in jail.

TIN OO: retired general, co-founder and emeritus chairman of the NLD, detained for many years.

WIN THEIN: veteran member and co-founder of NLD.

WIN TIN: dissident journalist, founder member of the NLD, jailed for nineteen years, died in 2014.

KYI MAUNG, deceased, provisional leader of the NLD who was arrested after the party's election victory in 1990.

Burmese Democracy Activists outside the NLD

MIN KO NAING (a nom de guerre which means 'Conqueror of Kings'), leader of the 1988 uprising.

KO MYA AYE, another leading activist in 1988, a Muslim.

ZARGANAR, one of Burma's leading comedians.

The Government, 2010–2016, and their Military Allies

PRESIDENT THEIN SEIN: former general, elected by Parliament in 2010, served 2011–2016.

YE HTUT, President Thein Sein's spokesman.

THURA SHWE MANN: former general, President Thein Sein's bitter rival, Speaker of the Lower House of Parliament in Naypyidaw, de facto ally of Suu in Parliament.

EX-GENERAL HTAY OO, replaced Thura Shwe Mann as head of the USDP in 2015, a known conservative and public mouthpiece of former strongman Than Shwe after the latter's retirement.

GENERAL MIN AUNG HLAING: Senior General of the army, successor to Than Shwe.

THAN SHWE: formerly Senior General and chairman of SLORC/SPDC, Burma's generalissimo, in power until March 2011.

LIEUTENANT GENERAL KHIN NYUNT (RETIRED): protégé of Ne Win; head of military intelligence, purged on orders of Than Shwe after attempting to broker a peace deal with Suu in 1994. Now runs an art gallery in Rangoon.

BRIGADIER GENERAL THAN TUN: member of Khin Nyunt's staff; negotiated with Suu in 2004.

NE WIN: general who seized power in coup in 1962, de facto ruler of the country until 1988; died while under house arrest in 2002.

Non-NLD Burmese politicians

KHUN HTUN OO, a leading politician from Shan state.

SAN TIN KYAW, a Muslim candidate in Rangoon during the 2015 election.

MYO KHIN, independent candidate in the 2015 election, ex-NLD.

DAW KHIN KHIN WIN, wife of Myo Khin.

Foreign Diplomats and Politicians

HILLARY CLINTON, Secretary of State in President Obama's first administration, co-author of the 'pivot to Asia' and friend and admirer of Suu.

DEREK MITCHELL: first US ambassador to Burma in decades.

KURT CAMPBELL: President Obama's head of East Asian Affairs at the State Department in his first administration, helped broker improved relations between Naypyidaw and Washington.

SUSILO BAMBANG YUDHOYONO, better known in Indonesia simply as SBY, former army general then civilian president of Indonesia.

ROBERT GORDON: British ambassador in the late 1990s.

UN Human Rights Envoys

IBRAHIM GAMBARI: UN Deputy Secretary General in the mid-1990s.

RAZALI ISMAIL: UN envoy in the early 1990s.

TOMÁS OJEA QUINTANA, the UN Special Rapporteur on Burma in 2015.

Nationalist Monks and Politicians

ASHIN WIRATHU, the 'Buddhist Bin Laden'.

PAR MOUNT KHA, anti-Muslim abbot near Rangoon.

NAY ZIN LATT, founder of the National Development Party (NDP), a new extreme nationalist party.

AUNG HTWE, vice chairman of the NDP.

Nationwide Ceasefire Negotiators

AUNG NAING OO

HAN NAUNG WAI

At the *Myanmar Times*

ROSS DUNKLEY: Australian entrepreneur and journalist, co-founder of the *Myanmar Times*.

SONNY SWE (Myat Swe in Burmese): Dunkley's business partner at the paper's launch, son of Brigadier General Thein Swe, later sentenced to jail like his father.

GEOFFREY GODDARD, Dunkley's right-hand man.

DR TIN TUN OO: regime crony; chief executive of the *Myanmar Times*; the publisher of a number of Burmese language magazines and at the time vice chairman of the (regime approved) Myanmar Writers and Journalists Association; known in the office as TTO.

KHIN MOE MOE: Dr Tin Tun Oo's wife.

Others

MAUNG ZARNI: sociologist and activist.

AUNG WIN, Rohingya activist in Sittwe.

MA KHIN AYE, Muslim victim of attacks in Meiktila.

SITAGU SAYADAW, one of the most revered Buddhist teachers in the country.

PHOE THAR AUNG, farmer in the Irrawaddy Delta.

DAWT PEN, seventy-six, and Ni Kil, seventy-eight, elderly women of Nabual village, Chin state.

EINSTEIN MC KING SKUNK, punk, aka Satt Mhu Shein.

HTIN LIN OO, NLD's former information officer, expelled from the party.

KEITH WIN, Anglo-Burmese son of a senior Burmese policeman, founder of Myanmar-British Business Association, former associate of David Cundall.

In May 1989, Burma's military junta abruptly changed the names by which the country and many of its cities, towns and natural features were to be known internationally: 'Burma' became 'Myanmar', 'Rangoon' became 'Yangon', 'Pegu' became 'Bago', and so on. Aung San Suu Kyi and the National League for Democracy have never accepted the new names because they were imposed without democratic consultation by a body with no constitutional legitimacy. For that reason, although some of these names have become more current in recent years, in this book the older forms are retained.

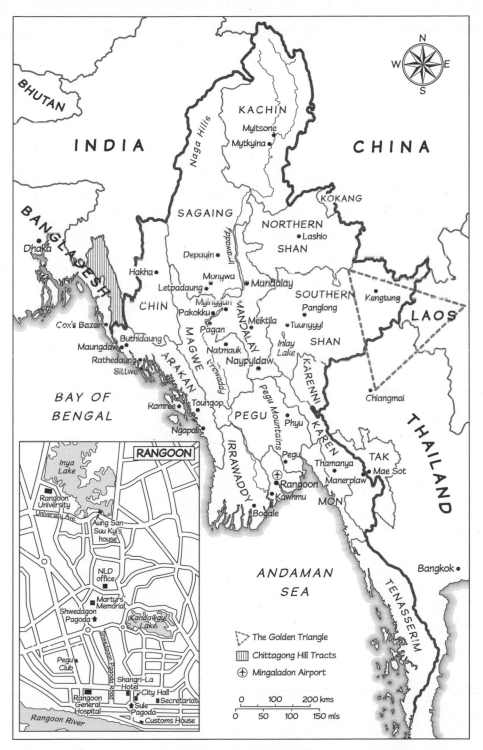

MAP OF BURMA

INTRODUCTION

Give us our country back. It's the cry of the oppressed and the dispossessed everywhere.

As I write we hear that cry most urgently from the people of Syria, their land torn apart by foreign militias, the machinery of the state turned against them, forced to flee for safety to anywhere that will take them. They are suffering dispossession of the most absolute type.

But there are other ways a people can be dispossessed. The Burmese feel they had their country stolen by the army more than fifty years ago. Since then they have been doing everything to get it back. They have protested in the streets and been gunned down, they have fled to the borders or into exile to fight the army from outside, they have fallen in behind a leader who promised to free them from their chains and give them back what they had lost, and twice they have voted overwhelmingly for that leader to take power. The first time the vote was simply brushed aside and normal dictatorial service resumed. The second time was on 8 November 2015. The result was the same as the first, an overwhelming mandate for Aung San Suu Kyi and her party to form a government and banish the tyrants. Unlike the first time, the military, closely watched by the international community, agreed to abide by the rules. By the time you read this we will know if they stuck to that commitment, what form the agreement has taken and how far the wishes of the people have been followed.

Then, of course, there are the years ahead, with all their vast uncertainties.

But what can be said with confidence is that on 8 November 2015 the Burmese people spoke with just about as unanimous a voice as is conceivable in an election, brushing aside the threats, bribes, inducements, the chauvinistic warnings and all the other devices seized on by the military to try to tilt the result its way, and gave Aung San Suu Kyi and her National League for Democracy an overwhelming mandate to rule, with nearly 80 per cent of the seats in both houses of parliament. As anyone who was present will agree, it was an ecstatic moment of national catharsis, comparable to the fall of the Berlin Wall and the other events that heralded the end of Soviet hegemony in Eastern Europe twenty-five years ago. Burma will never be the same again.

*

Burma is the in-between country. Its size is imposing, larger than France, a little smaller than Texas, with a population of 53 million, but because it is squashed between India and China, and so much smaller than either, it seems by contrast a diminutive land and its default posture is defensive. In skin colour the Burmese people are typically neither as dark as some Indians nor as pale as the Han Chinese but somewhere between the two. They are full of prejudices about both giant neighbours, while sharing much of the cultural heritage of both, notably Buddhism. Being in-between, they avoided being a destination, which was often a blessing: the British East India Company tackled Gujarat and Bengal and slowly took over India but it was the 1880s before Britain got around to completing the conquest of Burma, and it remained an afterthought to the Raj until the end of the colonial period. During the Second World War the imperial Japanese didn't want Burma per se, they needed it in order to get their hands on India; but in the end Burma was as far as they were to get. The independence of Burma from British rule became inevitable after India got its freedom, but again there was a sense of it tagging along behind.

This vulnerability of Burma to developments beyond its borders has also given it the tendency to roll up like a hedgehog when the neighbourhood becomes too lively: to shut itself up when the Vietnam War threatened to spill across South East Asia, to spurn for decades the (pacific) advances of its South East Asian neighbours, to prefer garrisoned poverty to the risks of foreign investment, to reject ideas like democracy as if they were toxic. But the Burmese people are not as paranoid as their leaders have been over the past half century. Nor are they content to remain an impoverished and oppressed in-between place, the private domain of strutting soldiers, a country becalmed in ignorance and fear while all around other peoples and countries discover new destinies. For decades now the Burmese have been much braver than the men (all men) who arrogated control of their destiny. They dared to dream. This book is the story of how, against considerable odds and even greater resistance, some of those dreams began to come true.

*

At the same time, and for the same reason, it is the story of how the dreams of Aung San Suu Kyi began to come true. I call her Suu, which is simpler than the full mouthful, and not intended disrespectfully: when she had more time for journalists, her first words to them were often 'Call me Suu' and it is what she was called by friends and family throughout her years in Britain. This is the second book I have written in which Suu is the principal character, so it is a particular pleasure that my story in this volume ends with the staggering success of her and her party in Burma's first respectable general election in more than half a century, which leaves it standing – at the time of writing – on the brink of a peaceful handover of power which cannot now be denied without a full-scale demolition by the military of all that has been achieved; a return of the hedgehog instinct that would take the country back to square one. This is not inconceivable but it is unlikely, and by writing that hypothetical and horrible possibility down in black and white, I hope in some talismanic fashion to make it even more so.

Suu's greatness derives from the fact that for her there was never anything 'in-between' about Burma. She was the child of the man, General Aung San, who put the country on the map and made it an independent reality – martyred before independence could be declared, but the author of that achievement, and universally recognised as such. From her earliest years, Suu's sense of herself was bound up with that achievement, the pride and the sorrow of it: pride in what he had wrought, sorrow at his assassination by political rivals before he could finish his work; pride as Burma took its place as the most promising ex-colony in South East Asia, sorrow as that project was hijacked by General Ne Win, sending her mother Daw Khin Kyi into gilded exile as Burma's ambassador to India when Suu, who accompanied her, was barely into her teens.

If her parentage gave her pride, her youth and adulthood abroad gave her perspective: appreciation of the achievements of India, which had absorbed the colonialists' culture without sacrificing its identity, and had cleaved to democracy through every temptation of secession and tyranny; budding awareness, during her years as an undergraduate at Oxford, of the values of the European enlightenment and how they fostered tolerance and secularism. Now she had experience of two great democracies from the inside; some years in New York working at the United Nations gave her direct knowledge of a third. And all the while her own country, which had begun its independent life so bravely, was festering away, a pretentious and squalid military dictatorship masquerading – it fooled no one – as a pioneer of something called 'the Burmese way to socialism'. Ne Win ruled the country through the Burma Socialist Programme Party (BSPP), an entity he created from scratch as a way to deflect responsibility for political and economic decisions away from the army and onto civilians, and to avoid becoming the subject of a personality cult, Mao-style. There were elections but no other parties for voters to choose from, so obviating Indian-style democratic chaos. Thus did Burma steer a course between the policies of its neighbours. But the economic disasters of the Ne Win years showed that in politics the Middle Way does not always lead to Nirvana: far from it. By the late 1980s Burma, still in reality a military dictatorship, had stagnated so thoroughly that it applied for and obtained UN status as a least-developed nation, on a par with Somalia, Eritrea and Sudan.

Britain relinquished control of Burma in 1948, but forty years later the Burmese realised they had lost their country again, and that this time it had disappeared into the pockets of military men whose only claim to legitimacy was the proclaimed need to wage endless war on the borders: against the Chinese-backed Communists, against the Shan, against the Christian Karen and Kachin and Chin, against the Muslim Rohingya. The military must stay in power to protect the nation from disintegration: that was the mantra. But the wars were never won but dragged on and on, so there was neither cause nor opportunity for the military to return to their barracks. Burma was in a permanent state of civil war, and this justified every form of abuse and repression.

This was the desperate land Suu returned to in March 1988 when her mother was hospitalised after suffering a disastrous stroke. Suu came back to nurse her. That was the only reason for her return, but by chance it was during these months that the oppressions of the BSPP government provoked the angriest protests yet against its rule, which continued month after month. Suu was the diligent and devoted mother of two sons, Alexander and Kim, then aged fifteen and eleven, the wife of an Oxford scholar, Michael Aris, a self-described housewife with modest academic ambitions – she was in the early stages of a part-time postgraduate degree at London University's School of Oriental and African Studies in modern Burmese literature – and firm domestic roots in the soil of Oxfordshire. Her ideas, never more than hazy, of somehow complementing or completing her father's work in her native land were as good as forgotten. But Burmese journalists and intellectuals caught up in the revolt appreciated the 24-carat value of her name and bloodline and besieged her with appeals to lend her name to the democracy movement.

After months of resistance and long discussions with her husband, who had brought the boys over for the summer holidays, Suu agreed to speak out in support of the revolt. It was the most momentous decision of her life. Despite her inexperience in public speaking and political engagement, she addressed a huge rally in Rangoon with stunning effect, demanding 'free and fair elections . . . as quickly as possible'.[1] She was hailed overnight as the democracy movement's figurehead – 'a star is born, something like that'[2] as a co-founder of the NLD later put it. At this point the protest movement was so strong, and the regime so shaky, that Michael and Suu fancied that the revolution would be all over by the end of the year, and the family reunited in a brave new democratic Burma.

The reality was very different, and the long attrition of her detention, totalling fifteen years, the regime's cruel and deliberate destruction of her family ties by refusing practically all their visa applications, Michael's early death from cancer – these sad events were narrated in my previous book, *The Lady and the Peacock*. The regime expected Suu – in their eyes a frail woman, after all – to crack under the pressure and fly home to her family. Instead they discovered they were up against a force of nature, a person whose commitment to the democracy movement, entered into so late and so apparently casually, was as hard as alabaster. She would not be moved. In the end the regime compromised with her as the only way of rebuilding relations with the West, which had loaded her with honours, including the Nobel Peace Prize, and had come to regard her as an incarnation of political sanctity in the mould of Gandhi, Martin Luther King and Nelson Mandela. *The Lady and the Peacock* culminates in her final release from house arrest in November 2010.

This volume describes what happened next.

*

There was never in history a country called Burma until the British declared it to be one. It was a colonial invention, in the same way that India was. China, as the Chinese often like to remind us, has a history as a unitary state going back thousands of years. By contrast what we now call Burma was, like India, a patchwork of competing petty kingdoms until the colonialists with their modern weapons and big ideas came to call.

It is a mysterious country, even now. Hundreds of miles south of Rangoon it tails off into a group of tropical islands with the idyllic appearance of the Maldives. In the far north it comes up against the wall of the Himalayas and borders Tibet: there are Tibetan villages here, where they follow Tibetan-style Vajrayana Buddhism, not the Burmese version, and where the sad, dwindling remnant of the Taron, the only known race of Asian pygmies, was discovered.[3]

The Taron were – or are, if any of them remain alive – one of the smallest and most obscure of Burma's huge and baffling array of tribes. Following the scheme of the colonial British, those obsessive pigeon-holers, the Burmese government accords 135 recognised ethnic groups within the grander scheme of eight 'national ethnic races', of which the Burmans, also known as 'Bamar', are much the largest. But these classifications were open to challenge even when the British made them, and today they are extremely problematic. Tribe was defined by mother tongue, but in an appendix to the census of 1931 entitled 'A Note on Indigenous Races in Burma', J. H. Green wrote, 'Some of the races or "tribes" in Burma change their language almost as often as they change their clothes . . . Races are becoming more and more mixed, and the threads are more and more difficult to untangle.'[1]

This rainbow of racial groups may have presented a fascinating problem to British ethnologists and administrators but to Aung San and his colleagues, taking up the task of ruling a democratic Union of Burma, there was nothing academic about the challenge: their task was to make the newly independent nation work; yet the condition of Burma at independence bore less resemblance to, say, the United Kingdom, than to Britain after the departure of the Romans, with Celts, Angles, Saxons and Norsemen battling for land, gold and resources. No sooner were the British gone than the so-called Union started to fall apart, with groups like the Karen in the east fighting to secede, and the China-backed Communist Party doing its best to smash the whole flimsy edifice.

It is therefore not surprising that, after ten years of this, the army stepped in; first at the invitation of Prime Minister U Nu, then in 1962, of its own accord and by force. The British had held Burma together by force; the Burmese army would do likewise. But while it suited the mercantile needs of the colonialists to rule Burma as a ragbag of races, the Burmese army saw its task as welding the nation into a single unit under Burman domination; a resumption, in other words, of the predatory behaviour that preceded colonisation, but with the benefit of modern weapons and the justification of standing proud as a nation-state among other nation-states.

The attempted Burmanisation of the non-Burman portions of the country describes the past fifty years of the nation's history, and it is fair to say that it has been a fiasco. The discrete bits of the country remain as stubbornly distinctive as ever but united with the Burman population in one respect: their hatred of the army. According themselves many of the privileges of the recently departed colonialists, the army today finds itself at least as thoroughly despised as the British were, perhaps more so. The massive turnout at the November 2015 election, and the almost equally massive mandate given to the National League for Democracy, was in one respect a peaceful way for the nation to chant, in unison, the rallying cry of the great colleague of Suu, U Win Tin, who died in 2014: back to the barracks!

The great achievement of Suu's epic struggle against the military is this: that after twenty-seven years she has succeeded in uniting Burma under her leadership as it has never been united in its history, neither before independence nor since. The figures for the election of November 2015 speak for themselves. The NLD gained a total of 405 seats in the two houses of the Union Parliament, in the capital, Naypyidaw (if we include the 15 seats won by its Shan ally, the Shan NLD). All the other ethnic parties between them won only 55 seats. Despite the fact that Suu is herself Burman and has faced criticism since 2010 as representing the new face of the Burman ascendancy, the ethnic rainbow doesn't see it that way. Her party also dominated in the regional assemblies, winning three-quarters of all seats and twenty-one out of twenty-nine posts for ministers of ethnic affairs.

That is the scale of her victory. How are we to understand it?

Like the Burma Socialist Programme Party which preceded it, the Union Solidarity and Development Party (USDP) which ruled from 2010 was a Frankenstein creation, the handiwork of the army, with no political roots in the population. It rigged the 2010 election, when Suu was still in detention and the NLD did not compete. But in the free and fair contest of November 2015 it won only 42 seats, one-tenth as many as the NLD.

The USDP's ranks were dominated by former army officers, and like the BSPP its job was to do the army's bidding while deflecting from the army the political flak that resulted. The fate of these two parties, both dubious inventions, was the same: twenty-seven years apart, they were both mortally wounded, and the army humiliated.

The difference this time is that the army has back-up protection in the form of a constitution, endorsed in a rigged referendum in 2008, which guarantees and perpetuates its predominance: a central role in government, a major stake in parliament, and if all else fails the right to declare martial law and take over directly. This constitution is fiendishly difficult to amend. And it bars anyone whose husband or child has a foreign passport – someone like Suu, for example – from becoming president, which is where executive power resides.

In other words, after the debacle of 1988, when Burma came closer than at any time before or since to a revolution, the army evolved a strategy for clinging to power by making the central organs of state siege-proof. It guaranteed that even if they failed to win the election they would still be substantially in charge.

The 2015 election was thus seen by the Burmese less as a contest between political parties than a battle between the people and the army. The people were united behind a single leader – but the army had bunkers to retreat to. In the event of a landslide victory for the people, the army in its constitution-bunker would remain in control.

That was the situation after the election results were published, and it presented Suu, the unchallenged winner, with a predicament. Would she try to flush the army out of its bunker or leave it where it was? Would she go all out for a constitutional revolution, however difficult that might be, which would culminate in sending the troops back to their barracks? Or would she seek an accommodation with the army, ruling with their consent and accepting their interference?

The danger of the second option is that she could find herself hobbled by the generals, tainted by their continual meddling in government, watching her precious political capital dwindle as her mantle of democracy heroine became tattered. There were already signs of that happening after she became an MP in 2012 and worked alongside former military figures, and on one or two occasions stunned protesters by coming out in support of the army's position. To go further down that road would be to risk frittering away all she has worked for, with such sacrifice – the people's trust.

The danger of the first option is impasse. As mentioned, the 2008 constitution is siege-proof. It was made in such a way as to be very hard to change. If Suu determines that no other reforming work can be done until the constitution is changed, Burma could find itself seriously stuck. That, too, would damage her reputation, both at home and abroad.

Whichever choice she makes – or if she is ingenious enough to find a third way, avoiding the perils of both – her personal and political resources will be tested as never before.

*

In the five years after her release in 2010, Suu grew from being a heroine who was largely unknown except for her suffering and courage to a fully fledged politician, but one about whom many people had serious doubts. That evolution is in large part the story this book tells; and the failings and limitations she revealed in the eyes of her former supporters in the West – her failure, in particular, to live up to her reputation as a champion of universal human rights – are closely examined.

The story has a twist in the tail: if Western commentators, including this one, came to have misgivings about her, it turns out that the people of Burma did not share them. Buddhist, Muslim and Christian, Burman and non-Burman, urban and rural, rich and poor, they overwhelmingly backed her. For the people who really matter, in her first five years of freedom she did not put a foot wrong.

It is hard to believe that some of the quirks and foibles that I and others have identified will not present problems as she moves to exercise power over her 53 million people. She does not delegate. She has no obvious successor. She has shown no interest in or capacity for sharing power in the party: it's all about her. Her party's manifesto is a string of vague good intentions.

But who knows? She has astonished everyone, friends and enemies, for a long time, by her resilience and determination. Now she stands on the brink of achieving her great goal, she may do so again.

1
SUU KYI FREE

O N 21 June 2012, after the most extraordinary ten months
in independent Burma's history, Aung San Suu Kyi stood
on the top step of an ancient hall by the Thames in London.

A man who had fought for his country's independence had
stood near this spot eight centuries before. William Wallace,
Scottish patriot, was found guilty of high treason here in 1305.
He was hanged, then cut down alive and disembowelled; his
head and his limbs were cut off, and pieces of his body were
sent back to Scotland to show the price of rebellion.

Time moves on, perspectives alter. Charles de Gaulle,
Nelson Mandela and Barack Obama had more recently stood
here and spoken. But the invitation to do so is a rare privilege,
as John Bercow, Speaker of the House of Commons, said in his
introduction: 'This hall has hosted many events over the past
900 years. In recent times only a few international figures . . .
have spoken here. Today, Daw Aung San Suu Kyi will become
the first figure other than a head of state, the first woman from
abroad, and the first citizen of Asia to do so.'

Her audience included the prime minister of Great Britain,
David Cameron, the leader of the Opposition, Ed Miliband,
and hundreds of British political and cultural grandees. Mr
Cameron, who had met Suu for the first time two months
before at her home in Rangoon, was the only begetter of the
occasion. When he had proposed it, there were rumours of
dissension from the precedent-mad people at Westminster:[1]

the man in charge of the House of Lords, known as Black Rod but real name Lieutenant General David Leakey, was reported to have insisted that only heads of state, actual or former, were entitled to address a joint session of Parliament; for Suu Kyi, a common-or-garden Burmese MP, and a newly elected one at that, such a forum was out of the question. The prime minister was 'apoplectic', the *Telegraph* reported, and insisted on the event going ahead.

Suu alluded to the controversy in her speech. 'I understand that there was some debate,' she said, 'as to whether I should speak here . . . or elsewhere in the Palace of Westminster.' It may have amused her that the person trying to put her in her place was a senior military man, just like at home.

This is the way Suu's life has proceeded: long periods of stasis, then sudden dizzying leaps. Years becalmed in comfortable north Oxford as wife, mother and faintly frustrated writer and scholar – then, within a matter of months, a fully formed political career conjured from nothing, leadership of the most potent mass movement in her nation's history.

Long years of house arrest, years of total seclusion and isolation that would test the sanity of a holy ascetic – then, as if by magic, here she stands at the head of Westminster Hall, addressing both houses of the British Parliament, no longer as an enemy of the state, a convicted rebel and unrepentant dissident but as an elected member of the newly constituted Burmese Parliament.

'The courage of our guest is legendary,' Mr Bercow continued. 'She has withstood the unimaginable suffering of separation from her family and her people with the dignity, fortitude and resolve that most of us can barely conceive. Her connections with the United Kingdom, reinforced in Oxford yesterday, are intimate. She has been *the* symbol of resistance to a regime which, even in an imperfect world, has been exceptional in its barbarity . . .

'As the United Nations has documented – and from my own research I attest – this is a cabal guilty of rape as a weapon of war, extrajudicial killing, compulsory relocation, forced labour, deployment of child soldiers, use of human minesweepers, incarceration of opponents in unspeakable conditions, destruction of villages, obstruction of aid, and excruciating torture. Burma has become a beautiful but benighted land where fear runs through society like blood running through veins. One woman has now defied a dictatorship of such depravity for two decades. That's why Daw Aung San Suu Kyi, a leader and a stateswoman, is here in Westminster Hall this afternoon.

'It is my pleasure,' the ringmaster of the Westminster circus declared in conclusion, 'to welcome the conscience of a country and the heroine of humanity, Daw Aung San Suu Kyi!'

*

Aung San Suu Kyi had been locked up, mostly in her own home, for more than fifteen years before she was released in November 2010. She was far more famous as an absence, a suffering victim, than when she was the active leader of her party and Burma's democracy movement, a phase that lasted less than a year. When they confined her to her home for the first time, on 21 July 1989, a spokesman for the regime, which had recently branded itself SLORC, the State Law and Order Restoration Council, said she was to be detained for at least a year[2] for 'committing acts designed to put the country in a perilous state'. But there was no trial, no legal process of any sort: extra-legal caprice was the way the regime terrorised its subjects. Her first spell of house arrest lasted to July 1995, a few days under six years.

Over the next fifteen years she was locked up and released, locked up and released as the tides of power among the ruling generals ebbed and flowed. She was never free long enough to resume a normal life. She never knew when her freedom would be taken away again.

But in 2010, we were told, it was all going to be quite different. Burma had a constitution now, which the people had endorsed in a (deeply flawed) referendum. The constitution meant that there were going to be elections to a new parliament, and the country was going to be run by civilians. True, all of them had been senior generals until five minutes before, but the optics would be different, the new rulers' hands would be tied by the rules they had signed up to under the constitution; and the freedom of the most famous woman in the country was part of the new deal.

Nonetheless, people were highly sceptical. Even some of her closest colleagues in the National League for Democracy (NLD) did not believe Suu was going to be freed. I remember the electric anticipation as the hours and minutes to her appointed liberation ticked by, shot through with poisonous anxiety.

I was in Mae Sot, on Burma's border with Thailand at the time. I had been expelled from Burma a few days before the election, having been exposed as an undercover reporter. Mae Sot, with its large population of Burmese refugees and political exiles, was the closest I could get.

I passed the time at the Mae Sot office of the NLD, a two-storey detached house with a lawn on the southern edge of the town. These people had been exiles here for years. In 1990 the NLD had trounced the military junta's proxy party in a general election, but the generals simply ignored the result and threw as many MPs-elect in jail as they could lay hands on. Those who managed to escape fled, many of them eastward, towards Thailand. They had remained here in limbo ever since.

For two decades Burma appeared to be completely stuck. Political repression was total. The political prisoners – in 2010 there were more than 2,100 of them – remained locked up in the regime's primitive jails where many had languished for years. Those who had gone into exile remained abroad.

But this time her release was not the fruit of autocratic caprice, not a stunt for the international audience, but a carefully planned event in the junta's bid to remain in power while gaining diplomatic credibility. The new constitution endorsed in the carefully stage-managed referendum of 2008 was envisaged as a step in the creation of what the military called 'discipline-flourishing democracy'. The general election that had just been held was equally controlled and carefully cooked; it was the next step on the junta's road map. And Suu's release was the next step beyond that. The entire process was sober, methodical and even, by the regime's standards, relatively transparent. Clearly somebody new was in charge.

The new emphasis on due process had first come into focus the previous year. In May 2009 a middle-aged American crank called John Yettaw had turned up on Suu's doorstep, demanding to be put up for the night. Suu had obliged, doubtless aware that by doing so she would be breaking the terms of her detention. Both Yettaw and Suu (and Suu's two maids) were put on trial, and an extra eighteen months was added to Suu's sentence. That term had now expired. She had done her time. She was due for release.

But that didn't mean the Burmese believed it was going to happen. They had lived with the arrogant caprices of the generals for too long to believe anything they said. When a country has two exchange rates for its currency, one of them a hundred times greater than the other, who can place their trust in the state? Ne Win, Burma's generalissimo for a generation, had de-monetised high-value banknotes without warning, turning millions of his countrymen into paupers overnight. His successors had called an election then tried to claim it wasn't an election at all. They said they were going to release the Lady. Perhaps it was another of their cruel tricks.

But then on the afternoon of 13 November 2010, workmen appeared without warning in University Avenue – a crowd numbering hundreds had already gathered – and began dismantling the barricades that for twenty-one years had barred access to Suu's home. The crowd quickly swelled to thousands. At the party's office in Mae Sot, where the scene was transmitted live by satellite television, the exiles watched in silence. Then at 5.30 p.m. Suu Kyi's head and shoulders suddenly appeared above the battleship-grey steel fence of her garden. The crowd roared, and did not stop roaring for five minutes.

'When people like me were released, it was like pouring water in a flower pot,' U Win Tin, a founder member of the NLD and a close colleague of Suu's, had told me a few days earlier when I interviewed him in Rangoon. 'But if Suu Kyi is released, it will be like the coming of the monsoon.'

*

There was the euphoria of her release, her triumphant return to her party's headquarters, where she gave an impromptu speech to the happy crowds at the entrance. The office, which resembles a cattle shed, and which had been in suspended animation for years, was brought back to life, and Suu's office on the first floor decorated to make her welcome: it was the only room in the building with wallpaper, the only one with a carpet and decent lighting and air conditioning, and in the first days after her release she gave a succession of interviews there to people like the BBC's John Simpson. (My own attempt to get back into the country and take my place in the queue fell flat when Burma's Bangkok consulate returned my passport with the word 'DEPORTEE' stamped on the visa page.) But once the international media had fed their fill and flown away, there was a sort of void. And this was both new and strange.

In the past when she was released she had always seized the initiative. In 1995, after her first spell of detention, she had taken to conversing with the crowds over her garden wall. For a while this became a fixture in the city's life, and foreign tourists turned up to gawp. The next time she was released, she tried to leave Rangoon, but the regime repeatedly stopped her from doing so. The time after that she travelled all over the country.

But this time, after the initial burst of activity, she did none of those things. 'When is she going to travel again?' people asked. That was seen as the big test of the regime's sincerity, its compliance with her freedom, the measure of whether she was free or merely on a sort of unofficial parole. Travelling was what had made Suu famous and beloved. Now she stayed home and kept quiet, and her people hardly saw her. True, there were modest signs of official relaxation: as if keeping her mouth shut and staying home were the price to be paid for small favours. Her younger son Kim obtained a visa and came to see her, bearing a puppy. For anybody who knew the family story, the pictures taken upon his arrival at Rangoon's airport were almost unbearably poignant: mother and son reunited after so many years.

Soon after Kim's arrival, Michelle Yeoh, the Chinese Malaysian film star, came to call. The kung-fu heroine had been cast as the lead in a film by Luc Besson about Suu's tormented decision to place her political ambitions above her family. Although Suu has rebuffed practically all attempts to get her to open up about her private life, the doors of 54 University Avenue swung open for Michelle, and they spent a day together. Journalists who had struggled over the years to get access of any sort to the Lady wondered what Michelle Yeoh had that they lacked. Eventually it emerged that Besson had had the good idea of engaging Suu's son Kim as a consultant on the film. (Ms Yeoh returned in June but was turned around at the airport and sent home, with the official explanation that she was on a blacklist.)

Still Suu went nowhere, merely shuttling between home and party, a journey of twenty minutes. The one exception was a brief holiday with her son Kim to the ancient city of Pagan; her first holiday in three decades, for the Burmese media it was characterised as a pilgrimage. Whatever you called it, there was no politics, and although the crowds pressed around her and dogged her heels, she gave no speeches. And when the NLD did something mildly provocative, the official reaction was fierce. A party statement arguing that international sanctions, while having little negative impact on the economy, were keeping the authorities under pressure, was met with a blistering commentary in the *New Light of Myanmar*, the official daily. 'If Daw Suu Kyi and the NLD keep going the wrong way,' the piece, published in February 2011, ran, 'ignoring the fact that today's Myanmar is marching to a new era, new system and new political platforms paving the way for democracy, they will meet their tragic ends.'[3]

Had Suu been intimidated into immobility and silence? She gave no explanation. But when I returned to Burma in March 2011 and visited the NLD's headquarters, she seemed resigned to staying where she was.

I discovered that a stage had been set up on the ground floor and the room had been converted into a modest sort of auditorium: party delegates were arriving from different parts of the country for deliberations with Suu and her central committee. After so many years incommunicado, it was important for her to meet those who had stayed loyal all that time, often at great cost to themselves. She was clearly aware of this need. But instead of travelling around the country as she had done to such extraordinary effect in 1989, she had the party come to her.

It was a very obvious second best, but it was the most she was permitted. She appeared to be in excellent health, no older-looking since our previous encounter eight years before, and I heard no rumours that she was ill. Despite the rigours of travelling in Burma, back in 1989 she had relished the opportunity to travel to every corner of the country from which she had been separated for so long, and hundreds of thousands of ordinary people flocked to join the party. So the only explanation for her immobility was that she was under orders from the authorities. But if so, she said nothing about it – this woman who in the past had never been short of a crushing put-down for her captors.

But then, in these months following her release, Suu said nothing much about anything.

*

It was on Sunday 14 August 2011 that things began to change. She left her home in a Japanese saloon car and headed north-east out of Rangoon to the town of Pegu, sixty-five miles away, in the scrubby deforested hills where fifty years before a communist insurgency had held out for years against the military government.

In colonial times, Pegu (now officially named Bago) was famous for its club and its club cocktail. For Suu the memories of the town were warm: back in 1989 she and her convoy had driven north from the Irrawaddy Delta where the authorities had harassed and abused them, arresting her supporters and firing guns in the air to deter local people from greeting her. But once over the line into Pegu, their problems melted away. As her then assistant Ma Thanegi wrote in her journal, 'The minute we crossed into Pegu Division, all harassment stopped. Just over the border, we saw trucks and cars and thought it was more harassment, but it was crowds welcoming us.'[4]

So coming back to Pegu was like the good old days. Friendly crowds thronged the streets. Photos of her legendary father were hoisted in the air. Local schoolchildren waved placards of welcome. She paid her respects in the local monastery, pouring tea for the abbot. In her old way, fluent, smiling, chatty, she spoke without notes from the first-floor balcony of a shabby old wooden building, home of the head of the Pegu chapter of the NLD, to a couple of thousand local people, who cheered her loudly and chanted her name. 'The last time I came here,' she told the crowd, 'it was the day of the World Cup final. But even then people came out to greet me. Win Tin asked them why they were not at home watching the World Cup. They said they could watch the World Cup every four years, but I had only come here once in eleven years . . .'[5]

She gave a donation for the relief of victims of a recent flood. She snipped ribbons to open two new libraries, named in her honour. Then, at a decent hour of the afternoon, she climbed back into her Japanese car and drove home. And that was that.

What was it all about? Her earlier visit to Pegu, like all her dozens of stops around the country, had taken place in the context of a great popular uprising. Every stop along the way was another kick in the teeth – administered with a gracious smile – to the military junta. Every stop added thousands to the NLD's membership roll, which by mid-1989, on the eve of her arrest, stood at 3 million. Every town Suu visited was another battle won by the party for the soul of Burma.

This time her visit to Pegu was a parody of that, a pale imitation. There was no context. She was alive. She was free. And now, once again, she could climb into a car and drive out of Rangoon like any other privileged Burmese. All these were good things, as the people of Pegu duly acknowledged. Of course she was popular, of course she was beloved: that went without saying. But what was going to happen next?

Myat Hla, the head of the local NLD branch, tried to elicit an answer. The newspapers had revealed that a few days before she had had another meeting, the second since her release, with Aung Kyi, the government minister and former general who had been assigned to liaise with her. What was that all about? he wanted to know. She would 'disclose more details at the appropriate time,' she told him.

And by the end of the week he had his answer.

*

On Friday 19 August 2011, five days after this enigmatic trip to Pegu, Aung San Suu Kyi paid her first visit to Naypyidaw, Burma's new capital, at the invitation of President Thein Sein, Burma's new head of state.

It was her first visit to Burma's newest and strangest metropolis. When in 2005 it was announced that Burma was to have a new capital city, the response was widespread consternation, especially from the civil servants required to uproot themselves from Rangoon and move there. It was no more than a clearing in the jungle, people said, it was in the middle of nowhere. It was the greatest folly yet perpetrated by the military junta. It was rumoured that the reason for building it – deep in the countryside – was to give Senior General Than Shwe better protection in case the United States launched an Iraq-style 'shock-and-awe' invasion to topple him.

With the passage of time, however, Naypyidaw began to make more sense. Two hundred miles due north of Rangoon, it is roughly in the centre of the country. In the old days, Burma's kings often created new capital cities, a solid and impressively expensive way of legitimising their rule, and keeping their rivals on the hop. Than Shwe, the poorly educated former postal clerk who had emerged as the head of the junta, had no legitimacy beyond the titles conferred on him by his army peers, so a vast new city created from scratch was a way to establish a link to the heroic, hereditary leaders of the past. Naming it Naypyidaw, 'Abode of Kings', and adorning it with oversized statues of the most illustrious Burmese monarchs, rammed home the point. Burma's military rulers also craved the respect of their peers across South East Asia: a capital untainted by colonial buildings or memories was a step in that direction.

Inviting Suu to visit the president in Naypyidaw was clever. All the regime's previous approaches to her had taken place in official guest houses in Rangoon, territory that was neutral for both parties. Bringing her north to the capital put her in the role of petitioner. It would also bring home to her the dramatic ways in which her country had changed during her absence from the scene.

The journey from Rangoon to Naypyidaw is like no other in Burma. Slicing through the featureless scrub of the Burmese heartland, it declares loud and clear that this is the new Myanmar, and that the people behind it are fully in command. The Road to Mandalay was never like this. Each furlong on the way to Naypyidaw – is Burma the only country in the world that still uses furlongs? – is marked by a cement marker. Built of concrete, the highway varies from four to eight lanes in width, with a strip of vermilion-coloured flowers in dusty beds between the two carriageways. Admonitory signs punctuate the journey: IF YOU DRIVE DON'T DRINK, IF YOU DRINK DON'T DRIVE – YOUR SAFETY OUR AIM, YOUR COMFORT OUR REWARD. It is a toll road, and drivers pay between 1,000 and 6,000 kyats, depending on how far they go. And that explains the other curiosity about this structure: there is practically no traffic on it. You can drive for a miles without seeing another vehicle.

Naypyidaw is a few miles east of the highway. Even after you have arrived in the city it is hard to appreciate the fact because there is simply a series of mesmerising, empty ring roads from which new hotels, shopping malls, housing estates and a park can be spied, all glinting in the distance.

The city's unique feature is the Parliament complex. It appears to float in the middle distance, but unlike the hotels, the shopping malls, the park, and so on, which are eventually reached, Parliament constantly seems to recede, like a city in a dream. The public is not allowed to approach it. Special permits are needed and a Mercedes hire car has to be taken from the only firm with the parliamentary contract to get through the gates. This arrangement is eloquent. A respected nation requires a parliament, it says. Parliament is the crystallisation of the popular will, expressed through the ballot box. But as the Burmese military remember all too well, this is a high-risk process. Putting Parliament not only in the middle of nowhere and barring public access is, to the military mind, the least unsatisfactory solution to a most regrettable necessity: democracy.

The man who summoned Suu to Naypyidaw was at the time almost unknown outside a small circle of ambassadors and Burma obsessives. President Thein Sein had been elected president in March, becoming in the process Burma's first constitutionally legitimate ruler since the fall of Ne Win in 1990. The outside world had paid little attention because the election that produced the Parliament that voted him into office, packed with former soldiers and dominated by the military's proxy party, the Union Solidarity and Development Party (USDP), had been so blatantly rigged.

Like his patron Than Shwe, Burma's recently retired military strongman, Thein Sein was a former general. The only remarkable thing about him at first glance was how little he resembled Central Casting's idea of a general. Aged sixty-eight, he was short and short-sighted, bald and physically slight. But however unsoldierly his appearance, that is what he was. And most people's reaction to his election as president was a cynical shrug. Here, it appeared, was yet another Burmese army officer in the long line that had abused and misruled their country since Ne Win's coup d'état of 1962.

So the first good look that non-Burma compulsives had of him was on Friday 19 August 2011. It was a photograph that made one look twice. President Thein Sein and Daw Aung San Suu Kyi stood together under a photograph of her late father, Aung San. For most Burmese, the presence of the three of them in a single image was startling. General – *Bogyoke* in Burmese, pronounced 'bo-joke' – Aung San was the founding father of the independent Burmese army, the father equally of the modern Burmese state, who negotiated Burma's independence from Britain and would have become its first independent prime minister had he not been assassinated in 1947, a few months before independence.

Aung San Suu Kyi's life has been dominated by the weight of that legacy. It was his myth-like life, cut short in its prime, that conditioned her urge to play a role in Burmese politics. Her strong physical resemblance to her father helped guarantee a hero's welcome when, in 1988, she spoke before a vast crowd in Rangoon and overnight became the de facto leader of the popular uprising.

Aung San fulfilled the same sort of role for Burma that Gandhi played for India: the legendary figure to whom all paid obeisance, the one from whom the nation's sense of its integrity derived. But as his daughter criss-crossed the country in the first half of 1989, whipping up support for her new-founded opposition party, the Aung San brand turned to poison for the military. Every town had its Aung San street and its Aung San statue. The kyat, the national currency, bore his image, the day of his murder was a national holiday. But now everything connected to General Aung San also reminded people of his daughter. So now the military sought to change that, to shuffle the great man slowly off stage. His old house, which had been turned into a museum, was closed to the public and fell into disrepair. The special regular classes for the nation's schools in Aung San's story were abandoned. On account of his troublemaker of a daughter, he was in the process of being expunged from the historical record.

Then suddenly Aung San was back – in the office of the president. With his daughter and ex-General Thein Sein in the same frame.

Thein Sein's patron and predecessor Than Shwe was known to storm out of meetings with foreign envoys if the Lady's name was so much as mentioned. His wife and the wives of other top soldiers were said by Rangoon gossips to do the Burmese equivalent of sticking pins into a Suu Kyi wax doll. Than Shwe had gone so far as to orchestrate an attempt on her life in 2003 that had nearly succeeded. When his deputy General Khin Nyunt, head of Military Intelligence, reached a tentative agreement with Suu that would have brought the NLD into a power-sharing agreement with the junta, Than Shwe rejected it outright and subsequently put Khin Nyunt on trial for treason.

But here she was, under a picture of her father, alongside Burma's new head of state. The president's spokesman let it be known that Suu had been received in Thein Sein's Naypyidaw residence, and had eaten supper cooked by the president's wife.

Besides the photograph and the supper, nothing has leaked out about this meeting. We do not know in any detail what they discussed. But less than a year later, unfazed by all the fuss, Suu stood in the Mother of Parliaments, accorded honours only ever given – Black Rod was quite clear on the point – to heads of state. A new age had arrived.

Or had it?

*

One man couldn't bring himself to believe it. U Win Tin, co-founder with Suu of the National League for Democracy, was to many Burmese the bravest person in the country, and the conscience of his party.

Finally released in 2008 after nineteen years, he was the longest-serving political prisoner in Burma. And though unshakeably loyal to Suu, he never changed his opinion that the reforms that brought her into Parliament were superficial, and that the army was still running the country behind the scenes.

After his release, he joked about Suu's relatively emollient attitude to the army. 'Some of us would like to push the military into the Bay of Bengal,' he said. 'She only wants to push them into [Rangoon's] Kandawgyi Lake.' Of 2010's election he said: 'We shouldn't be fooled by this . . . The military are firmly in control; it's liberalisation without democratisation. The army must go back to the barracks.'[6]

Born in 1930, schooled during the last, chaotic and contested years of British rule, Win Tin's adult life encompassed all the phases of independent Burma's short history. He belonged to that now dwindling generation of elderly Burmese who had direct experience of voting for a government, before the coup d'état of 1962.

As Suu told it, the passion of the Burmese for democracy had survived all the decades of repression. Describing the enthusiasm she had encountered while campaigning in the by-election that put her into parliament, Suu told her Westminster Hall audience, 'Apathy was certainly not a problem: the passion of the electorate was hunger for something long denied . . .' She went on: 'Following Burma's independence in 1948, our parliamentary system was of course based on that of the United Kingdom. The era became known in Burmese as the Parliamentary Era [and] lasted more or less until 1962. [It] could not be said to have been perfect, but it was certainly the most progressive and promising period up to now in the short history of independent Burma. It was at this time that Burma was considered the nation most likely to succeed in South East Asia.'

Win Tin was one of the beneficiaries of that 'most progressive and promising period'. One might say it was the making of him. Burmese further education still functioned well in 1948, the year of Burmese independence, when he turned eighteen. He took a degree in English literature, modern history and political science at Rangoon University, and retained his fluency in English all his life. As a student he worked as a translator and also did night shifts as an editor for Agence France-Presse. Later he won a scholarship to train as a journalist in the Netherlands, and hitchhiked around Europe during the holidays.

'He was an instinctive journalist,' wrote Rosalind Russell, who interviewed him about his younger years. 'If there was information, Win Tin wanted to share it.' In the Netherlands, receiving letters from home about strikes and insurgencies and economic collapse, he decided to share the news with fellow expatriates. He tracked down a company in Germany that produced typewriters with the Burmese script and bought one, then typed up a four-page newsletter on it, duplicated copies and posted them to all the Burmese abroad whose addresses he could find. 'Even if people lived in the same house or the same room I would send them their own copy by name,' he told Russell. 'When you are abroad, it is nice to get something addressed especially to you.'[7]

Win Tin's life traces the tragic arc of independent Burma's short history. He returned to Rangoon from Europe in 1957 and soon became one of his country's most prominent journalists and editors. He made no attempt to disguise his radical views, and in 1968 he was forced to move from the capital to Mandalay, where the authorities thought he would cause less trouble. By then the parliamentary era was six years in its grave but Win Tin survived professionally because U Ne Win, the army chief who had seized power in 1962, found the freewheeling ideas of this well-travelled intellectual fascinating. 'Each time [Ne Win] came to Mandalay,' Russell wrote, 'the general would invite the journalist for dinner . . . "It was a great safeguard for me," Win Tin said. "Because the authorities knew of my contact with Ne Win, they didn't dare to be too harsh."'[8]

As a result he was spared imprisonment or marginalisation long after other outspoken colleagues had been silenced, and became the head of the Journalists' Union. But his charmed life came to a sudden end in 1988 when he joined the swelling democracy movement and was among those who persuaded

Suu to get involved too. They went on to create and lead the National League for Democracy. Then in July 1989, when Suu was under house arrest, Win Tin and all the party's other core members were arrested and jailed. And from the outset, Win Tin was singled out for harsh treatment. Even before his first court appearance he was brutally beaten. His upper teeth were knocked out, and the purple welts all over his body betrayed the brutality of his beatings.

He was sentenced to three years in jail for 'spreading anti-government propaganda'. But the generals were well aware of the respect in which he was held by the democratic opposition, and in 1991, before the sentence expired they attempted to win him over to their side.

'They took me out of my cell to an exhibition,' he later told a fellow prisoner, 'called "The Real Story under the Big Waves and Strong Winds". The exhibition's aim was to denounce the 1988 uprising as a riot created by destructive elements and terrorists.' A poster at the entrance of the exhibition declared: 'Only when the Tatmadaw' – the Burmese Army – 'is strong will the nation be strong.' The exhibition highlighted the role of the army, with the underlying message that it was the only force that could keep the country safe. 'Sovereign power is only deserved by the generals,' Win Tin told his cellmate. 'That was the final conclusion.'[9]

The junta's agents asked their celebrity prisoner for his opinion on the exhibition, and if he would agree to switch sides. They gave him pen and paper and told him to write his views. 'I wrote down my criticism,' he later recalled. 'I used twenty-five sheets of paper. My comments were blunt. I made my commentary in a spirit of sincerity and openness. But it irritated them severely . . . In the end I came straight to the point: the army must go back to the barracks. That will make everything better in Burma.'[10]

Now the regime authorities were seriously angry with him. They added new charges to those for which he had already served time, increasing his sentence by ten years. 'They put him alone in his cell,' his jail comrade Zin Linn recalled. 'It was 8.5 feet by 11.5 feet. There was only a bamboo mat on the concrete floor. Sleeping, eating, walking and going to the toilet were all done in the same space . . . The authorities created an atmosphere of persecution to pressure the writer's spirit to submit. But it was in vain. Win Tin would not alter his beliefs to escape this severe hardship.'[11]

During his years in jail, Win Tin suffered spondylitis, a hernia, heart disease, failing eyesight, urethritis and piles. Despite this he contributed to every issue of a magazine his fellow political prisoners brought out secretly every month. When guards unearthed magazines during a raid in 1996, Win Tin and the rest were harshly interrogated over the course of a week. During the subsequent summary trial for producing the magazine, he and the others were confined in a tiny enclosure known as the dog house. On conviction an extra seven years was added to his sentence.

While locked in the dog house, Win Tin made a speech about democracy. 'He had to shout the speech in order for us to hear it,' Zin Linn remembered. 'When he had finished we clapped and sang the national anthem in unison. I still remember some of the words of his speech. '"The junta put us in the dog house to crush our morale, but by doing so our spirits have been hardened and tempered," he said. "It is a pity that they don't even know the law of nature." He also said, "True politicians are like a gardener who plants a tree. He may never have the opportunity to taste the tree's fruit, but he must tend it for the benefit of future generations."'12

Win Tin was finally released on 23 September 2008. His discharge from jail was delayed because he wouldn't relinquish his uniform blue shirt. Throughout his nineteen years in jail he had refused to compromise and never gave up hope that things would change and that the army would go back to the barracks, as he had advised them back in 1991. But once on the outside again, his scepticism about the reforms set in motion by President Thein Sein was insurmountable.

Win Tin embraced the life of a dissident democrat as fiercely as if it were a religious vocation. In the years after his release I twice visited him at his home at short notice, and both times he made me feel genuinely welcome. He lived in a shabby house by a busy road in a suburb of Rangoon consisting of two small rooms. His lack of concern for the material aspects of life was immediately apparent. 'I am a single person,' he said. 'I have no family life. Most of my life I have lived for my work as a politician and a journalist. That has consumed my life. Since the age of about nineteen I have lived as a public man. By that I don't mean as a well-known person. I mean that my life belongs to society, and society is my life.'13

He could never be shut up, whether locked in a prison cell or at large in the country whose freedom, he insisted, was still a long way off. Less than two months before his death he travelled north to Mandalay – the city where many years before he had experienced a mild form of internal exile – to visit the jingoistic Buddhist monk who had emerged as the voice of pious Burman[14] chauvinism, with a particularly virulent line on the menace of Islam. In addition to those views, Ashin Wirathu, a tiny man with cupid-bow lips and a prissy voice to match, also opposed changing the constitution to allow Suu to run for president. This was the issue on which Win Tin wished to change his mind. There is film of the encounter. They sit on office chairs in late-afternoon winter light in the leafy courtyard of Wirathu's monastery. Neither gives ground. Win Tin is old and already ailing. Wirathu is courteous. Both men smile. The meeting is an achievement of sorts, even if nothing is gained on either side: civil debate, in courteous language, from opposite sides of the political divide: the stuff of civilisation . . .[15]

*

During her years under house arrest Suu was given numerous honours in absentia. It started in 1990 with her election to an honorary fellowship of St Hugh's, her Oxford college. Soon afterwards the European Parliament awarded her the Sakharov Prize, named after the Soviet Union's most famous dissident. The Nobel Peace Prize followed soon after that. Then came dozens more from all over the world. The honours clattered around her like hailstones: honorary degrees, the freedom of this, that and the other city; India's Jawaharlal Nehru Award, the International Simón Bolívar Prize, the Olof Palme Prize, the Congressional Gold Medal, and many, many more.

In Oslo, five days before coming to Westminster, she told 'your royal highnesses, excellencies, distinguished members of the Norwegian Nobel Committee, dear friends' how strange – but sustaining – the award of the Nobel Prize had been, less than two years into the toughest, most challenging period of her years of seclusion.

In 1989, when my late husband Michael Aris came to see me during my first term of house arrest, he told me that a friend, John Finnis, had nominated me for the Nobel Peace Prize . . . I laughed. For an instant Michael looked amazed, then he realised why I was amused. The Nobel Peace Prize? A pleasant prospect, but quite improbable! So how did I feel when I was actually awarded the Nobel Prize for Peace?

. . . I heard the news . . . on the radio one evening. It did not altogether come as a surprise because I had been mentioned as one of the frontrunners for the prize in a number of broadcasts the previous week. While drafting this lecture, I have tried very hard to remember what my immediate reaction to the announcement of the award had been. I think, I can no longer be sure, it was something like: 'Oh, so they've decided to give it to me.' It did not seem quite real because in a sense I did not feel myself to be quite real at the time.

Often during my days of house arrest it felt as though I was no longer a part of the real world. There was the house [her old, rambling, ramshackle mansion on Inya Lake] which was my world, there was the world of others who also were not free but who were together in prison as a community, and there was the world of the free; each was a separate planet pursuing its own separate course in an indifferent universe.

What the Nobel Peace Prize did was to draw me once again into the world of other human beings . . . to restore a sense of reality to me . . . It made me real once again.[16]

Did all the other prizes and honours affect her similarly? Perhaps: she has not spoken about it in public. But once they were awarded to her there was the obligation, after she was again free to travel, to pick them up. And Suu has always been diligent about doing her duty.

Perhaps it was the spectacle of this woman, still beautiful and elegant, swishing around the world in her oriental gown with flowers in her hair, being feted and complimented and loaded with honours everywhere she went, that began to sow the first seeds of doubt, dislike and disbelief in the fickle mind of the great Western public. Could anyone – whatever she had put up with – really be that deserving?

The other seeds of public estrangement from a woman who for years had been idolised in the West were sown, in a coincidence for which there has never been a clear explanation, just as Suu was preparing to resume her foreign travels.

On 29 May 2012, one month before her trip to Oslo and London, Suu flew to Bangkok to participate in a seminar and visit Burmese refugee camps near the common border. This four-day trip to Thailand was her first overseas journey in more than twenty-four years. The previous day, a Buddhist woman had been raped and murdered by three Muslim men, reportedly members of the Rohingya community, in Arakan state, bordering Bangladesh in the west of Burma, where Muslims constitute a large minority. On 3 June, two days after Suu flew back in to Rangoon, ten Rohingyas were murdered by members of the Buddhist community in retaliation. The spiral of attacks and counter-attacks continued as she flew to Switzerland, the first stop on her European tour.

Suu drew the attention of her European audiences to these bloody events. In Oslo she said, 'Fires of suffering and strife are raging around the world. In my own country . . . to the west, communal violence resulting in arson and murder were taking place just several days before I started out on the journey that brought me here today.' Five days later in Oxford she said, 'In the west [of Burma], communal strife has led to the loss of innocent lives and the displacement of tens of thousands of hapless citizens.'

But although Suu had been an MP for barely a month, having been sworn in in May, and obviously held no office in the government, her name was swiftly linked to the violence. In July Moshahida Sultana Ritu, an associate professor of economics at Dhaka University in Bangladesh, wrote in the *New York Times*:

Last spring, a flowering of democracy in Myanmar mesmerised the world. But now, three months after the democracy activist Daw Aung San Suu Kyi won a parliamentary seat . . . an alarm bell is ringing . . . A pogrom against a population of Muslims called the Rohingyas began in June. It is the ugly side of Myanmar's democratic transition – a rotting of the flower even as it seems to bloom.

This is not sectarian violence; it is state-supported ethnic cleansing, and the nations of the world aren't pressing Myanmar's leaders to stop it. Even Ms Aung San Suu Kyi has not spoken out . . . Ms Aung San Suu Kyi, though not as powerful as the military officers who control Myanmar's transition, should not duck questions about the Rohingyas, as she has done while being feted in the West.[17]

Ducking the Rohingya question: it is an accusation that has been repeated many times by many people, both Muslims and non-Muslims, and it has dogged her ever since.

Perhaps the timing was not merely bad luck: perhaps a trap had been set for her by her enemies in the old regime, still powerful behind the scenes. One of the canniest Western observers of Burma over many decades, the Swedish journalist Bertil Lintner, believes that these apparently unrelated events – Suu's journey to the West and the anti-Rohingya violence in Arakan state – were closely connected. In June 2012 he said:

> The violence is clearly well orchestrated and not as spontaneous as we are being led to believe. The government is very worried about the support commanded by Suu Kyi. It wants to force her into a position where she has to make a pro-Rohingya public statement that could damage her popularity among Burma's Buddhists, where anti-Muslim sentiment runs high. On the other hand, if she remains silent she will disappoint those who support her firm stand on human rights.[18]

Another long-time observer of the Burma scene commented, 'Suu Kyi is damned if she does and damned if she doesn't. She is in a very difficult situation, which could seriously damage her reputation and erode much of her popularity.'

Detention in her home, with the awards for being 'the conscience of her country' and 'the hero of humanity' raining down upon her, must have seemed in retrospect much more straightforward.

*

Suu was collecting honours and receiving accolades from those in Europe who had admired her from afar. In England she was also visiting places that meant a great deal to her emotionally, where she had been a student, got married, given birth to her children, settled down. At the Sheldonian Theatre in Oxford, which was designed by Sir Christopher Wren and makes one feel like a toy in an oversized doll's house, she recalled her student days, 'The past is alive, it never goes away,' she said. Surveying the students in her audience, she recalled how she was in those years, and her friends and contemporaries who were

carefree, happy, nice – look at their faces, no hidden agendas there, no reason to be afraid . . . At Oxford I learned respect for the best in human civilisation . . . It gave me a confidence in humankind and in the innate wisdom of human beings. This helped me to cope with what were not quite the best of humankind.

During the more difficult years I was upheld by memories of Oxford. The memories were actually very simple: going to the Cherwell with friends in a punt. Or reading on the lawn at St Hugh's, or in the library – not looking at a book but out of the window. But these are very happy memories because I had lived a happy life. And this made me understand so much better the young people of Burma who wanted to live a happy life but had never been given the opportunity to lead one.[19]

But although St Hugh's laid on a birthday party for her – she turned sixty-seven on 19 June 2012 – she was at pains to tell Oxford that she had not come back to wallow in nostalgia. 'The prizes and honours I received [in the house arrest years] were not so much a personal tribute as the recognition of the basic humanity that unites one isolated person to the rest of the world,' she said. In the same spirit, 'This journey out of Burma has not been a sentimental pilgrimage to the past but an exploration of the new possibilities at hand for the people of Burma.'[20]

She was not, in other words, a prodigal daughter of Oxford, finally back home in the bosom of her alma mater. No: she was just one Burmese out of 50 million, the one Burmese person the rest of the world, on account of her courage, her suffering, her eloquence, her perfect Oxford accent – and heaven knows on account of her great beauty, too – would listen to.

*

Suu's speech in Westminster Hall was plain and to the point after John Bercow's fancy introduction. She reminded her audience that she had just had her photograph taken at 10 Downing Street, where sixty-five years before her father had also had his photo taken, in his case with Clement Attlee, David Cameron's Labour predecessor, after negotiating Burma's independence.

Her father had succeeded, she said, because he was so practical,

> and I have tried to be as practical as my father was. And so I'm here in part to ask for practical help. Help as a friend and an equal in support of the reforms which can bring a better life and greater opportunity to the people of Burma who have been for so long deprived of their rights and their place in the world.

My country stands today at the start of a journey towards I hope a better future. So many hills remain to be climbed, chasms to be bridged, obstacles to be breached. Our own determination can get us so far. The support of the people of Britain and people around the world can get us so much further.[21]

*

On 21 April 2014, five and a half years after his release from prison, Win Tin died in Rangoon. The cause of death was kidney failure. The day of the funeral was fiercely hot. His coffin came rolling out of the hospital on a trolley; beneath the transparent glass top was the familiar rumpled, sardonic, stubborn face of the man who had been the backbone of the National League for Democracy wearing his black-framed glasses. And he was still dressed in his blue prison shirt. The shirt had become his emblem. He had worn it through his nineteen years in prison. And he continued to wear it after he was freed in memory of his comrades who were still inside, and in solidarity with the rest of his countrymen, too, because, as he put it to me, 'Burma is still one great prison.'

Hundreds of people came to see him off. A dense crowd of friends and comrades, party grandees, students, reporters and photographers milled around the coffin, muttering prayers, bowing and weeping above the body of the departed hero.

There is nothing solemn about a Burmese funeral: people were bellowing and waving their arms around and a man with a megaphone tried in vain to organise them. Photographers suddenly descended – a small army of them, shoving and squeezing to get up close, craning and angling their telephoto lenses over the coffin's curved glass lid. A host of women sat on the ground flapping fans. One had a small photo of Win Tin stuck to her forehead. Floral wreaths arrived, one after another; one huge wreath covered in small pink roses bore the letters NLD; the young woman carrying it cried helplessly as she walked along.

Then a grey Mitsubishi SUV rolled up. On the windscreen was a laughing photograph of Win Tin and fighting peacock stickers, the symbol of the NLD. There was more pushing and shoving and yelling, then the back door opened and a woman's face appeared, a world-famous face, and Aung San Suu Kyi slipped out of the car, and with her head slightly bowed and a grave, wide-eyed expression on her face she marched with her soldierly tread into the vestibule where the coffin had come to rest. A ragged cheer went up from the crowd.

It was remarkable that she wore no flowers in her hair that day. Over the course of many years, Suu Kyi has rarely been seen without fresh flowers in her hair. She wore a pink and grey top and appeared small and tired and somewhat frail. At the coffin she stopped, looked briefly into it, exchanged a few words with two of her oldest party colleagues, then prostrated herself before it.

Win Tin was gone. Coming nearly six years after the end of his own appallingly long and harsh incarceration, four years after Suu's release, two years into Burma's sudden and dramatic opening to the world, it was another watershed. He was no longer there to demand answers, but the questions he had never stopped asking hung there in the hot air above his coffin.

What has been achieved, really, with all the hoopla of constitution, elections, reform, Parliament? Some people have got rich, many of them people who were already rich before. Some have come home. Some have been let out of prison. Others remain there. Twenty-six years on, Win Tin was still asking, is Burma appreciably closer to the goals for which you and I, Aung San Suu Kyi, sacrificed our happiness, our freedom, your family, my profession, when we formed the National League for Democracy?

Two years before – as Suu, with a fresh passport in her handbag, flew out of her native land for the first time in more than twenty-four years, a free woman and a Member of Parliament – to many people the answer had seemed an unequivocal 'yes'. Win Tin himself had never ceased to doubt it, to pour cold water. Was he right all along?

Suu, by contrast, felt there was no option but to believe: to live and act and work as if progress were not only possible, but were actually under way; as if it were not – as Win Tin seemed to believe – a cruel stunt to bamboozle the outside world.

But Suu herself was under no illusions about the scale of the challenge. 'Burma is at the beginning of a road,' she told her audience in Oxford. 'But it's not smooth, it's not well made – it's not even there yet; we will have to create it for ourselves. Too many people are expecting too much of Burma. Many people think the Burmese road is like the road I took from London to Oxford, so smooth and straight that I was almost car sick.' Burma is not like that, she said. 'We have to make the road ourselves, inch by painful inch.'22

2

MAN OUT OF TROUSERS

ROADS are a challenge in Burma. Normally they are very bad: narrow, crude, often washed away by monsoon rains or mountain flooding. In the early years of independence, road travel beyond the outskirts of Rangoon in any direction was lethally hazardous because of communist insurgents, freelance rebels and ordinary bandits who lay in wait to ambush anyone reckless enough to set off on a journey. Even after General Ne Win seized power and stamped out most of the rebellions except those on the borders, the roads remained treacherous: the wealthy elite dodged the problem by air travel. For foreign tourists, flying was in fact the only mode of travel permitted. The poor used the rivers and coasts, or stayed in their villages.

When one of Burma's poor, rough, narrow roads started to disintegrate entirely, the local population was pressed into service to restore it. On my first visit to Burma in 1991, one year after the election won by the NLD but stolen by the military, I obtained a seven-day visa (the only type on offer) and travelled round the country in an ancient Fokker aeroplane. On side trips to see the countryside by bus we would have to squeeze past road crews patching the roads. The foreman was always a man; the labourers doing the heavy lifting were women, often with babies slung on their backs. Our tour guides, still seething at the way the army had flattened their democratic hopes, informed us that the road gangs were local villagers, forced to do this work and receiving no pay for it. The roads they built without machinery of any sort were crude. Young women squatted by the side of the road and bashed big stones with hammers all day long in the hot sun, reducing them to piles of pebbles.

Seventeen years later, outside the town of Pakokku, in central Burma, I saw roads being repaired in the same way. Nothing had changed in all that time, nothing had improved. Bad roads became a byword for bad government, oppressively bad military government that had no interest in making life easier for the ordinary people – that positively preferred the common people to be stuck where they were born, to be grounded. And despite the rhetoric of the Burma Socialist Programme Party, nobody in power cared enough for the public good to do a better job.

Long residence had accustomed Aung San Suu Kyi to Britain's modern roads. When she went home in 1988 she was therefore sensitive to the dreadful state of her country's roads in a way that those who had spent their whole lives in Burma could not be. On her release from house arrest the first time, in 1995, she went with party colleagues to the town of Thamanya, a day's journey south-east of Rangoon, to pay her respects to a famously independent-minded Buddhist priest who lived there, known as the Thamanya Sayadaw. After a bone-juddering, spring-shattering journey down from Rangoon, she found the road leading to the town was a 'smooth, well-kept black ribbon winding into the distance'.[1] Tens of thousands of pilgrims visited Thamanya every year. Building good roads and keeping them well maintained was a spiritual as well as a material task. So the Sayadaw taught.

The contrast between the state of Thamanya's roads and those of the rest of the country reflected a moral more than a material difference. It was not that Thamanya was a rich town. But roads meant openness, mobility, a welcome extended to others, a readiness to go where one had not been before. Countries where people had some faith in the future had good roads. For countries where the important thing was to protect what you had, to hide yourself away, to avoid the scrutiny of others, decent roads were a dispensable luxury. Speaking about roads to Britain's Parliament, of Burma being 'at the beginning of a road' and of the need 'to create it for ourselves' was a way for Suu to stay true to her father's memory, to be 'as practical as my father was'. Of course it was a metaphor, like the 'hills to be climbed, chasms to be bridged, obstacles to be breached' which she referred to in the same speech. But it was not only a metaphor.

*

President Thein Sein – the man who brought Suu in from the cold – is an army man. The army has been his life. Aung San was the father of the Burmese army, so while he was Suu's natural father, he was in a sense Thein Sein's godfather, as he was godfather to all of the first generation of army men.

That connection between them seems to hover in the air above their formal photograph. It is like a photo of long-separated siblings, improbably united under an image of the man, long dead, who connects their lives.

Like Suu, Thein Sein was born in the dying months of the Second World War. But while Suu grew up in a privileged household, Thein Sein tasted the everyday poverty of the countryside. 'I am from a very poor background, I experienced poverty first hand,'[2] he said.

After high school he was bright enough to be accepted by the elite Defence Services Academy. Joining the army transformed his prospects. Since Ne Win's coup of 1962, the army, or Tatmadaw, has steadily cemented its position as a privileged caste, like the armies of many other newly independent nations. Officers live in comfortable housing colonies, send their children to exclusive schools, have access to good doctors and hospitals. Since the abandonment of the disastrous socialist economy in the early 1990s, they have also had plentiful opportunities to grow rich, and to cultivate wealthy, semi-dependent cronies. Corruption is manifested in the fancy cars driven by these officers' spoiled children, by their neo-baroque villas in comfortable suburbs like Dagon township in Rangoon. Their wealthy friends own most of the country's hotels and resorts and hold dominant positions right across the nation's economy. For those willing to abuse their power, a military career can be the royal road to extreme wealth and political influence.

But while privilege is common to all the senior army men, corruption and self-indulgence are not compulsory. There are claims that Thein Sein is clean. 'He carried out orders like everyone else,' a 'prominent Burmese entrepreneur' told an American journalist in 2012, 'but every businessman in the country knows that he's clean – and that's why he was never that powerful.'[3] This may be true. Or it may be helpful whitewash by a wealthy man hoping to benefit from the president's warm opinion, and well aware of what the West wanted to believe about Burma's new strong man. Other evidence – of his friendship with drug lords in the Golden Triangle, the notorious heroin-producing region on Burma's eastern border, for example – suggests he had his nose in the trough like many others.[4]

Since stepping into the international limelight on becoming president in 2011, Thein Sein has severed his visible links to the military. In the photograph taken with Suu in August 2011, he wears the standard Burmese dress of collarless shirt and longyi (known elsewhere in South East Asia as a sarong). Many senior Burmese soldiers have made that change; they are known sardonically as *baung-bi chut*, 'men out of trousers' – those who have exchanged Western-style uniforms for traditional garb.

In older photos wearing his army uniform, Thein Sein does not cut a very dashing military figure. He looks somewhat puny, he is short, he wears metal-rimmed glasses with thick lenses. In recent years he was fitted with a pacemaker.

Doubt has been cast on how valiant a soldier he was, even when young. A recent guide to investing in Burma claims that 'throughout Thein Sein's four-decade-long military career he was considered a bureaucrat, not a combat soldier'.[5]

But that is pure public relations spin. In 1988 – when he participated in the bloody suppression of the democracy movement – Thein Sein was a senior officer in a hard-core combat unit.[6] His participation in the massacres, in which thousands of unarmed demonstrators were gunned down in the streets and which put Burma in diplomatic quarantine for twenty years, was confirmed in a diplomatic cable from the US Embassy that was subsequently leaked. 'Major Thein Sein served as commander of Light Infantry Division (LID)-55k, one of the elite organisations loyal to the Burmese Socialist

Programme Party,' the cable, sent in October 2004, reads. 'In that capacity, he distinguished himself . . . in the crackdown against the 1988 uprising in support of democracy.'[7]

Thein Sein stoutly defended the army's role in such actions in March 2011, during his inaugural speech as president. 'The Tatmadaw, with a strong sense of duty and loyalty, saved the country several times whenever [it] was close to collapse,' he declared. '. . . Also in 1988, the Tatmadaw government saved the country from deteriorating conditions in various sectors and reconstructed the country.'[8]

He must have satisfied his masters – notably General Than Shwe, the dominant figure in the regime from 1992 until his retirement in 2011 – that he was reliable and not troubled unduly with squeamishness, because in 1996, after several years working under Than Shwe as a general staff officer in the Rangoon war office, he was given one of the Burmese army's most difficult challenges: confronting the multiple overlapping insurgencies in the Golden Triangle.

*

It would be fascinating to hear President Thein Sein talk informally about his years in the eastern Shan Hills. Sadly that is not likely to happen, at least not within earshot of a reporter.

The most responsible and onerous job he was given was as commander of the Golden Triangle Regional Command, which he did for five years. Considering his subsequent rise to the very top – always under the patronage of Than Shwe – he must have acquitted himself well. But under different circumstances the work he did in that pleasant upland region might have landed him in the dock of the International Criminal Court in The Hague.

During colonial times, the British had dealt with the Shan Hills as they did the princely states of the Indian subcontinent: they left the hereditary rulers to govern their pocket kingdoms in peace as they had done for generations, perhaps watched beadily by a British Resident. This minimised administrative effort and was an assurance of stability in border regions where trouble was often endemic. Britain's war was with the Burma king whom they eventually defeated, deposed and deported, and the millions of lowland Burmans who were loyal to him. It was not with the Shan who in language and culture were much closer to Thailand, and who owed no loyalty to Burma or its king and indeed did not consider themselves Burmese at all. After centuries fighting and winning in India, divide and rule came as naturally to the British as breathing.

Independence, embraced by Burmese as liberation from the colonial yoke, made that easy-going political architecture impossible to sustain. The British had counted and documented 135 different ethnic groups in the colony, among which the Burmans, dominant in the central heartland, were much the largest. But now Burma was to be an independent, unitary state. Everyone within its borders would be considered Burmese, and required to be loyal to the – Burman-dominated – Burmese government.

Aung San, who had fought first the British and then the Japanese to bring independent Burma into being, understood the nature of the problem. How could the loyalty of such a wildly diverse population be secured? His solution, arrived at under pressure from the departing colonialists, was an agreement with the ethnic nationalities struck in the town of Panglong in southern Shan state, guaranteeing its ethnic signatories a degree of self-government. Granted the right to preserve their languages, customs, and cultural practices, the Shan, the Kachin and the Chin would be willing to leave the big issues of diplomacy, foreign policy and so on to Rangoon. Unity in diversity would be the theme.

With the charismatic, pragmatic and revered Aung San in charge it might have worked. It would at least have had a fighting chance. But after his assassination in 1947, the guarantee of a strong centre vanished, too. Within a few years of independence Burma began disintegrating, as a communist insurgency backed by China joined dozens of revolts on the borders while freelance bandits marauded in the heartland. The Shan Hills, the most significant opium poppy-growing area in Asia, wedged between Burma, China, Laos and Thailand, became one of the most lawless corners of all, part of the Golden Triangle where drug barons including the notorious Khun Sa, half-Chinese half-Shan, took the place of any more stable authority.

Thein Sein's new post took him to Kengtung, the capital of the Golden Triangle, where the Burmese army was fighting to assert its power over a patchwork of vastly different ethnic groups and a palimpsest of overlapping and often competing insurgencies. 'Kengtung state . . . was as big as Belgium,' wrote Bertil Lintner, who made an epic journey through this region in the late 1980s, much of it on foot.[9] 'It was sparsely populated and made up largely of remote, undeveloped hill areas with dozens of tribes and ethnic groups and a variety of outside influences.' Lintner was travelling with the army of the Communist Party of Burma (CPB), in the late stage of a long war of attrition with the Burmese army. 'We rested on a ridge overlooking a wide valley,' he wrote. 'In the distance below we could see the tiny rooftops of the town of Mong Yang and the nearby Burmese Army garrison. The [Burmese] government controls the town and the connecting road to Kengtung – while the CPB's area stretches over the surrounding hills as well as half the valley.'

Lintner had already spent many months tramping through these war-torn borderlands. He wrote:

> It had become increasingly clear to me that any outside power wishing to control these mountains would inevitably have to act through the traditional rulers of the land. . . . The present Burmese government is forever hobbled by the fatally flawed certitude that it stands as the sole representative of the country's multitude of ethnic groups; and, by extension, as the only legitimate political force. To this extent, it can never hope to win the struggle for the loyalty of these people.[10]

The kaleidoscope of ethnic groups passing before his eyes – Akha women in colourful costumes and elaborate headgear, Palaung wearing nothing but torn longyis, Shan Buddhist monks on horseback armed with old muskets, the wild Wa, headhunters until recent times, their fortified villages overlooking broad fields of opium poppies, as well as the local Chinese – underlined his point. The imposition of central authority by brute force would never work – and in the process of failing would cause endless misery.

Becalmed for some weeks in a bamboo hut in a tribal village, Lintner befriended a Burmese activist of Bengali descent called Chit Tan who had been forced by army persecution to flee to these borderlands in the mid-1970s. 'When I lived in Mandalay, I never dreamt that parts of Burma are like this,' Chit Tan told him. 'He made a sweeping gesture towards the distant mountains with their scattered Akha villages. "And if someone had told me the government's army could kill poor villagers in cold blood, force them to walk ahead of troops to clear minefields, burn down villages at random and pressgang civilians to become porters, I'd have never believed it. But here, it's everyday reality for most people."'[11]

That was the everyday reality into which Major Thein Sein had been promoted. And it is one whose underlying rationale he has never questioned in public. The military junta that ruled until 2010 'has built political, economic and social foundations necessary for future democracy,' he told a conference in June 2013. '. . . We sincerely thank . . . all service personnel for achieving peace, stability and the rule of law . . . instrumental to a democratic nation.'[12]

That message, delivered two years after the start of the reform process he launched as president, went down smoothly in Rangoon and Mandalay among those who, like Chit Tan before his exile, had no idea of what was going on at the border. But what it meant in practice – the means adopted by 'service personnel for achieving peace, stability and the rule of law' – was land confiscation, torture, arbitrary killing and rape. All of these things happened on Major General Thein Sein's watch, under his nose, and at least some of the time on his orders.

To gain control over disputed territory, the army often forced villagers to leave their homes and farmlands, which were then seized by soldiers. Usually villagers were given a few days' notice before the army moved in. But in some cases the soldiers ignored the deadline they had given, and attacked the villagers while they were on the move. Then real atrocities could ensue. A report published in 2002 records:

> There was a Shan family of five in a remote hut near a rice farm of Mark Kawk village when SLORC troops came and saw them . . . Their village was being forced to move to the Laikha relocation site, and they were on their way there, but for some reason had stopped at the place to rest. The troops tied the father up, suspended him to the beam of the hut with a rope and made a fire under him, roasting him over it. They then gang-raped the teenage girl and eventually killed her. A few days later, her father died after suffering much from the pain of torture.[13]

This was what an army insulated from criticism and far from the metropolis was capable of. Were their commanding officers, including the man in charge of the Golden Triangle region, ignorant of what their juniors were doing or simply complicit? All the evidence suggests they were complicit. The fact that hideous abuse – rape as a weapon of war – was carried out not only in the field but also within army bases, under the eyes and with the knowledge of all, indicates that the soldiers responsible had no fear of punishment.

To the west of Kengtung, in a Shan town called Lai Kha, two girls in the town's middle school spoke up during school assembly to complain about the forced relocation of villagers in the nearby countryside and the army's closure of the town's market. Before the head teacher could say anything, two soldiers on security duty at the school called the girls over and invited them to come to the local light infantry battalion's base and put their questions to the commander in person. Did the girls have any idea what was going to happen to them? Did their headmistress? The report is silent – perhaps they were unable to resist the army's intimidating demands. At the base the commander locked them in a room, then raped each at pistol point on successive nights. After four days and four nights of this, he sent a demand to their parents for a payment of 15,000 kyats to secure their release.

Thein Sein was the commander of the Golden Triangle for five years, until 2001. Nothing in the record and nothing in any of his statements suggests that he attempted to stop such abuses, to punish those responsible or to speak out about them. If this loyal subordinate and favourite of Senior General Than Shwe objected privately to what was going on under his nose – and there is no evidence that he did – he was careful to keep his opinions to himself.

One could go further: his complicity in such behaviour would have done much to reassure Than Shwe and his senior colleagues that Thein Sein was a safe person to promote. Not only did he have the precious ability to hold his tongue; he was himself so deeply compromised by the behaviour of the soldiers under his command that any temptation, at some later date, when he was his own master, to confront the bad things that the Tatmadaw had done, would rebound on himself. So the temptation would be resisted. And so, to date, it has proved.

In 1998 his role in these abuses was spelled out in a report published by the United Nations Special Rapporteur on Human Rights in Burma and delivered to the UN General Assembly. Describing the 'hundreds of thousands of persons ... forcibly relocated, without any compensation or assistance, to new towns, villages or relocation camps in which they are essentially detained' across Burma's borderlands, it details in particular an order issued by the then Major General Thein Sein for the confiscation of '13 plots of land and rice fields'[14] belonging to Kengtung villagers. In compensation they were to be provided with sufficient land to build a small house – for which they would be required to pay 11,000 kyats each. They would also, on the land the army took from them, be forced to grow crops for the soldiers.

With all this in his record – not only in the files of Shan state democracy activists but in reports presented to the UN in New York – Thein Sein's blessed future was assured: his boss Than Shwe – 'such an old fox!' as a former World Bank official described him – clearly felt intensely relaxed about setting him on the fast track to positions of serious power. Hence, on his return to Rangoon from the wilds of Shan, he was put in charge of military business interests in the War Office, then promoted rapidly up the ladder until in 2007, on the death of the incumbent, he was appointed prime minister.

*

It was important for Than Shwe to be sure of his man's reliability. Because the senior general understood that, if he and his colleagues and cronies were to enjoy a serene and comfortable retirement, they needed the help of Thein Sein or someone like him: a dependable colleague possessed not of mere foxiness, but proper, educated brains.

Than Shwe was extremely shrewd but no one ever accused him of being well educated. The highest he had risen in civilian life was as a post office clerk. 'Our leader is a very uneducated man,' was one Burmese view of him.[15] A Western diplomat said, 'There were many intelligent soldiers but he was not one of them.' 'You feel that he got there by accident,' was another comment. But Than Shwe seems to have been aware of his limitations, and he took steps to make up for them.

Thein Sein's rise to the top came after, and as a result of, the purging and legal humiliation of the other 'intellectual' in the junta, General Khin Nyunt. Suave and even good-looking by the senior generals' lowly standards, a man with an addiction to self-publicity and bold political stunts, Khin Nyunt was chalk to Than Shwe's cheese and for many years his bitter rival at the apex of the regime.

If Than Shwe was dour, secretive and inarticulate, Khin Nyunt, the head of Military Intelligence, was the opposite. One press conference he gave lasted for seven hours. He was the only general who tried to speak English, and who fraternised with foreign diplomats. 'He was the closest thing to an acceptable face that the regime possessed,' the former British ambassador Robert Gordon remembered. 'Often key visitors would be introduced to him, and he would make efforts to speak English – badly but intelligibly.'[16] On one occasion, Gordon's young son squirted the general in the face with his water pistol. The mighty general laughed it off, much to the ambassador's relief.

Khin Nyunt was also behind the regime's only serious attempt to negotiate with Aung San Suu Kyi. He was bright enough to understand, firstly, that Burma needed a legally binding constitution if the generals were ever to improve their dreadful standing in the outside world; and secondly, that given her massive popularity outside as well as inside the country, Suu had somehow to be brought on board.

Khin Nyunt's opportunity to do both things came in 2003. In 2002 Suu had been released from house arrest amid widespread hopes that the regime would now try to do a deal with her. These hopes were dashed the following year when a convoy of cars in which she was travelling outside Mandalay was attacked by a well-armed mob and many of her supporters were killed. Suu only escaped thanks to the courage and daring of her driver. It later emerged – from his own mouth – that the assassination attempt was ordered by Senior General Than Shwe himself. With its humiliating failure his stock plummeted; the West's long-standing sanctions against Burma were tightened further.

In an attempt to recoup, Than Shwe appointed Khin Nyunt, his chief rival, prime minister, and Khin Nyunt seized the initiative. In a wide-ranging speech delivered to his most senior colleagues in August 2003, he announced the revival of a stalled National Convention, which would lead by steps along a 'road map' to a constitution, on which the whole population would vote in a referendum. Once the constitution was passed, it would lead to the creation of a parliament and democratic elections. At the end of this highway, Burma would become 'a modern, developed and democratic nation'.[17] In a single speech this mercurial general had sketched his nation's path for the ensuing ten years. But Khin Nyunt was fated to play only a preliminary role in that story.

Aung San Suu Kyi had been locked up in the notorious Insein Jail in Rangoon following the assassination attempt, provoking Western countries to tighten their sanctions yet further. The National Convention had gone into deep freeze back in 1996, after Suu and her party walked out of it, claiming that it was an army stitch-up. It could not be revived, Khin Nyunt reasoned, without including the NLD and Suu herself. And on this basis he launched secret negotiations with Suu, who was now under house arrest again. The Burmese public first learned of these talks when Suu herself mentioned them in an interview six years later.

The chief negotiator was a confidant of Khin Nyunt called Brigadier Than Tun. Belying Suu's reputation for stubbornness, the two sides came to a secret agreement by May 2004: it envisaged the NLD re-joining the National Convention and Suu being freed and politically rehabilitated. But when Khin Nyunt presented this fait accompli to the Senior General, the latter turned it down flat. And within two months, when Khin Nyunt was away in Singapore, his enemies in the regime struck, raiding and eventually closing down Military Intelligence, and putting him on trial on charges of corruption. He was sentenced to forty-four years in jail, later commuted to house arrest. Suu's interlocutor Brigadier Than Tun was even more harshly treated, sentenced to 130 years. While Khin Nyunt was released in 2012 and now runs a small Rangoon art gallery, Than Tun was not pardoned and freed until July 2015. The price for making peace with Than Shwe's mortal enemy was very high.

*

Despite meting out such fearsome punishment to his rival, Than Shwe recognised that the broad lines of Khin Nyunt's planned reforms were the right ones. He and his junta colleagues needed an exit strategy. Burma remained the sick man of Asia, the only South East Asian economy that had failed to prosper in the previous twenty years apart from, communist ruled Laos, dwarfed by its booming neighbour Thailand. Hamstrung by the West's sanctions, Burma was more and more dependent on investment by China – but with its long, porous border and overwhelming size, China was a problematic trading partner, as its increasing domination in the north, especially in Mandalay, made obvious: memories of the proxy war waged on the Burmese state via the communist party were still raw. At the same time Than Shwe and his senior colleagues were growing old: the senior general had turned seventy in 2003. How could they arrange things so they avoided suffering the fate they had meted out to their former boss, General Ne Win, who had died under house arrest, or their colleagues General Khin Nyunt, now detained at the regime's pleasure, or General Saw Maung, purged in 1992 after suffering a mental breakdown? How could Than Shwe organise a soft landing?

He turned reflexively to Thein Sein: the docile and loyal brigadier twelve years his junior who had ordered the carrying-out of atrocities in Kengtung, who had supervised the military budget as adjutant general in the War Office without allowing the money to stick to his fingers, and who, while lacking in brawn, was clearly more blessed with brains than most top soldiers. On Khin Nyunt's downfall Thein Sein was given the job of reconvening the National Convention, with the aim of rapidly arriving at a new constitution. By common consent the ingredient which had proved indigestible to Than Shwe – the involvement of That Woman and her party – was omitted entirely: Suu, back under house arrest on University Avenue, was to remain practically incommunicado for the next six years, visited only very occasionally by diplomats and a general called Aung Kyi, who had been given the job of liaising with her. Once in a while her senior party comrades would be allowed to visit. But of participation in the new constitutional arrangements, let alone sharing power with the generals, there was no more talk. She was increasingly forgotten by the world. In the world's eyes she became, in the phrase Justin Wintle used as the title of his biography of Suu, the 'perfect hostage'. Solitary suffering on the margins of the land she aspired to lead: that appeared to be her sad destiny.

With hindsight, however, we can only admire Thein Sein's subtlety. Unlike Khin Nyunt, who had treated Suu like a formidable adversary whose favour it was necessary to obtain lest she lash out, Thein Sein seems to have understood from the outset that the junta's position was far stronger. They could lock her up for ever if they chose, and she knew it. But if the regime could construct the rudiments of a parliamentary democracy, however stylised and stunted, Suu could not oppose it indefinitely without losing her credibility in the outside world. If the regime offered her the opportunity for which she had sacrificed her husband, her children, her happiness – the opportunity, however limited and hedged about with restrictions, to play a role in the moulding of her country's future – she could not resist it for long. And meanwhile the NLD's absence from the National Convention, which it had essentially shattered in the mid-1990s by calling attention to its formalistic, top-down character, would make its task much simpler.

Summoning delegations from the nation's ethnic nationalities, marshalling its deliberations with military discipline, within two years the National Convention under Thein Sein had achieved what it previously failed to do in twenty: drafted a new constitution. In 2007 he was appointed prime minister, climbed out of his khakis and into civilian clothes, and set about rebuilding Burma's reputation in Asia.

That year Burma was again in the headlines for all the wrong reasons when hundreds of thousands of protesters, with Buddhist monks in the lead, took to the nation's streets to protest the sudden removal of government fuel subsidies. The outside world called it the Saffron Revolution – the first Asian cousin of eastern Europe's 'colour' revolutions – and for a season it was on everybody's lips: Burma seemed on the point of recapturing its democratic destiny by mass peaceful action.

So many illusions, so many vain dreams: the junta knew well how to suppress revolts of this sort and did so in the old style, going in hard and shooting and beating enough demonstrators, monks or not, to scare the rest back into their homes. As senior general, Than Shwe took the international flak for the violent suppression of the uprising; for the devout

Burmese it was the last straw, and confirmed their conviction that he would burn in one of the terrible Buddhist hells. His regime's pathetic approach to the Cyclone Nargis disaster the following year, in which more than 130,000 people died, consolidated the view that this was a regime on its last legs, so consumed by paranoia, so obsessed with protecting its own privileges at whatever cost, that for many days it barred entry to international aid organisations, thus hugely increasing the number of fatalities.

Thein Sein's involvement in both these debacles – the murderous suppression of the Saffron Revolution and the failure to deal with Cyclone Nargis – was largely missed by critics. The prime minister's self-effacing style, his Zelig-like ability to appear invisible even when sitting at the top table, often helped him during these bumpy years. The cyclone coincided with the regime's attempt to secure popular approval of the new constitution: despite the suffering of millions in the Irrawaddy Delta rendered homeless by the disaster, the referendum went ahead as planned, to international consternation. The desired result was obtained. And again Thein Sein, the Teflon premier, somehow sailed through the controversy with his reputation undamaged.

*

Burma held its first general election since 1990 on 3 December 2010. Seven days later, in a cunning choreography of the news agenda – blotting out the bad feelings generated by this horrendously rigged election – the regime released Aung San Suu Kyi from house arrest, on schedule. And seven days after that, an obscure Tunisian university graduate turned itinerant fruit seller called Mohamed Bouazizi set fire to himself in the town of Ben Arous in an impulsive protest against official corruption, setting in train what quickly became known as the Arab Spring.

Burma's generals were always sensitive to events in the Middle East. Despite all the obvious differences of culture and religion, these various regimes had much in common. Their countries had been freed from the colonial yoke within living memory. The colonial elite had often been smoothly replaced by a national army which arrogated to itself many of the privileges the imperialists had enjoyed. Democratic protest was brutally dealt with. The economy, dominated by corrupt regime cronies, unable to nurture native entrepreneurship or attract foreign investment, remained stagnant. Civil society was equally stultified, unemployment ballooned. The educated young fled abroad. Those who remained at home seethed with anger and resentment.

Could the virus of Bouazizi's rebellion jump 4,000 miles from the shores of the Mediterranean to the Indian Ocean? The conditions in Burma seemed promising for another mass revolt. The Saffron Revolution had confirmed the regime's rigid and punitive attitude to dissent. More than 2,000 political prisoners remained in jail. Both the referendum and the election had been blatantly fixed, as most Burmese were well aware. Releasing Suu was like opening a safety valve – might it not lead to a repeat of the nationwide rebellion of 1988? For Burma's generals this was a moment of great peril.

In the Arab world events took their dramatic course. On 14 January 2011, mass protests overthrew the government of Tunisia and forced President Ben Ali to flee the country. Less than a month later, President Hosni Mubarak of Egypt resigned in the face of massive demonstrations and handed power to the army's Supreme Council. A few days later, demonstrations erupted in Benghazi against the Libyan regime of Muammar Gaddafi. In early March the prime minster of Egypt, Ahmed Shafik, followed his boss Mubarak into the political wilderness.

It was against this tumultuous backdrop that on 30 March 2011 Thein Sein, wearing a dazzling white silk *gaung baung* turban and with the sash of office across his shoulder, gave his inaugural speech as president of the Republic of the Union of Myanmar.

The speech got practically no attention in the international media: so little was expected of Burma's phony new democracy, given the flawed constitution, dubious referendum and outrageously fixed election. Thein Sein was nobody's idea of an inspirational leader. The Middle East's revolutions – at the time still inspiring brave democratic hopes both inside and outside the countries involved – were much more interesting. 'To many Burmese democrats,' the Euro-Burma Observer think tank commented, 'nothing U Thein Sein said made any difference since he is perceived to be the faithful servant and puppet of Senior-General Than Shwe, former head of the State Peace and Development Council (SPDC) and, as many believe, still the power behind the throne.'[18] Yet the speech he gave was remarkable and in some ways marked a clear break with the past.

The constitution, the writing of which Thein Sein had himself supervised, was now at the heart of the nation, he said.

'All the representatives,' he told the huge and gleaming new parliamentary chamber, 'including me are all duty-bound to honour and safeguard the constitution . . . I would like to call on you to cherish and protect at risk to life the constitution and the democratic nation to be built in line with [it].'[19] With these words Thein Sein drew a sharp line between the present and the past. 'It may be unremarkable for a leader in a Western democracy to make such statements,' commented the Euro-Burma think tank, 'but this is quite remarkable in the Burmese context because it is the norm to swear allegiance to the army . . . Allusion is also made to a democratic nation, which is an anathema to Tatmadaw doctrine.'[20]

In a few words the president then sketched Burma's nightmarish first sixty years of independence. 'In the post-independence period, national races [became] involved in armed conflicts . . . due to dogmatism, sectarian strife and racism instead of rebuilding the nation . . . the people were going through the hell of untold miseries.'[21] Thein Sein knew whereof he spoke, having been personally responsible for putting some of the people through just such a hell.

He then lavished praise on the Tatmadaw, which had reared and promoted and rewarded him from the years of his earliest youth. He went out of his way to cite its performance in 1988 as worthy of honour. Anyone hopeful that this man might be ushering in real change would be forgiven for switching off at this point.

Yet hints of new thinking broke through the military boiler-plate, like frail grass shoots squeezing through concrete. To hold the country together, he said, 'our country needs three types of might'. And the first of these was not, as one might expect, the army, but 'political might' – 'Political might means national unity.' And: 'National solidarity is very crucial to our country, home to over 100 national races. If national unity is disintegrated, the nation will split into pieces. Therefore we will give top priority to national unity.'[22]

Already what one might term the bi-polarism of this career soldier turned democrat was becoming apparent. In the constitution Thein Sein had fathered, peeling away from the Union is expressly forbidden. 'No part of the territory constituted in the Union', states Article 10, 'shall ever secede from the Union.' 'Non-disintegration of the Union' is the first clause of Article 6. That absolute veto implies that any attempt at secession – and the Karen people, to take a single example, had been struggling to secede even before Burma became independent – will be resisted by military force; such, indeed, was the country's bloody and hideous history. Yet what did Thein Sein mean by the term 'political might'?

'Lip services and talks are not enough,' he said, landing a direct hit on the turgid boosterism of the *New Light of Myanmar*, the regime newspaper. 'It is required to build roads, railroads and bridges to overcome the natural barriers . . . and to improve the education and health standards; to lay economic foundations to improve the socio-economic status of national races. We have to improve the living conditions for national brethren, using the roads, bridges, educational institutions, hospitals and health centres.' The more of these things were done, the 'friendlier relations will be among national races'.[23]

More clichés from the development manual for beginners – but revolutionary stuff coming from a senior Burmese general.

Education and health budgets had been systematically starved ever since Ne Win's coup of 1962. Universities in particular had borne the brunt of the army's anger: one of Ne Win's first acts after seizing power was to blow up the Rangoon University Students' Union, with an unknown number of people inside it. Now suddenly social spending, including spending on schools and universities, came into focus as an alternative way to get people to be nice.

Later he enlarged on the theme. It was no longer enough to have a bloated, entitled, omnipotent military sitting tight in their paranoid new capital. The Than Shwe model had to be superseded. The people had to be given their head. According to Thein Sein: 'We need more and more human resources of intellectuals and intelligentsia in building a modern, developed democratic nation . . . Therefore, we will promote the nation's education standard to meet the international level . . .' The lessons of Cyclone Nargis had also been learned, at least in theory. 'We will work in cooperation with international organisations including the UN, INGOs and NGOs.'[24]

Already the new president was stretching credibility. What he said next elicited cynical guffaws. 'To safeguard the fundamental rights of citizens in line with the provisions of the constitution is high on our government's list of priorities. We guarantee that all citizens will enjoy equal rights in terms of law . . . We will fight corruption in cooperation with the people . . . We will amend and revoke the existing laws and adopt new laws as necessary to implement the provisions on fundamental rights of citizens or human rights.'[25]

The judicial system was another of Burma's rotten foundations, the institutions in place at independence having been eaten away in the subsequent decades by the imperious and often corrupt demands of the military. I remember making friends with a lawyer from Arakan state who had fled to Manerplaw, the jungle camp near the Thai border occupied by rebels following the ignored election of 1990. 'People no longer chose a lawyer who knew the law, but a lawyer who knew a judge, or they went straight to the township councils, or delivered a petition direct to Ne Win,' he told me. 'There is no law in Burma now. We Rangoon lawyers are supermen: we practise law where there is no law.'[26] Now President Thein Sein was proposing to upend that situation, to repair it from the ground up.

His last remarks have a valedictory tone: bidding farewell to the old days and the old ways, while offering those who had been in charge all this time the honour and respect due to them from one of their own. It is in the nature of such tributes that charitable exaggeration plays a part. 'The State Peace and Development Council has built political, economic and social foundations necessary for future democracy,' he said. 'We sincerely thank all the people, all the Tatmadaw members and all the service personnel for achieving peace, stability and the rule of law and building development infrastructures instrumental to a democratic nation. I urge the Pyidaungsu Hluttaw' – the houses of Parliament – 'to put such endeavours on record.'[27]

Yet, as Thein Sein understood perfectly well, the work was only half done, and much of what had been done would have to be undone and redone. And this meant doing things very differently – reaching out the hand of friendship to those who, with his military cap on, he would gladly have slung into jail and thrown away the key. 'Regarding national reconsolidation,' he said, 'there are so many individuals and unlawful organisations inside and outside the nation that do not accept the State's seven-step road map and the constitution. They are all citizens of our country . . . It is still necessary to show our genuine goodwill towards those who have not accepted the constitution . . . in order that they can discard their suspicions and play a part in the nation-building tasks . . .'[28]

Furthermore, for those awkward customers that did not accept Thein Sein's handiwork – now welcomed into the brotherhood of the Union – 'the people have been vested with the right to amend the constitution in line with procedures.'[29] These 'procedures' are some of the toughest in the world. There were obvious things that some of the dissenters he referred to in his speech would object to. There was the notorious Article 59 (f), for example, requiring that any candidate for the post of president should not have a child who is a 'citizen of a foreign country'. This eliminated Aung San Suu Kyi from consideration, her sons having US and UK citizenship respectively.

But there were more fundamental problems. Three of the most important ministers – of the interior, defence and border affairs – were to be directly appointed by the army. There was a new, army-dominated body, the National Defence and Security Council (NDSC), successor to the army councils which had ruled Burma since 1989. The army would no longer rule, as the SLORC and the SPDC had ruled. In fact the new body's day-to-day duties were hazy. But it sat in the clouds above Parliament, with the right to close it down on a whim and rule by fiat: to declare an emergency, disband Parliament and rule directly – to return, in other words, to the tyrannical and arbitrary state of affairs that had been in place since the 1988 uprising. All that required was for the head of the army to deem it necessary.

All these and many other oppressive articles in the constitution were locked into place by the fact that this constitution was deliberately constructed so that it was fiendishly difficult to amend: a supermajority of more than three-quarters of representatives in both houses would be needed for any amendment to be passed. And that was almost impossible, because one quarter of all MPs were serving soldiers, who attended in uniform. Changing the constitution would require both the support of every single non-military member of the house and the willingness of at least a single soldier to break ranks. And in the unlikely event that enough soldiers could be persuaded to defy the wishes of their commanding officers and vote for constitutional change, it would then have to be put to a national referendum, in which more than half of eligible voters would have to vote for it.

All this sounds like a tall order. But what do the experts say? In 2013 a committee to review the constitution was established in Burma, and the London-based Bingham Centre for the Rule of Law participated in many workshops across the country to encourage debate. In January 2014 the Centre published a working paper on its findings.[30]

It reveals that the military's entrenched role in the constitution is unique in the world. 'In countries where democracy has been established for some time,' the paper noted, 'military presence in the legislature is unheard of

. . . In fact a number of constitutions explicitly prohibit the military undertaking a political role.'[31] Of the 189 constitutions studied for the paper, only Uganda's 'specifies the appointment of military personnel to parliament'. And Uganda's situation is not comparable to Burma's because the number of MPs specified, ten, 'does not afford sufficient power to veto constitutional amendments'.

The effect of the military's presence in Parliament was that the military appointees 'hold a practical power of veto over constitutional changes even where such changes are supported by every elected member of the Pyidaungsu Hluttaw (i.e. houses of Parliament).' And this defect was unique. 'No constitution in the world, other than Myanmar's, has an amendment procedure which requires approval by more than 75 per cent of members.'[32]

That was the package President Thein Sein offered to his people: a hand of welcome to dissidents, to the minority nationalities, to those who had fled abroad – and in principle also to those still locked up in prison for their beliefs. Welcome to democratic Burma, where the people have the constitutional right to amend the constitution they have voted into force. And so what if it's the toughest constitution in the world to amend? The Burmese have always enjoyed a challenge.

3

SNAPSHOTS OF FREEDOM

WHATEVER President Thein Sein's limitations and whatever crimes he may have committed as a serving army officer, his country owes him a huge debt of thanks because, in the space of a few months, between August 2011 and April 2012, he ended an era of toxic isolation, repression, surveillance and arbitrary imprisonment that had gone on for so long it had become normal, and seemed likely to endure for ever. It's hard to appreciate the drama of this transformation unless you had spent time in the country before.

For many poor Burmese, especially the tens of millions in the countryside, the difference may have been slight, perhaps too slight to notice. But in the city, among those with some education and a little knowledge of the outside world, the change was like moving from night to day.

A few years ago, a mobile phone, known locally as a 'hand phone', was an expensive status symbol. A Burmese friend of mine who helped me set up interviews and trips in the bad old days, a university graduate with fluent English who had travelled abroad, possessed one and kept it in a sheath on his belt. It was only of use to make calls. After reform of the telecoms market, within a few months every teenager in Rangoon had a cheap smartphone and spent hours on it, texting and sharing photos and Facebooking and tweeting, like every teenager in the world.

Bad old Burma was the strangest place in the world for money. It had two different exchange rates: an official rate of around 7 kyats to the US dollar, and an unofficial rate of about one hundred times that much. If you were mad enough to change your foreign cash at a bank, seven kyats is what you would get for your dollar. So instead you changed it at your hotel for the black rate, or on the street for even more. The dual exchange rate enabled the generals and their cronies to grow obscenely rich, buying at the official rate and selling at the black rate and making a profit of 10,000 per cent on every transaction. This is a major reason why the economy refused to grow, why over time this immensely well-endowed country became the poorest in South East Asia: no foreign businessman wanted to sink their money in a country where they were certain to be ripped off.

Abolishing this racket and establishing a single, realistic exchange rate, which he did in March 2012, was the single most important reforming measure Thein Sein took. Overnight Burma became almost normal.

In the old days tourists and other foreign visitors had to bring large quantities of cash into Burma because credit cards were not accepted. There were no ATMs, and only a handful of luxury hotels accepted cards, charging punitive fees for the privilege. Cash didn't mean any old cash: American greenbacks were the only foreign currency notes that worked. And not all of them: they had to be immaculately clean, fresh out of the mint – smelling of the printing press, ideally. Any folds or marks or stains and they would be handed back with a disdainful glare. In return for your crisp, starched, ironed, high-value notes, the hotel receptionist or tout on the street would hand over a fat bundle of dirty, disintegrating kyats. Burma's miserable self-esteem seemed epitomised in that transaction.

*

I worked in Burma numerous times during the dark ages, but 'work' is not exactly the word because it was practically impossible to work as journalists work in other countries. I ducked and dived and learned what I could from furtive conversations and masquerading as an ignorant tourist and simply from keeping my eyes open.

Burma did not want foreigners poking their noses into things. The rule of thumb was that visas were not issued to journalists. The last exception to this rule was in the run-up to the election of 1990. The new military regime, known as SLORC, was still feeling its repressive way and making hilarious blunders in the process, which included holding polls that were free and fair and allowing foreigners to observe them. In time they realised the error of their ways, deporting the journalists, even those with the right sort of visa, and ignoring the election result when it delivered a landslide win to their democratic enemies.

One would have thought that they would learn from such errors, but right up to the dying days of the Than Shwe dark age they were capable of amazing incompetence. One of the complications was caused by the fact that visas were issued by embassies, which were controlled by the Foreign Ministry, while the black list of those permanently barred entry was in the hands of the Interior Ministry. A further hiccup was caused by the abolition of Military Intelligence after the purging of its boss, General Khin Nyunt, and with it the loss of all the agency's secret files. They had to start building up information all over again.

The author and human rights activist Benedict Rogers was a victim of this incompetence. The author of an extremely hostile biography of Than Shwe, he had been deported from the country once already. The issue of a fresh visa some time later indicated that the regime had changed their mind about him. He flew into Rangoon, got through immigration, doubtless with the usual sweating and palpitations that we all felt during this nerve-wracking rite, collected his bags and was climbing into a taxi when a frantic immigration official came rushing out into the forecourt calling his name and practically yanked him out of the car. He had been admitted in error, and was sent back to Bangkok on the next flight.

If you managed to get in, the next question was: what now?

*

Careful preparation meant one came armed with a list of guest houses in central Rangoon that were, or at least so it was claimed, surveillance-free: where not every move and phone call would be bugged and passed on to the Special Branch or the immigration police. Was this reliable? I think it was based on guesswork. Spies were everywhere. Burma, which had suffered greatly when it was occupied by the Japanese during the Second World War, had also learned from and adopted the micro-surveillance techniques developed by the Japanese and applied during the war years across South East Asia. This meant that every courtyard, every subdivision of every ward, every street and market and taxi rank had its paid informant: not a secret spy but a known funnel of information to the next level up.

Every step of the way you were under close watch. That was the feeling, and I'm sure it was true. Outside the airport, a woman with the state tourism agency would assign you a guest house. That meant it was certain to be bugged. But to ignore the advice and set off alone would immediately arouse suspicion. And anyway it could be assumed that taxi drivers were all spies, even if they spouted anti-regime slander along the way. And then inside the guest house: would it be wise to call contacts, carefully set up in advance, from the house phone? And if not, from where, given the absence of public phone boxes and the paucity of public call offices, where in any case there were always people lurking around and listening in?

Gradually, over a number of visits, you could build up a little tradecraft. The Internet was fantastically slow and unreliable pre-Thein Sein, but little Internet dens did exist all over downtown Rangoon, each presumably with its quota of spies. Many ordinary Burmese used them freely, and, in a country where other media were strictly controlled, the Internet became the major conduit of information about the outside world. I remember sitting next to a mother with two small children carrying on a long Skype call with her husband who was working in Thailand. But she was not at risk of deportation for activities incompatible with a visa, so she could afford to be relaxed. Gmail was for a long time the only mail-server that worked, and I used multiple accounts in fanciful names and never visited the same Internet cafe twice. I set up face-to-face meetings with local informants by means of brief, cryptic phone calls, arranging rendezvous in the depths of empty cafes, painfully aware that, while I risked expulsion, my Burmese contacts could end up being thrown in jail for years.

Then – because after all I am a journalist not a trained spy – I would drop my guard and make a mistake and something strange would occur that would force me to raise it again. Once from my hotel room I got lazy and used the house phone to telephone a senior member of the NLD to try to arrange an interview. He answered in person – he seemed panicked to hear a foreign voice – and said, no, it would not be possible. End of story – except that, the next time I went to order a cab at the front desk, instead of the usual beaten-up Datsun with collapsing springs and a door that didn't shut properly, a gleaming black Mercedes rolled up to collect me. Yes, this is your car. There were crossed Burmese flags on the dashboard. Where do you want to go? I told him. He took me there. How much is that? No payment required – do you want me to wait? I told him it would not be necessary. It was the subtlest, creepiest of warnings.

Then Thein Sein became president and over the course of the next year everything changed. In March 2011, the month he became president, the entrance to the head office of the NLD was still ringed by regime spooks who photographed every foreigner who went in and out. That had been the practice for years. Sometimes – it never happened to me – the foreigner would get back into their taxi and find they were being tailed on motorbikes. One undercover journalist recounts being driven all over town at top speed by her cabbie as he tried to shake them off.

When I next visited the office, some months after the reform process got under way, the sinister reception committee was no more. The spies had simply melted away, replaced by stalls selling Aung San Suu Kyi T-shirts.

Suddenly Suu was everywhere. It was like those old weather clocks: the rain man goes in, the sun comes out. For twenty years she was a rumour rather than a real person: in those years only a single grainy newspaper photograph of her was published when, in 1995, the generals took it into their heads to invite her to a vapid, content-free summit. She was a secret that people shared but could never mention, and so rarely seen that she was like Sleeping Beauty or the Fairy Queen, an object of love and longing that owed more to the realm of myth than to grimy everyday life. I remember visiting the home of dissidents in Mandalay. They kept a painted portrait of Suu upstairs in the kitchen, at the back of the house where outsiders did not penetrate.

Then Thein Sein met her in Naypyidaw and their joint photograph was published at home and abroad, and along with other relaxations came word that the Lady could now be brought out of the closet. And suddenly her beautiful, feminine features, only very slightly aged in twenty-five years as if there were indeed something genuinely magical and otherworldly about her, were on every magazine cover. Local journalists lined up to interview her, editors competed to publish the most charming photographs. Book publishers raced to bring out trashy cut-and-paste biographies. My own book about her began to circulate in pirated form.

It was a shift from Burmese exceptionalism to normality. In almost all countries it is normal to use ATMs to get your money, for a currency to have a single exchange rate, to choose your hotel without fear of having your movements logged, to telephone friends without having to worry if you will be deported or they will be jailed. Thein Sein ironed out all the weirdness that had marked Burma as strange and different for fifty years. And it began to assume the lineaments of any other, impoverished, messy, devout, Asian country.

Now when I go to report from Burma I email my trusty fixer, agree on dates and a rough plan of action, meet him in the lobby of a Rangoon hotel and go to work. On the last two occasions I was formally invited by the Ministry of Information, and issued with a business visa. The spooks are still around, but they don't get in the way. After a bout of anti-Muslim bloodshed in the central town of Meiktila, we went looking for people whose homes had been burned down and who were staying temporarily in camps. We found some and interviewed them. Four or five men in smart longyis stood around listening. 'They are Special Branch,' my fixer told me. 'What do they want?' I asked him. 'Nothing. But they don't have any other work.'

My trusty fixer: that's new, too. In the bad old days, foreign snoopers like me were toxic. The only people who were at least in theory in a position to help us were licensed tour guides: university graduates from elite families who enjoyed the rare privilege of travelling and perhaps even studying abroad, and who spoke English as proficiently as their parents and grandparents, brought up under British rule, and who passed the required exams. Only they had the opportunity of mixing with foreigners: but as a result they were even more spied upon, and consequently paranoid, than Burmese less exposed to suspicion. And as a result they were effectively useless as fixers.

It wasn't always like that. In 1991, when Burma was still throbbing with anger at the theft of the general election one year before, guides could be cavalier about such risks. This was the year of my first visit, when the only way to see the country as a tourist, with a one-week, single-entry visa, was to join an official guided tour. A trip took us to the ancient city of Pagan on the banks of the Irrawaddy River, whose thousands of temples, built between the ninth and thirteenth centuries, constitute Burma's most spectacular historical site. On the way there our guide told us bitterly that we would not see much of the everyday life of the city because its population had been forcibly removed to make way for new hotels. I took the opportunity of a break to tell her that I was an undercover journalist: where could I find this decanted population? With no fuss she arranged for me to be met after dark at my hotel by a man with two bicycles; together we rode through winding, rutted lanes to the huddle of huts which was the new downtown for the lacquerware makers of old Pagan.

But years of repression, summary trial and long prison terms had put the guides in their place. Bennie (as he asked me to call him), who I finally plucked up the courage to telephone from my guest house, was a portly young man in a dark longyi who spoke English with an old-fashioned Tory drawl. I suggested we go somewhere to talk, so he took me to a scruffy tea shop, the sort of place where Burmese men spend many hours every day gossiping and philosophising over small cups of strong tea thickened with condensed milk, accompanied by glasses of green tea, provided free. The 1988 democracy uprising broke out in such a tea shop, from a dispute about the records playing on the jukebox. Here, I fancied, we could talk freely, if quietly, and lay out our plans. But Bennie, who was funny and nice and is still a friend, went completely blank when I tried to draw him out about dissidents, rebels, anti-government plotters – anything like that. He was happy to talk about himself: his frustration at giving up a promising academic career, his guilt about drinking beer when as a good Buddhist he should have renounced it, his scorn for many of his clients, his boredom with the job. I felt I was listening in to a conversation he was having with himself. Asked about the regime and its policies he looked blank and fell silent. The only contact he was able to offer me was to meet another tour guide, in Mandalay.

By this time – 2008, seventeen years after my first visit, one year after the Saffron Revolution – state repression had penetrated deeply into the brains of the intellectuals of Bennie's generation. The terror tactics of authoritarian regimes everywhere – imposing mental uniformity through surveillance, summary trial and harsh imprisonment – had done their brutal work. You could leave, and many thousands of Burma's brightest did so, and stayed away indefinitely, often barred from coming back. But if you stayed, like Bennie, you battened down the mental hatches.

But by now, in the early years of the century, a new generation was coming up, twenty years younger than Bennie, who was in his late-thirties when we met. Burma, however fierce and long-lasting the regime's repression, however tight their ship, was springing leaks and beginning to take on water. As in the Middle East and all across the developing world it was down to the Internet, which sprang up wherever a computer and a signal could be put together. It had the effect, in a state run like a prison camp, of boring many small tunnels to the outside world. It was like introducing a thin stream of oxygen into a dungeon where those imprisoned are on the verge of dying from suffocation. In a word, it was life-giving. Witness the teenagers crammed into every Internet cafe in Rangoon, where for a few kyats, with the patience and ingenuity of starving people who had stumbled on something they could eat, they sat out the electricity blackouts, waited hours for some kind of a signal, however feeble, to be restored, then once it had come back they wormed their way through all the obstacles set in place by the regime until they connected with the outside world.

Young people were desperate to connect. And this desperation, this sense that connection was possible, gave them the courage that Bennie's generation, those that remained at home, so palpably lacked. Fifteen and more years before, young people who could no longer bear to live in Burma, either because they risked jail or had already spent time in jail or because they could not tolerate the intellectual stultification, went away: across the border to Thailand, to India, to the United States and Australia or Britain and Norway.

Like Win Tin in the 1950s with his Burmese script typewriter and his Cyclostyled newsletters, some of them decided to bring news of the outside world – also news of Burma which the authorities did not want known – to their

81

fellow countrymen. The results of this urge included the Irrawaddy, a news website edited in Chiang Mai, and the Democratic Voice of Burma, a multi-media operation based in Oslo, which had a magazine and an online presence and eventually a satellite television station that broadcast into Burma. It was on DVB's satellite channel that I followed, from Mae Sot in Thailand, the scenes at University Avenue in 2010 when Aung San Suu Kyi was released from detention.

Fired by their determination to connect, the kids of Rangoon and Mandalay made Internet contact with the older generation based abroad. The editors at the Democratic Voice of Burma knew what was missing from their coverage: reports from inside Burma that showed what was really going on. The tiny new video cameras on the market made it possible with practice to shoot news practically unseen. Burma was an unreported land at this point, as it had been for most of the preceding half-century. The would-be video journalists flew to Bangkok and were trained to use the tiny cameras, which they then smuggled in and went to work. They filmed family and friends, simple, innocuous footage, then spread their wings, making short, surreptitious films about land confiscation, forced labour, beggars, official bullying. These early ventures were to get their hands in, not for broadcasting, which would mean instant arrest, repression, probably jail, but merely to learn what doing this kind of work involved.

So when in September 2007, following scattered protests about the sudden removal of fuel subsidies, angry Burmese took to the streets, the young video journalists were ready to record the unfolding events. Buddhist monks, who depended for their daily bread on the generosity of ordinary householders, were keenly affected by soaring fuel prices, and in the town of Pakokku joined in the protests. Police beat some of them up and tied them to trees as punishment. The monks demanded an apology – assaulting monks is a serious matter in this devout country. No apology was given, so the monks, too, returned to the streets in their maroon robes and bare feet in larger numbers, and the numbers swelled day by day until these armies of austere, shaven-headed figures were moving down the main streets of every town and city in the country.

It made incredible television – but there was no television. There were no accredited foreign journalists in the country, and state television was very busy looking the other away: to judge by the regime's media, these events were not even happening. But the Democratic Voice of Burma's video journalists were ready and waiting. With awesome courage they shot the whole thing, and uploaded it to DVB in Thailand, from where it made its way to CNN, the BBC and everybody else. And then, bizarrely enough – the regimented military system was already cracking up in unpredictable ways – the footage was beamed back into Burma: I covered the uprising for my newspaper from the extreme south of the country, the town of Kaw Taung, and I was able to watch extended reports of the protests on CNN, at a local open-air tea house.

Some of the video journalists suffered drastic punishment for their boldness, sentenced to dozens of years in jail. But those who escaped the net were not deterred. The following year, in 2008, when Cyclone Nargis tore apart the Irrawaddy Delta and the regime responded by sitting on their hands, thousands of ordinary Burmese raised funds and bought essentials and packed them into small boats and delivered them to the cyclone's victims down in the Delta. And the video journalists went with them, recording the whole way, providing the outside world with vivid images of the conditions of those who had lost everything, and of a military regime indifferent to their suffering.

My brilliant assistant Han Thar was one of many young Burmese reporters inspired by this unusual and testing school of journalism. And when, in late 2011, President Thein Sein removed the necessity to have all material cleared by the censorship board before publication, and started issuing foreign journalists with visas, he and his colleagues were ready.

*

The president's meeting with Aung San Suu Kyi on 19 August 2011 appeared to be a run-of-the-mill Burmese regime media stunt, very much like the meeting she was summoned to by Than Shwe and Khin Nyunt in 1995. No context was provided: it dropped from the sky like some enigmatic extraterrestrial object, exciting the wonderment and puzzlement of observers. Was this the beginning of something or the end of something? Or the middle? Had it, as Hillary Clinton claimed in her book *Hard Choices*, been preceded by other cosy 'at homes' with the actual First Lady cooking dinner for the unofficial First Lady while the president looks benignly on? (Answer: yes, at least one.[1]) Or was it a one-off, with no meaning beyond its power to startle and bemuse? Five weeks later, the question of

84

what the meeting meant received a startling and unequivocal answer.

*

Topographically speaking, Burma climbs smoothly up from the sea-level paddies of the Irrawaddy Delta via the hot scrubland of the central regions to the rugged mountains of Kachin state in the north, and so on up to the Himalayas, from where, with their Tibetan blood and Tibetan-related language, the Burman race is believed to have arrived.

Like the people in Burma's other borderlands, the Kachin have, for many of the years since independence, been fighting for their autonomy and against attempts by the government to Burmanise their distinctive culture. The struggle began after Ne Win's coup d'état of 1962, which prompted the creation of the Kachin Independence Army. Guerrilla warfare persisted until a ceasefire negotiated by Khin Nyunt in 1994.

But Kachin's semi-independent condition, its prosperity dependent on the smuggling of jade and drugs across its long border with China, was an offence to the patriotic imperatives of Burma's new, notionally civilian president, for whom the first commandment was, 'Thou shalt not secede.' Kachin state had gone too far along the primrose path to secession for the Burmese army's liking, and in June 2011, less than three months after President Thein Sein's inauguration, the conflict erupted again when Burmese forces attacked Kachin fighters, breaking the ceasefire. This is the bare background to understanding the first declaration by Thein Sein that really made the outside world sit up and take notice.

One of the central grievances in the re-ignited war between the Kachin and the Burmese state was a joint Burma–China project to build a huge dam called the Myitsone Dam at the headwaters of the Irrawaddy River, 500 feet high, creating a vast, 300-square-mile reservoir which would displace thousands of Kachin villagers.

There were a number of problems with this project. One of them, the most obvious to the Kachin, was its imposition by the hated Burmese state, at the expense of impoverished Kachin farmers: yet another example of how remote Naypyidaw was from the concerns of people on the borders. Anger at the project had produced a robust campaign to halt its construction.

But the dam was a problem for many other Burmese, too. Financed and promoted by China, it was a glaring example of the increasingly lopsided relationship between the newly affluent, expansive and resource-hungry Central Kingdom next door and its poor, much put-upon, one-time tributary state, Burma. The impetus, the capital, the engineering knowhow and most of the workforce for the dam were Chinese. The scale of the thing, too, was stereotypically Chinese: it would not be, as the BBC claimed, 'one of the world's tallest dams' – there are more than forty taller ones, half of them Chinese – but it was vast: it was a glaring and humiliating example of the way the heavy-handed, top-down Chinese model of development was being imposed on Burma, which, with large-scale corruption and (thanks to sanctions) the economy's disproportionate dependence on trade with China, seemed to have lost all ability to resist Beijing's will. The proof of that one-sidedness was the fact that practically all the electricity generated by the dam was earmarked for China – despite the fact that most parts of Burma were supplied with electricity for only a few hours every day.

Myitsone, in other words, was a project that could only have been promoted by an oligarchic government in hock to its powerful neighbour and with the barest concern for the needs of the ordinary people. And there was one more thing: the Irrawaddy, which carves a broad swathe from the far north of the country to the south, is as much a symbol of Burmese nationhood as the Mekong is for Vietnam and the Ganges for India.

All these factors had contributed to making opposition to the dam a national issue. Aung San Suu Kyi, in one of her first political declarations since her release from detention ten months before, had written an 'Irrawaddy Appeal', for inclusion in a book on the river to be published by the NLD, urging the government to reconsider the project. Perhaps it was this that decided things: at this delicate juncture, a new mass protest movement with Suu as its figurehead was the last thing Thein Sein needed to crown the first year of his presidency.[2]

We can only guess which of these many considerations weighed most heavily: the shift from out-and-out military rule to notional democracy has done little to remove the dense curtain of secrecy behind which Burma's rulers take their decisions. But at the end of September 2011, a letter from the president was read out in Parliament making his position on the issue clear: the dam's construction was to be frozen.

'We have a responsibility to solve the worries of the people, so we will stop construction of the Myitsone Dam during our current government,' the letter ran. 'As our government is elected by the people, we have to respect the will of the people.'[3]

It was the first sign that the ringing phrases in Thein Sein's inaugural speech – all that stuff about 'equal rights in terms of law' and the 'fundamental rights of citizens', which upon delivery back in March had sunk like a stone in the stagnant waters of apathy and disbelief – might actually mean something. It was the first step along a new road.

And it was just the beginning. Over the next four months, as Thein Sein signed off one reform after another, Burma's image in the outside world underwent drastic renewal. At this point the nation's image was about as bad as it could be. And wrapped up in this reputation of badness was the well-founded belief that nothing would ever really change; the conviction that repressive stasis was all that the generals, whether in or out of trousers, could or ever would deliver. So Thein Sein – a military man to his fingertips – had the advantage of surprise. And he set about delivering one ambush after another.

In September the creation of a National Human Rights Commission was announced. The ban on access to foreign news websites such as the BBC and the Voice of America was lifted. Internet bans on many other sites were lifted, too. The main subjects still restricted were confined to national security, alcohol and drugs, and practically anything relating to sex.

And then there were the traditional media. Until Thein Sein's inauguration, every article intended for publication in every newspaper and magazine in the country – and there were many hundreds – had to be cleared by the Ministry of Information's Press Scrutiny and Registration Division in advance. Already this laborious process had been relaxed, allowing magazines whose content was obviously innocuous to censor themselves. This relaxation continued in phases, until in August 2012 it was lifted entirely.

In October 2011, one of the opposition's main grievances was partially met when more than two hundred political prisoners were released. They included Zarganar ('Tweezers'), one of the country's most popular comedians, who had been given a fifty-nine-year jail sentence in 2008 after criticising the junta's response to Cyclone Nargis. And in the same week, trade unions were legalised for the first time since 1962. The legislation to do so was drafted following discussions with the International Labour Organisation – almost as dramatic an initiative as the law itself, given Burma's longstanding allergy to involving foreigners, Westerners in particular, in its affairs. The NLD pronounced itself 'satisfied' with the legalisation, because labour rights had 'improved from nothing to something'.

In December 2011, peaceful anti-government protests were legalised. The following month, a ceasefire was signed in Shan state, where Thein Sein had been a commander in the 1990s. In January, many of Burma's most famous political prisoners were released, including Min Ko Naing, 'conqueror of kings', the charismatic leader of the 1988 uprising, and many of his comrades. And in the same month, the government also signed its first-ever ceasefire with the rebels of Karen state, who had been fighting for autonomy for more than sixty years.

The reaction of the outside world to this cascade of unexpected good news was stupefaction and disbelief, rapidly followed by loud applause, a standing ovation, and the granting of a number of the most important things the president had been angling for. In October, the UN's point man in Burma, Tomás Ojea Quintana, described the release of Zarganar and other political prisoners as 'an important further step by the authorities in Myanmar to respond to international concern and advance political reconciliation in the country'.

In November, ASEAN, the Association of Southeast Asian Nations, gave Thein Sein a major international boost, announcing that Burma would be given the rotating chair of the body in 2014, two years ahead of schedule. Then, on 1 December 2011, Thein Sein hooked the big one. Hillary Clinton came to call.

4
THE CLINTON CLINCH

THEY were both wearing white. It was one of the colours, along with black and red, that the Secretary of State had specifically been advised not to wear, in the department's briefing on cultural norms. Hillary chose to give that the go-by. And then Aung San Suu Kyi shows up in white, too. Everyone laughed. The ice was broken.

That first meeting was in the home of the American chargé d'affaires on Inya Lake in Rangoon, which has been the playground of choice for Burma's ruling elite for a long time. The lake is near the broad meandering boulevard that takes the visitor from the international airport down into the city, but it is far enough away and at a sufficient altitude that the air is sweet and the city noise muted. Once upon a time there were plentiful fish and birdlife in and around the lake but poverty and hunger brought that to an end years ago. Following the murder of her famous father, the government provided Suu Kyi's family with a large detached ex-colonial house on the lake. That house, at 54 University Avenue, became Suu's childhood home, then her home again on her return to Burma in 1988, and after her house arrest in 1989 it became her prison.

General Ne Win had a home on the lake, too, and like Suu he had also been locked up in it, and had died in detention there in 2004. So the mood around Inya Lake's glassy waters is suffused with what has been and what might have been, with the crimes and the sufferings of the people who aspired to lead the country. During Suu's years in detention, young people would gather on the opposite shore, from where her crumbling cream stuccoed villa is visible far away, and play guitar and sing songs or just hold hands and look over to where she lived out those years of solitude. 'Dukkha, 'suffering' in the ancient Pali language, its causes and its relief, are the insights at the heart of Buddhism. 'Dukkha!' Burmese exclaim when they hurt themselves or when something goes wrong. The air of Inya Lake is full of dukkha.

But not only dukkha. The 'lovely old colonial home' – Hillary's words – where the two women met had been the residence of the American ambassador to Burma, when Burma rated an ambassador; and Hillary Clinton's presence here, on the first visit by an American Secretary of State since John Foster Dulles in 1955, was an augury of what might be, if this and other meetings went well.

On the evening of 1 December 2011 Suu was driven the short distance around the lake to meet the Secretary of State. There to greet her were Kurt Campbell, the head of East Asian Affairs at the State Department, and Derek Mitchell, also an Asian specialist, who would go on to become America's first Burma ambassador in many years. Dr Campbell, a stocky, irreverent, pugilistic academic, the sort of straight-talking, no-nonsense diplomat that only the United States seems able to produce, had met Suu twice in 2010 while she was still in detention. The meetings took place at a government guest house; at their first encounter they had retreated to the garden to avoid having their conversation recorded. The photograph of them talking intensely under umbrellas went around the world. At the end of his trip, Dr Campbell had released a highly undiplomatic verdict on the regime's preparations for the election, declaring 'our profound disappointment in what we have witnessed to date'.[1]

Much had changed since then: enough to make Hillary Clinton's visit thinkable. Now Suu was free, and had established a working relationship with President Thein Sein, who had enacted one reform after another with military despatch, and now she was face to face with a woman whose career resonated with her own. There was the campaigning activism of the political idealist; the thrusting, charismatic male – Hillary's husband, Suu's father – from whose shadow one must eventually emerge, and trust to one's own intelligence and determination; the frustrations and reversals along the way. One of these women had already tried and failed to become her nation's head of state and was now its most senior diplomat; the other was a Nobel Peace Prize laureate and a living legend. Which was more in awe of the other? We only have Hillary's account of the meeting – cryptic and sketchy – but both must have realised at the time that it was the stuff of history.

'The first time I met Aung San Suu Kyi . . . we were both wearing white,' Clinton wrote in her memoir, *Hard Choices*. 'It seemed like an auspicious coincidence. After so many years of reading and thinking about this celebrated Burmese dissident, we were finally face-to-face . . . We sat down for a private dinner on the terrace of the chief US diplomat's residence in Rangoon . . . a lovely old colonial home on Inya Lake. I felt as if we had known each other for a lifetime, even though we had just met . . . soon we were chatting, strategising and laughing like old friends.'[2] They talked – Suu, a lifelong vegetarian and teetotaller, doubtless merely nibbling at what was offered in her usual fashion – for two hours. And by the end of the dinner, Suu had confided to Hillary her intentions, about which up to this point the world had been in the dark.

Suu told Hillary that she no longer wanted to be an icon: she wanted to be a politician. 'Suu Kyi told me that she herself would run for Parliament,' Clinton wrote.[3] Suu's only previous experience of an electoral battle had been somewhere between the farcical and the tragic: herself locked in her home, permitted to vote from there in advance of election day, her party forbidden to campaign but winning a landslide victory anyway, one which the paranoid generals then merely ignored. This time around, by contrast, it would be the real thing, more or less. 'After so many years of enforced solitude, it was a daunting prospect,' Hillary wrote.[4]

Hillary told Suu about her own first election. Then Suu explained how, despite the years of detention, she still had a sense of connection to the generals who had imprisoned her, on account of her father and her childhood among kindly, affectionate soldiers. 'We can do business with them, she said confidently . . . She was determined to change her country, and after decades of waiting, she was ready to compromise, cajole, and make common cause with her old adversaries.'[5]

Suu did not fool herself that she was ready for the fray. 'She asked me many questions about the preparation and process of becoming a candidate,'[6] Clinton wrote. And the American warned her what would happen. 'Get ready to be attacked,' she told her.[7] It is a theme – the serene certainties of the activist versus the obligatory pragmatism required by the practical politician – that Clinton has returned to several times since then. 'Aung San Suu Kyi, like Nelson Mandela, would have been remembered in history for ever if she had not made the decision to enter politics,' she told the Women in the World conference in New York three months later. 'She knows that when she crosses into politics, even though it is ultimately the way change is made that can last, she moves from being an icon to a politician. I know that route. And I know how hard it is to be able to balance one's ideals, one's aspirations, with the give and take of any political process anywhere in the world.'[8]

It was, therefore, an important conversation for both women, but especially for Suu. And yet, despite Hillary Clinton's hints about what passed between them, a nagging question remains.

Five months before, answering questions after her first Reith Lecture, which Suu had delivered to BBC cameras at her home and which had been broadcast live in London, she had addressed the question of why her party had refused to participate in the general election of November 2010, immediately before her release from house arrest. There were three reasons, she said.

> The first was that if you were to contest the elections, you have to sign an undertaking to protect the 2008 constitution. Now this constitution gives the army a right to take over all powers of government whenever they feel it's necessary. Secondly, we couldn't accept the condition that we would have to expel all members of our party who were in prison. And thirdly, we would have to wipe the 1990 elections off the political map of Burma. That also we were unprepared to do.[9]

In the months between delivering that lecture and dining with Hillary Clinton, Suu had met and established working relations with President Thein Sein. Political prisoners had been released. Censorship had been eased. But the question of the 1990 election, and the NLD's triumph at it, had sunk without trace; no one mentioned it any more. And, far more significantly, the constitution of 2008, which vested ultimate power with the military, was unchanged. Yet that same constitution was now no longer a problem for Suu: she had decided – on the basis, it is said, of an ad hoc agreement reached with Thein Sein at their meeting in August – to enter politics through the front door. And there is nothing in the record to indicate that Secretary of State Clinton warned her about this; warned her that, thanks to the constitution, she might be entering a blind alley.

Because at that point the stakes for the United States were far greater than one dissident heroine's political career. The Obama 'pivot to Asia', which was becoming a media catchphrase, now focused on normalising relations with Myanmar as fast and as smoothly as possible. And if Suu saw her future course as passing through Parliament – if this was her price for consenting to the normalisation process – there was nothing to be gained from warning her that she could be making a mistake.

Suu was discovering the delicious yet ultimately treacherous sensation of being love-bombed by a powerful American. Over dinner, Hillary told her, 'You have been an inspiration . . . You are standing for all the people of your country who deserve the same rights and freedoms of [sic] people everywhere.' The Secretary promised her new best friend that the United States 'would be a friend to the people of Burma as they made their historic journey to a better future'.[10]

But as well as being an inspiration, Suu was suddenly part of a large and complex machine, powering the boldest new direction in American foreign policy in a generation. She could either be a small cog in that machine, or she could be a spanner, to stop it working. She decided in haste to become a cog; she would have all the leisure in the world to repent.

*

Asia is the past America cannot forget, and the tantalising future it turns to when the rest of the planet looks forbidding. And in December 2011 the biggest obstacle to America fulfilling its Asian destiny took the shape of the nation of Burma.

It was Pearl Harbor that dragged the United States into the Second World War. Europeans may remember Monte Cassino, the Gothic Line, the GIs who were 'over-paid, over-sexed and over here', D-Day and the Marshall Plan. But etched more deeply in the American psyche are Iwo Jima, Saipan and the other terrible battles for the Pacific. It was the crushing of Japan that put the seal on American post-war pre-eminence. Never did America play the imperialist with more impressive Yankee swagger than when General Douglas MacArthur towered over Emperor Hirohito – he had just stripped him of his divinity – amid the ruins of post-war Tokyo. Korea by contrast was no more than half a success story, thanks to the intervention of China; Vietnam a long, cruel debacle to be dropped into the memory hole. Japan, recovering at blinding speed under the American nuclear umbrella, stole march after march on its enemy turned protector turned commercial rival: transistors, motorbikes, cars: 'Japan as Number One' was the bogey of the 1980s. And then on Japan's coat-tails came rising China – ten times bigger, and possibly just as clever; a country with which the United States had had only hostile relations since the Communist victory in 1949.

But one American president and his intrepid envoy had shown a way forward with China, and in the most unpromising circumstances: not with weight of firepower and Cold War menaces but with deep historical knowledge, an open mind and a keen eye for the way the world's power balances were shifting.

Kissinger and Nixon's diplomacy with Mao was the single most remarkable initiative in America's foreign relations since the war, but now it was forty years in the past. In those decades, and with increasing momentum since the first Gulf War, the Middle East and its woes had begun to box America in. The end of the Cold War, despite the first President Bush's hubristic declaration of 'a new world order', only aggravated that tendency: the bitter and apparently unappeasable enmities of Iran, Iraq, Saudi Arabia and Israel, in a context of abundant oil and religious fundamentalism, were the explosive materials that constrained and defined the ambitions and obsessions of the remaining superpower. And the twin debacles of Iraq and Afghanistan, each in their way unpleasantly reminiscent of the Vietnam quagmire, intimated that America was going nowhere fast.

For the newly elected President Obama, born in Hawaii, partly raised in Indonesia and a declared opponent of the

Iraq War, this was unacceptable. Hillary Clinton felt no less strongly about it. Freshly appointed Secretary of State, in February 2009 she mulled over where to make her highly symbolic maiden overseas trip. To Mexico, like Colin Powell? To the Middle East, into which billions had been poured, most of it in military materiel, since the 9/11 attacks? To the NATO allies, traditional bedrock of American diplomacy?

Clinton decided instead to go to Asia. She and her team would visit America's treaty partners, Japan, South Korea, the Philippines, Thailand and Australia and reassure them that, as she put it, 'America was back'.[11] They would make initial approaches to China: its economy storming ahead at a rate of 8 per cent or more a year; after what Chinese called the 'century of humiliation', the 'Middle Kingdom' was entering a phase of stunning growth similar to that of Japan in the 1960s and 1970s, and rediscovering its central place in the Asian neighbourhood. And they would also 'reach out to Indonesia,' as Clinton put it. 'After a decade of focusing on the areas of greatest threat, we had come to a "pivot point",' she later wrote, using the word that Obama had introduced into the discussion. '. . . It was . . . time to do more in the areas of greatest opportunity.'[12]

Indonesia was intriguing in many respects. With a population of more than 250 million, it was a rapidly growing regional power. It was the biggest Muslim majority nation in the world, yet held fast to the basic principle of the Non-Aligned Movement, keeping out of exclusive alliances and maintaining functional relationships with countries as diverse as Saudi Arabia, Russia, China and Japan as well as the United States. Indonesia was also the home of the Association of Southeast Asian Nations (ASEAN), and the dominant voice in that organisation, which includes the communist states (and historic American enemies) Vietnam, Laos and Cambodia as well as the economic powerhouses of Malaysia, Singapore and Indonesia itself.

These were all countries with which the United States could hope to improve relations and thereby improve trade. And the growing power and ambition of China made those American aims of far greater interest than before to the ASEAN nations themselves.

As much the largest country bestriding East and South East Asia, China had for millennia been the hegemonic power, expecting and if necessary demanding tribute from the petty countries clustered in its skirts. Those that disdained such a lopsided relationship – Japan in particular – removed themselves from China's orbit altogether. Because relations with China could never be anything but lopsided. And now that the dogma and hysteria of Mao's Great Leap Forward and Cultural Revolution had been swallowed up by the hard-headed, market-oriented, pseudo-capitalist common sense promulgated by Deng Xiaoping, China was throwing an ever larger and more menacing shadow over its ancestral neighbourhood. Some countervailing influence in the form of that other Asian power, the one across the water, the one with much the world's biggest defence capability and navy, would be much more welcome to the nations of South East Asia than it had been in the recent past. In the achievement of that aim, Burma was a small but glaring problem.

The nature of the Burma problem is reflected in the bruising experience of a man called Susilo Bambang

Yudhoyono, better known in Indonesia simply as SBY. Today he is Indonesia's elder statesman, after two terms as head of state during which he did more than any other individual to put Indonesian democracy on a solid footing. But for the first half of his adult life he was a career soldier, removing his lieutenant-general's uniform finally in 1999. He was then appointed the government's Energy Minister, and five years later, in 2004, won the presidential election.

Like Burma, Indonesia had been under the military's thumb for most of the years since independence, but SBY believed that those days were over. 'Since 1998, the military has decided to stay out of day-to-day politics,' he said in 2000. 'The basic idea of military reform is to go back to the role and function of the military as a defence force and move them away from politics systematically. [There will be no] so-called dual function of the military . . . no so-called social function in the military.'[13]

By 2004, Burma was groping in the same direction. General Khin Nyunt, the nice guy, relatively speaking, in the ruling triumvirate, had the previous year announced the now-famous 'road map', intended to culminate in 'discipline-flourishing democracy'. It was logical to suppose that this would involve the all-powerful Tatmadaw stepping aside, or at least mutating into civilians. It was equally logical to suppose that Senior General Than Shwe, the primus inter pares of the triumvirate, was signed up to this programme.

It was with such reasonable thoughts as these that the new Indonesian president came to call on Than Shwe – effectively his Burmese counterpart – in March 2005. He must have imagined he could give the generalissimo some pointers about democratic transformation. Because, despite being Muslim, not Buddhist, Indonesia was in a better position than any other country to offer friendly advice. It was not geographically too close; there were no strategic or historical elephant traps to be negotiated. And it was the home of ASEAN, of which Burma had very belatedly become a member – thirty years after its foundation – in 1997. As the association's most populous member, Indonesia carried a lot of clout.

The United Nations envoy Razali Ismail, who as recently as 2003 had seemed on the point of negotiating a democratic breakthrough, had been refused entry the following year, but SBY was granted a visa: an encouraging sign. Even better, he was granted an audience with the generalissimo.

But an audience, in the literal sense, was what it turned out to be.[14] The meeting lasted thirty minutes, according to a diplomatic source; the first twenty-eight minutes were taken up with a monologue by the Burmese leader on why the military was so central to the life of Burma. SBY had two minutes to make his case. It was not long enough.

*

Burma may have been a member of ASEAN but it was not collegial. With its fellow members it shared some or all of the following: Buddhism, an historic sacred monarchy, tributary relations with China, recent domination by a European imperial power, invasion by the Japanese, mayhem and massacre in the Second World War, independence and membership of the Non-Aligned Movement, an assertive military caste, democratic activism, abundant natural resources. There was much to share, much historical experience, many modern challenges to be confronted that might better be confronted together.

But Burma was not interested. With its immediate ASEAN neighbour and fellow Buddhist country Thailand, relations had always been frosty if not downright bellicose. Burmese tended to look down on Thailand as a country of bumpkins and paltry cultural achievement. And Thailand's soaring growth rate from the 1960s on, attracting hundreds of thousands of illegal Burmese migrant workers, added injured amour propre to the toxic mix.

Burma's other two neighbours were giants, India and China. With the memory of wars fought and lost against Britain only a couple of generations away, Burma's leaders knew all too well that they lived in a dangerous neighbourhood. 'Burma is a tender plant between two cactuses,' U Nu, the first prime minister after independence, once said.[15] A wry Burmese saying goes: 'When China spits, Burma swims.' So when war erupted in Indochina in the 1950s, Burma's reaction was to slam the door and pull down the blinds. This country had enough problems of its own with secessionists and communist insurgents without getting involved with other people's. Thirty years on it was being tempted out of its bunker. But resistance remained strong.

The three years after SBY's failed attempt at dialogue saw Burma slipping back into ever-greater isolation. Only the cactuses offered companionship. China took advantage of Burma's isolation to muscle in, buying up much of Mandalay, dominating business in the north-east, building dams in

Kachin. India, once vocal in its condemnation of attacks on Aung San Suu Kyi and her party, fell silent on such matters. The United States and Europe stayed away, repelled by the regime's seemingly endless detention of Suu, its relentless persecution of other democrats, its refusal to improve. And ASEAN, after SBY's humiliation in 2005, made all the right angry noises but was unable to make any difference: the bar in its constitution against interference in the internal affairs of member states tied the association's hands.

The violent suppression of the revolt of the monks in September 2007 once again put ASEAN under pressure to do something about its rogue member. But what? At the association's summit meeting in Singapore that November, the UN Secretary General's new envoy to Burma, Ibrahim Gambari, was invited to give a briefing on the situation in the country. Like the briefings given by his predecessors, its content could only be highly critical. But it never happened: the man fated to become Burma's reformist president, Thein Sein, who was then prime minister, stopped it in its tracks at the opening dinner by issuing a veto: decision-making by consensus was 'a basic principle' of ASEAN, he insisted; Myanmar did not consent to the hostile briefing, so it could not be allowed to happen. That was all it took to cow and humble an organisation whose founding charter commits members to defending democracy, freedom and human rights.

To mark 'thirty years of friendship' between ASEAN and the United States and strengthen the rather flaccid ties between them, George W. Bush's White House had floated the idea of inviting the leaders of its member states to his ranch in Crawford, Texas for an informal summit. But the killing of the monks and the extension of Suu's house arrest cast a fatal shadow over the proposal. If the ASEAN summit went ahead, Burma's leaders would have to be invited along with the rest, and there was no stomach for that, and no political capital to be gained from it. Even if Dubya had wanted to buck the mood, he would have encountered formidable opposition across the breakfast table from his wife, Laura, who had made Suu's fate and the larger questions of the regime's bestiality a personal crusade. Instead Bush ordered sanctions to be tightened further if the regime continued to ignore calls for a democratic transition. 'It will be very difficult,' said Douglas Paal, a former Bush administration official, 'no matter whether in Texas, Singapore or elsewhere, to persuade the President to sit down with the junta leader who used force to kill demonstrating monks and their movement for freedom.' A White House insider was quoted by Singapore's *Straits Times* as saying that Mrs Bush 'will put her foot down again and again against a Burmese leader entering her house'. The Crawford summit never happened.[16]

*

A petite woman in a royal-blue trouser suit with a blonde bob and sparkling earrings stands on a stage in Jakarta in February 2009. There is a freshness about Hillary Clinton in this video: this is only the third stop in her first foreign trip as Secretary of State, right at the start of Obama's first term: there is a palpable sense of possibility, of new perspectives, new roads to be taken. Disengagement from Iraq, pulling out of Afghanistan, closing Guantánamo Bay, all those horrendous errors of the previous regime still wait to be rectified: the Iraqi blowback in the form of ISIS, the agonies of Syria's civil war and the Libyan implosion, the stalemate over Guantánamo, all these complications and unexpected consequences lie over the horizon. For now the sky is full of hope and possibility. And Hillary Clinton, despite the rings under her eyes, is as fresh as a young girl, personal, almost intimate with her audience of Indonesian grandees as only an American politician could dream of being.

> We have a democracy, I have a political party, I have people telling me I am going to win – but it doesn't turn out that way. Well – I've had that experience! [cue laughter; a disarming toothy smile from the defeated ex-presidential candidate] I was the most surprised person in the world when President Obama asked me to be Secretary of State but I knew that it was part of my commitment to our country and my belief in our shared agenda that told me to say yes, what an honour and a privilege.[17]

President Obama has already killed off the Bush phrase 'the war on terror'. The odour of American Islamophobia is lifting, and Clinton adroitly praises Indonesia's counter-narrative. 'As I travel around the world over the next years I will be saying to people, if you want to know whether Islam, democracy, modernity and women's rights can coexist, go to Indonesia.'[18] And President SBY, given such short shrift by Senior General Than Shwe four years back, senses that this turnaround in Washington can be a watershed for his country and for South East Asia. When Hillary Clinton becomes the first American Secretary of State to visit ASEAN's headquarters, the association's Secretary General greets her with a bouquet and the words, 'Your visit shows the seriousness of the United States to end its diplomatic absenteeism in the region.'[19] And while the cosy warmth of Hillary's welcome is a great start, reflecting the fact that her boss, the most powerful man on the planet, went to school here, SBY knows what must happen if the relationship is to prosper: the stone in the shoe must be removed. Or, in the metaphor President Obama adopted on the eve of his first presidential visit to ASEAN, a few days after Hillary's tête-à-tête with Suu: 'We're not going to let the Burmese tail wag the ASEAN dog.'[20]

Clinton later recalled that, in their first conversation, the Indonesian President 'encouraged me to pursue a new approach toward Burma . . . Yudhoyono had met twice with Burma's top general, the reclusive Than Shwe, and he told me that the junta might be willing to inch toward democracy if America and the international community helped them along.'[21]

Thus in 2009 was the seed planted. Three months later Aung San Suu Kyi was in the dock in a court inside Burma's most notorious prison, accused of breaking the law by allowing an American intruder, John Yettaw, to stay in her house overnight. She was sentenced to three more years of detention for this crime, reduced by half thanks to the personal favour of Than Shwe, who in a written message brought in by hand explained to the court, and the foreign diplomats attending the trial, that this act of leniency was on account of Suu being the daughter of Aung San, 'who sacrificed his life for the independence of Myanmar' and in order that 'there be no obstruction to the path of democracy'.[22]

More bizarre whimsicality from the world's second weirdest regime after North Korea; what path to democracy, after all? But as practising politicians know, change doesn't come easy. 'We're still sorting out everything we've inherited,' Clinton told the House Foreign Affairs Committee in April 2009. 'We are trying to shift this gigantic ship of state.'[23] And somewhere in the depths of Myanmar's absurd new capital, someone was trying to do the same thing.

By November 2011, Burma's president had succeeded. On the island of Bali in Indonesia on 18 November 2011, President Obama acknowledged as much: 'After years of darkness, we've seen flickers of progress in these last several weeks. President Thein Sein and the Burmese Parliament have taken important steps on the path toward reform.'[24]

5

INTO PARLIAMENT

D EMOCRACY: it sounds like a fine thing. But only Burmese people over seventy years old, who remember the last normal election of 1960, have a relatively clear idea of what it's about.

'People don't understand what it means,' a well-travelled Burmese told me. 'They think it just means doing what you want.' It can be taken to mean simply the opposite of the prevailing state of affairs, where you could only read and watch what the junta ordained, you could not stay in a relative's home without informing the authorities, you could be kicked off your land by some powerful person without any recourse; if you were on the border you could be forced to become a porter for the army or a human landmine detector or a rape victim.

Things like that – people were aware – did not go on in the rich democratic countries, so democracy must mean getting rid of all such trials and terrors. It meant – everyone who had been around in 1990 knew this – declaring what you wanted in secret, where you could not be spied on, and then what you wanted coming to pass, in a magical kind of way. When in 1990 the NLD swept the board at the election, and the army ignored the whole procedure, locking up those MPs-elect who had not fled the country, it proved how terrible army rule was, and by contrast how wonderful democratic rule would be.

These were dangerously vague and idealistic views of democracy which Suu, campaigning in 1989, worked hard in her speeches to dispel. 'You've got a head,' she told the great crowds that gathered to hear her, 'and you haven't got a head to nod with, you've been nodding for twenty-six years. The head is there for you to think.'[1] And the country people laughed and cheered and clapped, and chose to believe, contrary to what she was saying, that when they elected Ma Suu, all would be well. 'Expectations are so high that it is going to be hard for anyone to satisfy them,' a senior diplomat in Rangoon told me in May 2015. 'A lot of people think that if Daw Suu is in charge of the country then a lot of problems will very quickly be resolved and people's lives will get better.'

This simple view of politics ensured that Suu's first experience of campaigning for a seat in Parliament was a great success. The by-elections held on 1 April 2012 were the first fruit of the historic accord between Suu and President Thein Sein. They were the first palpable sign that the ex-general was not only prepared to speak and be photographed with the army's great adversary, but to give her a chance to join the ruling class.

In Burma's system, Members of Parliament who are promoted to the cabinet must vacate their parliamentary seats, triggering by-elections. Forty-five MPs had been promoted, so that number of by-elections was held simultaneously. It was Suu's first true electoral test ever, and the first for her party since 1990.

Like many of the initiatives launched by President Thein Sein, including the constitution itself, the by-election was cunningly crafted. It was timed to take place while the memory of the reforms already enacted was still fresh, thereby reflecting yet more credit onto his presidency. Like the election of 1990, and in contrast to that of 2010, it was carried out with sufficient probity and openness to satisfy the foreign observers who – in another striking first for Burma – had been invited to attend. It would help Burma to shuck off the evil reputation that clung to it; it would heap pressure on the West to remove the sanctions that had been in place ever since 1988. It would allow Burma to hold up its head again in the world. Yet at the same time – because of the small number of seats to be contested, fewer than one-tenth of the total – it would have negligible impact on the quasi-civilian government's ability to control events.

It would give Suu official status for the first time in a career of insurrectionary activism that had lasted – allowing for fifteen years of house arrest – twenty four years. And without giving her even a scrap of power, it would bring that insurrectionary career to a full stop.

If Suu had understood the president's calculations, they did not deflect her from her aim. 'We're going to work towards national reconciliation as we've always intended,' she told reporters, diplomats and observers at an eve-of-poll meeting at her home, 'and we hope that these by-elections will be one step further in that direction. If I'm going to be used [to give the government legitimacy] for the sake of the nation, that's fine by me.'[2]

*

Suu decided to stand for the constituency of Kawhmu, a town thirty kilometres south of Rangoon in the Irrawaddy

Delta which had been ravaged by Cyclone Nargis four years before. Probably she could have stood for practically any constituency in the country with excellent hope of victory. But Kawhmu was carefully chosen.

It could be reached from her home in the city – admittedly on poor roads – within a couple of hours. It was a good symbol, both of suffering Burma, having been ravaged by the cyclone, and of the callousness and incompetence of the military, whose sluggishness in organising relief for the cyclone's victims had exposed the hollowness of their patriotic pretensions. Conversely, in this and other crippled towns around the Delta, the NLD had been the only political organisation to make a difference after the disaster, both in bringing immediate relief and in long-term reconstruction.[3]

Two hundred years ago the Delta was a huge malarial swamp, a wilderness of no use to anybody. But after being drained during British times it became the rice bowl and melting pot of the nation, home to hundreds of thousands of Burmans and Karen, and many Hindu and Muslim migrants from the subcontinent as well. Watered by Burma's greatest river, the immensely fertile soil provided a living to farmers willing to brave its fierce climate and wandering watercourses. But the Delta is too close to the sea ever to be really safe – as its inhabitants discovered in May 2008.

The cyclone that Asian meteorologists called Nargis – a Hindi word meaning Narcissus – made landfall in the town of Pyapon, the biggest township in the Kawhmu constituency, at six o'clock on the evening of 2 May 2008. 'We heard the warning on the radio,' a young man in the office of the NLD told me, 'just thirty minutes before it arrived. The government said it was travelling at 40 to 50 mph. But DVB [the Democratic Voice of Burma, an alternative broadcaster with underground correspondents all over the country] said it was moving at 120 to 150 mph. It moved through the Delta like a snake. At 7.30 a huge wave crashed through the town. The eye of the cyclone came swirling through the town.'

It was a disaster Burma was ill-prepared for. Civil defence was a long way down the ruling military's list of priorities. After recent Asian disasters, notably the Indian Ocean tsunami of Boxing Day 2004, the machinery of international aid had quickly gone into overdrive and had made a massive difference. But a sudden influx of military aircraft from all points of the compass was not something Burma's ruling generals were ever likely to smile on, given their extreme paranoia.

The official death toll from the cyclone was 138,000, though many believe the true figure to be much higher.

*

The wounds inflicted by Nargis have healed now. But the pain and the memories endure. Five years after the disaster, I took a boat trip through the Delta's waterways to hear the tales of survivors and to find out how they were coping.

We drove down into the Delta from Rangoon to the town of Bogale along a single-track lane fringed by banana and rattan palms. In few places does Burma look more idyllic than the Irrawaddy Delta. There is water everywhere: the stream that runs alongside the road, crossed by bamboo bridges, ponds full of ducks or pink lotus flowers, a river where black water buffalo wallow in mud to their shoulders. The flimsy wooden farmhouses, each with its big glazed pot to collect rainwater, are fronted by gleaming paddy fields and framed by coconut palms. Everything one's eye falls on shrieks of life and fertility. In Bogale, where children bathe in the Gone Nyin Tan River, its waters chocolate brown with silt, we boarded a long-tailed motorboat and headed south towards the village of Sat Saw, a two-hour journey through a vast web of rivers.

Little has changed here in half a century of military rule. A fisherman throws his net from the stern of his small, sleek rowing boat. More rowers propel a boat stacked with logs upstream. On the breeze comes the smell of burning rice stubble.

As we headed away from the Delta's small towns towards the sea, activity both on the shore and the water dwindled. Then on the southern bank at the far end of a narrow inlet gleamed the roofs of the little village of Sat Saw.

Along the village footpaths – there are no motorable roads and no wheeled vehicles – we are taken to meet a man called Phoe Swe, aged fifty, in the dingy rattan hut that is home to him and his surviving children.

'Nargis hit this village at 8 p.m. and it washed many people into the sea,' he recalled. 'I ran out of my house with my family to take shelter in a nearby monastery. But after an hour another big wave came and smashed the monastery's pillars, so with one of my children on my back and two others in my arms I climbed a tree. We stayed up the tree all night and when the morning came we saw that everything was destroyed.' Amazingly, eight of his nine children survived up that tree, clinging to each other. But his wife and their ten-month-old baby died.

For the next four or five days they survived on coconuts. After that, help arrived from a Buddhist organisation. And the army? 'They didn't help at all,' he says. 'We didn't even see them in the village.' Five years on, he says, 'I'm still struggling. It's hard to get back to a normal life. The year after Nargis we had no rice crop because the fields were soaked in saltwater.'

In a hut nearby, fifty-six-year-old Thein Win tells of his lucky escape. 'We were all sleeping over in our hut by the paddy field when the cyclone struck,' he said. 'The cyclone didn't hit us there. But our house here was destroyed, and five of our friends who were staying in it all died.' In all, 530 villagers, more than one-third of the population, lost their lives. 'It's because our village is so close to the sea,' explains Tun Lin, who owns a store in the village. 'We are in the front line. Even now if it rains hard, the children get scared and hide under the blankets.'

The military junta was slow to respond, slow to release information – and slow to the point of criminal about admitting the foreign aid agencies that were clamouring to help. They released bizarrely detailed casualty figures, posed in front of surreally immaculate camps for the displaced for the cameras of the state-controlled media. But the simple, vital task of bringing aid to desperate people, hundreds of thousands of whom were clinging to life without food or fresh water, seemed somehow beneath them. They were to pay for their arrogance in the by-election.

Instead Burmese civil society, almost wiped out through the decades of army repression, leapt into the breach, with dozens of ad hoc groups organising missions to bring food, water, medicine and other necessities to the devastated communities. The Buddhist monks' organisation which saved the lives of Phoe Swe and his children was one of many groups taking the initiative. The most celebrated was the flotilla of boats organised by Zarganar, the nation's most popular and subversive comedian, which took aid to forty-two remote villages. The following month he spoke to foreign media about the plight of millions of survivors in the Delta left to fend for themselves. For that he was arrested, put on trial and sentenced to fifty-nine years' imprisonment for 'public order offences'.

Some of the larger international agencies eventually prevailed on the generals to let them in. In the village of Sat Saw their legacy is plainly visible: solid concrete bridges over the waterways, courtesy of Care International; a new primary school, built on stilts to double as a refuge in the event of another disaster, thanks to UNICEF. The Swiss Red Cross provided mosquito nets, a Japanese NGO gifted a water tank. The NLD, though at the time still a persecuted and semi-legal party, dug a drinking-water pond, helped rebuild village houses and concreted the main pathway through the village.

And the military government? What was their contribution? 'Nothing,' says Tun Lin, the shopkeeper, who is today the head of the local branch of the NLD, established in December 2012. 'On account of Nargis, they didn't tax the rice harvest that year. But they taxed us double the next.'

Kawhmu had suffered from the cyclone in similar ways to Sat Saw and as a result a man in a monkey mask could have stood on an NLD ticket with a good chance of winning. Instead they got the woman regarded by millions of Burmese as a living Buddha, and the nation's legitimate ruler. On

1 April 2012, Aung San Suu Kyi obtained 99 per cent of the vote.

*

One year and four months after her release, Suu was finally on her way. The long, stuttering, tormented march of the NLD to the sunlit uplands of power had finally arrived somewhere.

When the results were published on the day after polling, more than a thousand supporters gathered outside the NLD headquarters in Rangoon, waving the party's Fighting Peacock banners, pumping fists, holding up 'I LOVE DEMOCRACY' scarves. Some wore bandanas on their heads with the same image, others Daw Suu T-shirts. 'Does the victory mean she could become president?' one of them asked Myo Win, a party official. 'There is more of a possibility of that now,' he replied. 'The army has changed now, they are more lenient.'

Suu's first-ever opportunity to celebrate an election victory was notably restrained: far from whipping her supporters into a lather of triumphalism, she did all she could to cool them down. 'I would like all NLD members to ensure that the victory of the people is a dignified victory,' she told the crowd. 'Words, behaviour and actions that can harm and sadden other parties and people should be avoided . . . It is natural that NLD members and their supporters are joyous at this point. However it is necessary to avoid manners and actions that will make the other parties and members upset. It is very important that NLD members take special care that the success of the people is a dignified one.'[4]

But she was in no doubt about the meaning of the result. Twenty-two years on, the NLD was clearly as popular as it had been in 1990. And now that the country's rulers had sanctioned its existence – now the party was not fighting merely to survive, defying the will of an all-powerful army – they could finally get down to work. She told the crowd, 'It's not so much our triumph as a triumph of the people, who have decided that they must be involved in the political process in this country. We hope that this will be the beginning of a new era when there will be more emphasis on the role of the people in the everyday politics of this country. We hope that all other parties that took part in the elections will be in a position to cooperate with us to create a genuinely democratic atmosphere in our nation.' The elections, she said, were 'a foundation stone for the future of democracy in Burma'.[5] Supporters shouted 'We won, we won!' and waved party flags. They burst into cheers and danced in the street.

The victory was, for her party's supporters, the perfect prelude to Thingyan, twelve days later: the annual festival at the stifling peak of the hot season when Burmese dump their inhibitions, get riotously drunk and drench all and sundry with water for days on end, to the accompaniment of deafening music. During Thingyan, all the rigid social protocol of this hierarchy-ridden country is thrown out of the window. It is the one week in the year when people say exactly what they think to one another, with no fear of the consequences. It is also, for the majority of the population, a blessed and total holiday from work. For those who prefer to resist the bacchanalian mood it is the ideal opportunity to retreat to a monastery for a few days' meditation.

It is not, therefore, the obvious moment to do serious political business in Burma, but David Cameron swept aside any cultural qualms his advisers may have mentioned to pay the first-ever visit by a serving British prime minister to independent Burma during the festival, tacking it onto the end of an Asian trip which saw him, in his own words, 'load up an aeroplane full of business people to fly the flag for Britain'.

Leaving aside the risk of getting very wet and finding nobody indoors, a minor controversy erupted when Mr Cameron showed up in Rangoon with a fair sprinkling of those business people in tow – despite the fact that economic sanctions had barred British business from having anything to do with Burma for more than twenty years. Downing Street did its best to cram this small complication back into its box before it caused too much trouble. 'It is not a trade mission,' the *Guardian* was told. 'We are going to Burma for reasons of geography and the recent elections, which led to a positive outcome. The government policy on Burma is to discourage trade. That remains the case. Around ten members of the business delegation will come to Burma. They will have a cultural programme. They will be like tourists.'[6]

First Mr Cameron flew to Naypyidaw, that great non-place, where he met President Thein Sein 'in a grand hall that could accommodate a tennis court or two'; the meeting, Nicholas Watt of the *Guardian* felt, was 'cordial, if slightly stilted,'[7] as Cameron metaphorically patted the ex-general on the head for the political reforms he had pushed through. Then it was back on the plane and down to roasting, sopping wet

Rangoon and a trip to the house on University Avenue that Suu had occupied for the best part of twenty years.

After meeting Suu inside the house, the two emerged for a press conference in the garden, as the throbbing drums and bass of Thingyan rock music rolled across Inya Lake. And then Cameron pulled his surprise.

Sanctions were the issue on everyone's mind: imposed in the wake of the massacre of demonstrating students in 1988, they remained the most glaring obstacle to the normalisation of Western ties with Burma – and over the years Suu had consistently spoken in favour of maintaining them, despite criticism that she was thereby robbing poor Burmese of jobs.

Suu remained by far the most famous symbolic victim of the former regime's sins; now, with her election victory, she was becoming the poster girl for its reforms. But at this early date – with so far to go before Burma could claim to have been transformed – would she go along with the removal of the one weapon at her disposal, the one tool she possessed to put pressure on the generals?

Cameron was able to tell her that Britain was under great pressure from its European Union partners, especially Germany, to lift sanctions altogether: at a summit nine days later the issue was to be discussed by European leaders, and given the extent of Thein Sein's reforms – including the release of political prisoners, a ceasefire with the Karen and the licensing of Suu to enter politics – there was no doubt that sanctions would go. But now, thanks to his idea of braving the water festival and tacking Burma onto his Asian tour, the British prime minister was in a position to make Suu an offer she would find hard to refuse: he proposed persuading the European Union not to *remove* but merely to *suspend* its sanctions on Burma – which could then be re-imposed at a later date if Burma began backsliding. By making this announcement here and now, in Suu's garden, with Suu at his side, he would underline how central the Lady was, in Britain's eyes, to the reform agenda (Germany, he may have been blunt enough to tell her, was far less convinced that she mattered). And at the same time Burma's president would be left in no doubt about her international heft and her helpful commitment to his programme, which would put him under a debt of gratitude to her for this splendid contribution to the nation's economic revival.

Cameron thus demonstrated the sleight of hand which had enabled him to become Britain's youngest prime minister since Lord Liverpool in 1812. The idea of 'suspending' rather than lifting sanctions had the world's media scratching their heads, as it was not a notion that had been discussed before. But as the *Economist* noted, in effect it was the same as removing them: it just sounded less definite.[8] Whichever word was preferred, re-imposing them later would be a major political challenge.

Suu is a highly intelligent and sophisticated woman, but she had never had much exposure to the intellectual shenanigans of the world's rulers. And here she was, with two masters of the dark political arts, Thein Sein and David Cameron, one on either side, both at the top of their game. Her deficit of political cunning showed. With the assurance that sanctions would be merely suspended rather than cancelled, she tossed away the only weapon she and her party possessed. She walked blithely into Cameron's neat little trap. If, in the following days, she had listened to U Win Tin, her party's great contrarian, and come to the conclusion that, yes, perhaps it was a little early to be giving the former general, now president, who had come to power via a rigged election, this ringing endorsement before the cameras of the world, she would have been able to do absolutely nothing about it. (But there has never been much evidence that Suu is a good listener.)

Mr Cameron and Suu emerged from her handsome but decrepit house and ascended the platform. In his most mandarin and ruminative of tones, he told the journalists assembled in the garden, 'I think there are prospects for change, and I think it is right that the rest of the world responds to those changes. Of course we must respond with caution; we must be sceptical, because we want to know those changes are irreversible, but I think it is right to *suspend* the sanctions.'[9]

Suu replied that she welcomed Cameron's decision. 'I support the idea of suspension, rather than the lifting of sanctions, because this will be an acknowledgement of the role of the president and other reformers,' she said. 'It will also make it quite clear to those who are against reform that, should they try to obstruct the way of the reformers, then sanctions could come back.'[10]

The icing on Cameron's cake for Suu was an invitation to her to return to her 'beloved Oxford' in June, for the first time in almost twenty-five years. She replied graciously that she hoped to be able to accept the invitation. 'Two years ago I would have said, "Thank you for the invitation but sorry." Now I am able to say "perhaps", and that is great progress.'[11]

Aung San and his wife Daw Khin Kyi with Suu as a baby: photo in Aung San Memorial Museum in Natmauk, upper Burma.

A young Suu with her diplomat mother in India: photo in Aung San Memorial Museum.

Aung San's birthplace in Natmauk, now a museum.

Survivors of Cyclone Nargis in Irrawaddy Delta, five years on.

Heat haze over parliament in Naypyidaw.

Above: The large symbolic *patta* or alms bowl at the entrance to parliament.

Right: The gleaming marble halls of Burma's parliament.

Below: Politicians in uniform *gaung baungs* (turbans) in parliament.

President Thein Sein (centre) at a conference in Rangoon in 2014.

Suu's Naypyidaw home where she stays when parliament is sitting.

shin Wirathu: firebrand Buddhist leader in
s monastery in Mandalay.

Abbot U Par Mount Kha: 'Buddhism is weak
because of Islam'.

ung Win, a Rohingya activist, outside his home on the outskirts of Sittwe, Arakan state.

Above: Ma Khin Aye, a Muslim of Meiktila, who lost her home in the violence.

Above left: Devastation in the town after the communal violence of March 2013.

Left: Many Muslim-owned shops in Meiktila were burned out.

Below: One of several mosques destroyed by mobs in Meiktila.

The ruins of the neighbourhood where Ma Khin Aye lived with her mother.

There were victims on both sides – displaced Buddhist families receiving food parcels.

Above: Suu in a crowd of MPs and visitors in parliament, 2015.

Right: With censorship lifted, Suu's face appeared on many magazine covers.

Below: Suu did not baulk at wearing many different outfits for NLD calendars.

Outside her gates, Thingyan revellers rumbling past in lorries did their best to pour cold water on the whole proceedings. But Mr Cameron and the Lady were out of reach.

*

One week later, as Rangoon dried out under the hot sun, Suu and her forty-three triumphant MPs-elect presented themselves at Naypyidaw's parliament complex to begin their official parliamentary careers. But there was a problem – one which someone might have foreseen. Before taking up their seats in the Lower House, they had to swear to safeguard the constitution.

Suu and her colleagues objected to this oath. They hated this constitution. It had been foisted on the nation by a rigged referendum. It gave the army the power to rule for ever, under the pretence of bringing democracy. The NLD was determined to change it. But here they were, with the high doors of the Pyithu Hluttaw or House of Representatives – Parliament's Lower House – barred to them unless they swore to 'safeguard' the thing.

They appealed to the Speaker of the Lower House to allow them to change the wording of the swearing-in oath from 'safeguard' to 'respect'. The appeal was rejected. As a result, on 21 April, the party informed the world that it planned to boycott Parliament until its appeal/demand was accepted. 'We won't say we are not attending parliament,' Suu explained. 'We will attend after the oath [is amended]. Regarding changing the phrase, it is in accordance with the constitution . . . I hope there will not be a problem with this.'[12] She pointed out that, when her party had re-registered with the authorities after her release from house arrest, the requested change in wording was accepted. All the NLD wanted was to extend the exemption to Parliament.

But Parliament refused to budge. All the representatives had to take the same oath. As one newspaper said, it was 'the first sign of serious discord between Suu Kyi and the reformist regime' since the by-elections.[13]

Suu and her colleagues sat tight. One is reminded of the times in the mid-1990s when Suu, freed from detention, had tried to leave Rangoon by car to resume her countrywide tours but had been stopped shortly outside the city limits and had remained in her stationary vehicle in a battle of wills with the junta, which demanded that she return home. But each time – one of these stand-offs went on for a week – it was Suu who was eventually forced to back down, defeated by the enemy's superior resources.

And so it proved this time. After an impasse lasting ten days, Suu, once again in her garden in Rangoon, this time with UN Secretary General Ban Ki-Moon at her side, announced that she and her colleagues would reluctantly do as required and swear to 'safeguard' the constitution. She did her best to present the volte-face as a victory for her party's reasonableness. 'We have always believed in flexibility, in the political process, throughout the years of our struggle,' she told reporters. '[Swearing the oath] is the only way in which we can achieve our goal without violence.'[14]

It was an ominous start. The battle was a pointless one: however unattractive the constitution, it was by its rules that the NLD had won election, and whatever they swore or did not swear they would be obliged to 'safeguard' it until they were able to change it. It was a battle they were bound to lose. As such, it was a cruel demonstration of the tight limits to the party's power, now it had joined the system. And if Suu had imagined that President Thein Sein would step in to force Parliament to compromise with her, she was to be disappointed. Sanctions were gone, Thein Sein was away in Japan, where Prime Minister Yoshihiko Noda was expected to announce that it would write off Burma's debt and re-start a long-suspended aid programme.

Suu had served her purpose.

6

OPEN FOR BUSINESS

Aung San Suu Kyi's long disillusionment with President Thein Sein and his commitment to reform began at the gates of Parliament, with the humiliating spat over the swearing of the parliamentary oath. But elsewhere, suddenly there was a palpable buzz over this obscure country in the middle of Asia which couldn't decide what it was called, and which had been closed for business for sixty years.

This excitement did not find its focus on Suu. She was the heroine of the hour, sure, but somehow this role did not seem to suit her as well as sacrifice and solitude. Sleeping Beauty is more interesting before she is kissed; Cinderella is more *simpatica* when being abused by her sisters than on the arm of Prince Charming. Human beings are fickle that way. She was about to begin a long series of journeys to collect the awards she had been honoured with in absentia. The smiles on the faces of her Western admirers grew somewhat glassy as she did so. It might have been more interesting if she had sent one of her sons to collect them, or some young Burmese boys or girls who had never travelled before.

But it was not to be. The editor of a British national newspaper examined a new photograph of her during these months. 'Hasn't had much *work* done,' he remarked.[1] After all she was sixty-six now, extraordinarily well preserved, but no one would doubt that she was a grandmother. It has never been easy for women over sixty-five to set the public's pulse racing. Instead the West found something else to symbolise the return of this semi-mythical country to the international community: buried Spitfires.

David Cameron made two main points to the media in Suu's garden in April 2012: the suspension of sanctions on Burma, and an invitation to his hostess to return to the UK for a visit. But the other theme of the trip – announced by his press officer – made for much better headline material. 'Spitfires "lost" in Burma could fly' was the Press Association's headline.[2] 'Twenty "lost" Spitfires that were buried in Burma during the Second World War could return to the skies, it has been revealed,' the story ran.

'. . . Mr Cameron raised the fascinating find when he met Mr Sein [sic] for talks yesterday,' it continued. 'Officials said the president was "very enthusiastic" . . . A Downing Street source said: "The Spitfire is arguably the most important plane in the history of aviation, playing a crucial role in the Second World War. It is hoped that this will be an opportunity to work with the reforming Burmese government, uncover, restore and display these fighter planes and get them gracing the skies of Britain once again."'

But no sooner was this patriotic prospect raised than it was plunged in controversy. One of the British businessmen accompanying the prime minister on his Asian circuit was Steve Boultbee Brooks, the rugged, toothy owner of a Mayfair property investment company. An aviation nut in his spare time, he claims to have been the first person to fly a helicopter from the North Pole to the South, and to drive a vehicle across the frozen Bering Strait from Alaska to Siberia. He was also the owner of the Boultbee Flight Academy, based at Goodwood Airfield in West Sussex, which offers a thirty-minute flight in a Spitfire over the English Channel for £2,750, including VAT.[3]

The reason for Mr Boultbee Brooks's interest in Spitfires was plain enough. 'Pilots dream of experiencing the thrill and the emotion involved in climbing into the seat of a Spitfire,' the Academy's website notes. But 'with only 35 flying Spitfires remaining out of more than 21,000 built, and only six two-seaters, it has been a pretty difficult box to tick to date.' If there were Spitfires buried in Burma, the Boultbee Flight Academy was where they belonged. That was clearly Steve Boultbee Brooks's view – and he had the ear of Number 10.

Within a fortnight, however, Mr Brooks had dramatically fallen out with his source for the discovery, the man who had made exhuming forgotten military aircraft his life's work, a Lincolnshire farmer called David Cundall. But who said these aeroplanes even existed?

The story goes like this. The Second World War ended abruptly in August 1945 when the Japanese surrendered after the dropping of the second atomic bomb, with a Soviet invasion of Hokkaido believed to be imminent. The Allies had no way of knowing that the Japanese were going to surrender – the fear was that they would fight to the last man. But surrender they did. So when twelve Rolls-Royce-powered Vickers Supermarine Spitfires arrived at Mingaladon Airfield in Rangoon, each carefully packed into a large crate, they were of no use to anyone. The war was over.

An American Construction Battalion – Seabees – had arrived in Burma the previous month with the task of extending Mingaladon's runway for use by American bombers.

VJ Day rendered this job unnecessary. Instead, we are told, they were ordered to dig a very large hole, then bury the crated Spitfires in it. The reasoning: it was too expensive to ship them home. They were redundant – the war was over. All available ship space was needed for demobilised troops and liberated prisoners of war. So they buried them.

Did this really happen? Would not the task have been logged by both the US and British military, so that, if and when questions arose – where are they? – a satisfactory explanation could be provided? But no such record has ever surfaced.

Instead what we have is the memory of a chance conversation in Jacksonville, Florida in 1974 between one of those Seabees and a dedicated British 'warbird' finder called Jim Pearce who had earned his stripes digging up bits and pieces of a Focke-Wulf FW 189 – a twin-engined German aircraft – in Russia. 'We did some pretty silly things,' the unnamed former Seabee told Pearce, 'but the silliest was burying some of your Spitfires.'[4]

For Pearce this was tantalising information. But in the 1970s the Ne Win tyranny was in its pomp. Burma was firmly closed to outsiders of every sort. The Englishman applied for permission to dig at Mingaladon – now the site of Burma's main international and domestic airport as well as a major military base – but got nowhere. In 1996 he passed the cryptic tale on to David Cundall, a member of the same flying club, and a man possessed like him of an unconquerable urge to dig up buried aviation treasure. Cundall had been looking for aircraft in Britain since the mid-1970s.

Cundall felt he did not yet have enough information to act, so he advertised in aviation magazines in the hope of obtaining more. Alerted by a friend who saw the ads, a former private in the Royal Berkshire Regiment named Stanley Coombe got in touch. Coombe had arrived in Burma in 1944 at the age of eighteen. On one particular day the following year he claims that he was on his way back to the base near Rangoon's military airfield when he saw a group of American Seabees lowering thirty-foot-long crates into a hole near the runway. The next day he was back at the airfield and asked an airman on duty, 'What's in those crates down there?' The answer was, 'Would you believe, Spitfires.'[5]

Coombe told the *Daily Telegraph*, 'I was amazed. But we were the last people to use that road. The next day they closed it . . . When we returned [to Rangoon] three months later, no one would have known anything was buried there.' Tiring of the incredulous looks his story prompted, Coombe said he ended up keeping the tale to himself. 'I got the sense people were thinking, "Oh here he goes again with his silly old boy's yarns." So I gave up telling them.' But David Cundall was all ears.

Cundall also flew to Florida with the hope of meeting the original Seabee source but he was too late – the man had died. But his family put him onto another Seabee who was still alive, if only just. 'He needed an oxygen pipe to breathe,' Cundall said. He confirmed the original Mingaladon story, 'Then he said, "But I buried a lot more, well over 100." I couldn't believe it. I asked him where. He said, "We buried 18 at Myitkyina. And there were other places, lots of -tins, -tuns . . . funny names."'

The Englishman was ready to go to work: each of these aircraft was potentially worth millions. And it wasn't only the money. 'I just want to honour the people who kept this country free,' he said later. 'I just want to hear twelve Spitfires roar down the runway and peel off . . .'[6] But there was one major obstacle: Burma – at the time one of the most hermetic autocracies in the world.

However, for a man called Keith Win, Burma was home, or one of his homes. The Anglo-Burmese son of a senior Burmese policeman, Win was born and raised in Rangoon in the years when it was impenetrable.[7] He then moved to London, qualified as an accountant and got a job, and in the mid-1990s founded the Myanmar-Britain Business Association, 'to promote the best of both worlds,' as its mission statement reads, 'and to build bridges.'

In those years, with thousands of political prisoners in jail and the military junta refusing to talk to the democratic opposition, the country was split into warring camps. But Win had friends and relatives on both sides of the divide and had been using his contacts to try to bring them together, with modest success. He was one of the very few people outside the regime who had been allowed to meet Suu while she was still under house arrest. He also had contacts with senior military figures, including General Khin Nyunt, one of the three top leaders of the junta.

David Cundall contacted Win via his business association and appealed for his help. 'Cundall approached me in 1997 and said, I'm involved in this project, we've been trying to get into Burma but without success,' Win said. 'He had heard that I might be able to open doors . . . I researched the Spitfire story but discovered it was based on hearsay and there was not much to go on. But I found it intriguing and worked hard to get approval. The aircraft were supposedly buried at an airfield shared with the Burmese Air Force. Cundall also wanted to take out a British television crew.'

Thanks to his meeting with Suu, Keith Win had acquired a certain cachet with the regime. During a chance encounter with Khin Nyunt he requested a meeting. The powerful general, chief of Military Intelligence, agreed. 'He must have thought I had come with a message from the British government,' Win recalled, 'because at the meeting in Khin Nyunt's office there was also the Foreign Minister and the Burmese ambassador to London lined up to greet me, and a TV crew and photographers. I explained the Spitfire project and they listened politely.'

Win had no great hopes that they would be granted permission. 'When you think about it, Mingaladon is a military airport, they've got MiG jets and whatever, it's shoot to kill for anybody wandering around. And here we are, Westerners, a TV crew, wandering around this airfield with special equipment looking for several buried airplanes – it really was mission impossible. But Khin Nyunt gave me his approval.'[8] And in a country infamous for corruption, all it took to swing it was a bottle of whisky and a book about the economy.

As a result, Cundall's door to Burma swung open. Win and Cundall went into partnership and Win threw himself into the research, trawling through army veteran websites for more possible witnesses to the alleged burial of the planes. And soon the hunt was under way: with permission granted and the hard-to-obtain visas issued, Cundall and Win came out with a team of experts and the backing of sponsors and began to survey, to excavate and to dig, all within a few yards of Burma's most sensitive military airfield, recorded by television cameras.

Nothing emerged, which only made Cundall's rhetoric fly higher. Loyal experts kept the faith. A PhD student in the geophysics and tectonics department of Leeds University tested Mingaladon with powerful electromagnetic equipment and reported: 'Discrete geophysical anomalies, two clear areas of high response, both indicative of buried metal.'[9] Another search located a buried crate, though the team was unable to determine what if anything was inside it other than mud.

But Cundall was sublimely confident now: he claimed that the aircraft were not only present, a few feet underground and in large numbers, but had been so carefully packed that they would soon be flying again. 'Hopefully they will be brought back to the UK and will be flying at air shows,' he told the *Daily Telegraph*.[10] 'We have had offers from British companies to restore them and put their logos on them, which is acceptable to me. It should take two to three years to restore them so we should see something in the next three years or so.' A piece about the hunt in the *Daily Mail* was accompanied by a grainy black-and-white photo allegedly showing 'one of the Spitfires being crated up in Burma ready to be buried'.[11]

So contagious was the excitement that it infected the British Foreign and Commonwealth Office, from where it was a short jump to Number 10. The British ambassador to Burma wrote to Keith Win in December 2012, 'We have spoken about your desire to recover British aircraft that you believe were buried in Myanmar in 1945. The Embassy would be extremely keen to see cooperation between the UK and Myanmar on such a joint heritage project . . .'[12] Within months it had become an item on the agenda of the first-ever visit to Burma of a serving British prime minister.

*

Keith Win had in fact parted company with David Cundall on the worst of terms a full twelve years before. Relations between the two men foundered in 2000 when Win says Cundall dumped him in Rangoon and vanished. 'He left me stranded,' he said.[13] 'He ran out of money and said he was going back to the UK to get some. I waited for him for eight days in a service apartment in Rangoon, and I couldn't contact him. Finally I realised he wasn't coming back.' He says he paid the expenses of $5000 out of his own pocket then spent years trying to get the money back.

Some of David Cundall's specialist collaborators have similar tales to tell. Malcolm Weale is a geophysicist and aviation archaeologist who runs a Norfolk-based company called Geofizz Ltd. 'I met Cundall in 2004 after I was involved in a dig for a Hurricane in London,' he said. 'I was out in Burma with his team for about a month, but I was pretty much left stranded: they just cleared off, leaving me with a debt of several thousand pounds to pay. I had to do a bunk from the hotel early in the morning.' In his work with Cundall in Burma, he said, '. . . we got some very interesting readings, but they could be lots of other things – buried pipes, metals and so on: you always pick up anomalies at an airfield, but they are just anomalies until you put a borehole down and take a photograph.'[14]

Cundall's working methods were part of the problem, Weale said. 'David seems a little bit erratic, he runs from pillar to post promising things to many different people. He's a dreamer – he wants to make himself out to be a bit of an Indiana Jones. Myself, I'm very, very sceptical about the story.' The words are echoed by Win.

As soon as you mention Spitfires to David Cundall, he's off, without doing proper research. During an earlier dig they claimed to have found a crate, but there was no picture of the crate and I'm thinking, we still haven't found any evidence. There's nothing concrete. Cundall's claiming there are 160 Spitfires, but the only picture released so far is of a British war veteran holding a framed picture of a Spitfire.

I did a hell of a lot of work. Jim Pearce told us that these planes were meant for 273 Squadron, so I researched 273 Squadron, I went to the National Archives at Kew, went through their log books and it shows there was nothing about new Spitfires being supplied for the squadron.

The only eyewitness they had identified, despite extensive appeals, was Stanley Coombe, the ex-private who had answered Cundall's advertisement. 'Stanley claimed he had seen six Spitfires being buried,' Win said, 'and it stuck in his memory because they were such large crates.' But the fact that he was the only eyewitness troubled Win. 'I thought, this still sounds far-fetched: why is it I can only find one individual – among hundreds of veterans, only one person saw the burial?' His doubts intensified when another veteran got in touch – after Coombe's claims were made public – to tell him Coombe was lying.

And then there was the meeting that would have persuaded a less passionately committed man than Cundall to throw in the towel. 'In 1997,' Win said, 'I contacted Brigadier Derrick Baynham, who had been the aide-de-camp to Reginald Dorman-Smith, the British governor of Burma at the end of the war.' Win's reasoning was that if this extraordinarily wasteful burial had taken place, it would have to have been authorised at a high level. Now he had found the man to tell him whether it was.

Baynham, who had been an officer in the SOE, Britain's Special Ops unit in the Second World War, could not have been more categorical. 'He said, "Look, this story cannot be true. I would have known about it. I would have seen all these sorts of documents." Because he saw everything. So you had people like him at a high level saying this is not possible, and the only person saying yes is a private.'

But no amount of cold water could put David Cundall off. After sixteen years of striving, more than a dozen trips to Burma and a succession of spats with disillusioned collaborators and sponsors, he had obtained the Holy Grail of treasure hunters, endorsement at the highest political level – only to see it whisked away from him by the elegant figure of Steve Boultbee Brooks. Cundall's rage knew no bounds. 'The President of Burma wants to do business with me,' he told the *Independent*. 'We were issued a permit to dig which is still a valid and exclusive agreement. Mr Brooks wants all rights handed over to him, including media rights, and if there's any money over he says he might pay me something. It's appalling!'[15]

And still nothing emerged from the ground. Less than a year after Number 10's declaration that it wanted to get the aircraft 'gracing British skies again', the world decided it had all been a colossal waste of time. But good fun while it lasted!

Cundall's latest sponsor, a video gaming company called Wargaming.net, which had promised to fund the search with $500,000, pulled out, with the damning message that it thought the planes did not exist, that accounts of the burial were a myth, and that it was 'almost impossible' that the crates had been buried in the first place, given the bad weather and equipment shortages at the time.[16]

On the Facebook page 'Burma Spitfires', one former enthusiast wrote, 'Reality check time.' Ric Gillespie, director of an American company that excavates historic aircraft, said, 'When someone says there are 15, then 30, then 60 planes, it looks like a case of a fish that keeps getting bigger. I hope they're right. But this smells.' Derek Tonkin, a retired diplomat and peppery commentator on Burma, dismissed it as 'A wild goose chase of mythical proportions.'[17]

Despite all the work, the broken agreements and the disappointments, Keith Win, who has spent more time on the quest than almost anyone, has not lost faith entirely, though his assessment is a long way from David Cundall's happy vision of 'Twelve Spitfires [that] roar down the runway, and peel off like this . . .' Win says: 'I think there might be two or three Spitfires, probably crashed, broken. They were used in that theatre. There are three airfields to look in . . .'[18]

The story of the buried Spitfires is a modern fairy story. This closed, forgotten land possesses buried treasure of incalculable value. To obtain it the land must be prised open, then the treasure located by back-breaking toil and maps and the recitation of magic spells ('They will be brought back to the UK and will be flying at air shows'). The treasure was buried by men from the seeker's own land, investing, in this dream-like way, a radiant symbol of their own genius and courage ('The most important plane in the history of aviation') in the soil of Burma. And now the time has come to claim it back and reap the reward.

The tale of the buried Spitfires of Burma is receding rapidly into the realm of far-fetched yarns. But the real-life attempt of Britain and its Western partners to return to the Golden Land and dig up some treasure was just getting under way.

7

THE WEST POURS IN

O N 27 September 2012, Prospero House, a conference hall in central London, was packed with business people for a 'one-day summit' on doing business with Burma. If the audience was braced for the bad news about the Asian country that people were calling 'the Last Frontier', they certainly got it.

Eminent figures including Sir Thomas Harris, vice chairman of Standard Chartered Bank, Anthony Nightingale of Jardine Matheson, the Asian trading house with its roots in the opium trade, and Lord Davies of Abersoch, who as Mervyn Davies had been the Labour government's Minister for Business, left them in no doubt about the challenges.

These included the fact that two-thirds of the Burmese economy was in the black market; that Burma was placed third from bottom in the Transparency International corruption index, above only North Korea and Somalia; that no credit ratings were available, and the legal system was in chaos. They also included the fact that, as no one had done business in the country for two generations, no one knew anything about it. 'The definition of a Myanmar expert,' as one pioneer put it, 'is a guy who knows his BlackBerry won't work when he gets off the plane.'[1] 'There is a massive problem with corruption,' one expert pointed out bluntly.[2] 'Any Western company has to be seriously concerned about its reputation.' 'It's a cash economy par excellence,' another explained, 'and

149

only 65 per cent of Burmese companies have bank accounts.' Due to 'the end of reliable higher education,' said a third, 'the only trained staff in the banking sector are over sixty – it is difficult to overstate how few competent officials there are in banking.'

But none of these awkward facts subtracted from the basic message of the meeting which, as Nightingale of Jardine Matheson summarised it, was that '[Burma] has emerged as a very important strategic country' and that as a result, as Lord Davies said, because 'We are well liked . . . Burma will become an incredibly exciting business partner for the UK.'

Philip Bouverat, Director of JCB, the bulldozer company, wowed the meeting with his company's vision of building 'an expressway from Mandalay to the Indian border, a corridor for Indian exports, then highways on to Thailand, Malaysia, Singapore'. In his mind's eye he saw 40,000 kilometres of new roads, 17,000 kilometres of new railway lines. And he warned, 'If we don't get our proverbial towels on the sunbed before the Germans, French and Italians, the Burmese will be buying from them.'

Sir Thomas Harris pointed out that Standard Chartered had been in Burma from 1864 to 1963. 'In 1995 we opened a representative office, but it was a false dawn,' he said. 'We were frustrated by sanctions and closed in 2004.' But today the situation was different. 'Two years ago I would have said to would-be investors, you couldn't or you shouldn't.' Not so now. Now his advice was, 'Cautiously go forward and prosper responsibly – invest in a responsible manner . . . There are opportunities in every sector.' Including, he might have said, that of the mass media – where one buccaneering Australian learned the hard way the rules of doing business when there are no rules.

*

The *Myanmar Times* is the best English language newspaper in Burma, and has a flourishing Burmese edition, too. When Ross Dunkley launched it in 2000 it was the first time since the military coup of 1962 that foreign investors had risked their money in a Burmese media start-up. As such, coming at a time when the junta had yet to show any serious interest in reforming and opening up, it might be seen as an inspiration to other entrepreneurs tempted to try their luck in this 'very important strategic country'. But its evolution tells a more alarming story.

Launched at a time when Suu was still in detention, thousands of political prisoners were still behind bars, and the blanket of media censorship suffocated free expression, Dunkley's venture got plenty of flak from critics of the regime. He never apologised for his decision to plunge into this virgin market. 'If you want to instigate change', he said many years later, 'you have to be on the field. Anyone who screams from the sidelines – it's just a shriek that's going off into the wilderness.'[3]

The reason he believed he could do the impossible and produce, to Western standards, a decent newspaper in the prevailing conditions was that he had an excellent partner. Everyone who considers doing business with Burma knows that that is the most important thing to have. But Dunkley's was a particularly happy choice: Sonny Swe (Myat Swe in

Burmese), who had been educated in America, was the son of Brigadier General Thein Swe, an army general serving in Military Intelligence, the powerful spy bureau headed by General Khin Nyunt. Dunkley had met the son by chance on holiday in California. 'Coming into a market like this you have to have a political umbrella,' he told me when I met him at the paper's newsroom in 2002. 'Our general is a diplomatic assistant to Khin Nyunt.'[4]

This gave the *Myanmar Times* a charmed life. Instead of having to submit all articles to the Ministry of Information's Press Scrutiny and Registration Board for approval before publication, Dunkley was allowed to send his material to censors at Military Intelligence, whose approach was less stringent and more sophisticated. 'I said [to Sonny], I will refuse to submit to censorship,' he told me. 'Sonny assured me it wouldn't happen . . . It's a question of how to put the right spin on things. Now it's a new ball game. We have to think about the right to press freedom or we cannot move forward. It's one of the fundamental rights. I see *Myanmar Times* as a litmus test to determine how fast [Burma] is moving forward. We're the first paper in the country to talk about the NLD, the first to talk about HIV/Aids . . .'[5]

Brash, fast-talking, chain-smoking, entirely bald, with sticking-out ears, thick glasses and a slightly clownish cast to his features, Ross Dunkley was raised on a cattle station in Western Australia, then drifted into journalism. While working for a Melbourne paper he won the Walkley, 'an award that recognises outstanding acts of courage and bravery in journalism' for his reporting of waterfront strikes. After trying to break into publishing and surviving bruising encounters with the big beasts of Australian journalism – 'I got screwed by the cartel of big publishers,' he said of his publishing experience in Australia, 'I learned a big lesson: you don't threaten the big boys'[6] – he moved to Vietnam, where in 1991 he became a partner in *Vietnam Investment Review*.

The publication prospered, and Dunkley sold out profitably to James Packer, son of the tycoon Kerry Packer, in 1994. 'In '99 I started to think what I was going to do next,' he told me. 'I had Myanmar in mind anyway. I came for a week in '99 to have a look around. It's a virgin market.'[7] With his Burmese business partner, financial backing from an Australian mining tycoon called Bill Clough and with the protection of the political umbrella of Military Intelligence, he established Burma's first recognisably modern newspaper.

In a market like this, connections count for an awful lot, and they help to explain why Dunkley's progress in the early years was relatively smooth. But in the long run the hazards spelled out at 2012's London summit – especially the lack of a legal system with any integrity – brought disaster. Dunkley and the *Myanmar Times* were entirely at the mercy of his patron. His patron, for his part, depended entirely on the survival of his boss, Khin Nyunt, and the perpetuation of the political status quo, which had allowed Khin Nyunt to rise to the top. When that suddenly changed, Dunkley and his organisation were horribly exposed.

*

Like any dictatorship, Burma was very vulnerable to the shifting rivalries of people at the top. Khin Nyunt, the personable, English-speaking, out-going member of the top trio, was enormously powerful, thanks to the spy agency he headed, which not only spied on and arrested and tortured the regime's enemies but also kept tabs on one and all, including fellow members of the military hierarchy. This gave him great power, but also ensured that his colleagues hated and feared him.

As described in Chapter 2, in 2003 Senior General Than Shwe, the top man in the regime, engineered an attempt to assassinate Suu, intending thus to eliminate the regime's biggest irritant. But the mass attack on her party's convoy at a place called Depayin, north of Mandalay, failed to kill her, thanks to the bravery of her driver. Suu ended up first in prison then back under house arrest; Than Shwe, who admitted his involvement, suffered severe loss of face and sanctions against Burma were tightened even further.

In the wake of these setbacks to the top man, Khin Nyunt was promoted to prime minister and consolidated his position by announcing a seven-step road map, designed to lead Burma from dictatorship to democracy via the adoption and popular ratification of a constitution.

This was, by local standards, both flamboyant and imaginative: brazenly lifting the 'road map' terminology from the Israel–Palestine road map for peace announced by President Bush in 2002, it showed a way for Burma to emerge from its long tunnel and reconnect with the world. Khin Nyunt seemed fated to eclipse Than Shwe and take the top job. But power shifts in Burma are very rarely bloodless. Khin Nyunt's 'road map' concept guided Burmese strategy from its announcement to the inauguration of President

Thein Sein in March 2011 and beyond. But its author is long gone.

Building on his achievements, Khin Nyunt decided to deal with Suu, the thorn in the regime's flesh, in a diametrically opposite manner to that taken by Than Shwe: not to liquidate but co-opt. Accordingly he sent a trusted deputy, Brigadier General Than Tun, to negotiate with her about bringing the NLD back into the National Convention, the body tasked with drawing up a new constitution, which Suu's party had walked out of in 1995. Despite her near-death experience at Depayin, Suu participated willingly if warily. The two held a number of meetings, and by May 2004 an agreement bringing the NLD back in the National Convention had been drafted. Khin Nyunt now had the awkward task of presenting the deal to Than Shwe. To Suu's fury, the senior general turned it down flat.

It was now open war between the regime's two top figures. Two months later, when Khin Nyunt was away in Singapore, officers of an intelligence agency set up by Maung Aye, the third member of the top triumvirate, and operating in parallel to Khin Nyunt's Military Intelligence, raided an MI depot in Shan state and claimed that it had found evidence that the network was involved in illicit trade. In retaliation Khin Nyunt ordered his top staff to compile incriminating dossiers on his rivals at the top of the regime – but before they could do anything with them he was purged. On 18 October 2004, state-controlled media carried a one-line announcement that, at the age of sixty-four, Khin Nyunt had been 'permitted to retire on health grounds'. Once Than Shwe and Maung Aye had got their man down, they proceeded to make sure that he was out for the count: he was put on trial, found guilty of corruption and sentenced to forty-four years in jail, later commuted to house arrest.

It was the biggest shock the regime had taken since the detention of Khin Nyunt's late patron, General Ne Win, a dozen years before. But Ne Win, the former dictator, was very old and had been marginalised years before that. Khin Nyunt by contrast was at the height of his power, so the collateral damage was correspondingly greater.

To ensure that the intelligence accumulated by MI could do the regime no harm, Khin Nyunt's senior colleagues were also put on trial and given colossal jail sentences. Than Tun, for example, was sentenced to 130 years and forced to serve his time at one of Burma's most remote jails, where he remained long after the great majority of anti-regime political prisoners had been released. And Brigadier General Thein Swe, father of Sonny, was sentenced to 152 years, to be served at the notorious Myingyan Prison, in central Burma, where many political prisoners had been tortured and some had died of starvation. (President Thein Sein pardoned him in 2014.)

With the arrest of Brigadier General Thein Swe, the *Myanmar Times*, Burma's most interesting newspaper, was left as naked as a new-born baby. Sonny Swe, Ross Dunkley's partner, was arrested at the same time as his father, and now the regime got its revenge for the special treatment Khin Nyunt's patronage had allowed the newspaper since its inception. Sonny was charged with publishing a newspaper without approval from the Ministry of Information's Press Scrutiny Board, convicted and sentenced to fourteen years in jail – seven years for the Burmese language edition and seven for the English one. His 51 per cent share of the business was transferred to his wife, but within a year she was forced to sell it to the man destined to become Ross Dunkley's nemesis: Dr Tin Tun Oo, known within the paper as TTO: a smooth, smiling, plausible character, the publisher of a number of Burmese language magazines and at the time vice chairman of the (regime-approved) Myanmar Writers and Journalists Association. He was also believed to have a close relationship with the Ministry of Information.

It was the beginning of a long battle for control of the newspaper during which Dunkley refused to let TTO into the office except for the monthly board meetings. 'He thinks he knows the way,' Dunkley told an undercover Australian film crew, 'I think I know the way best. [But] if I am running the company there is only one way and that's my way.'[8]

Things came to a crunch in 2010, as Burma's first general election in twenty years approached. The crisis at the newspaper was caught by the Australian film crew's cameras. In August of that year TTO resigned from his post with the regime's tame writers' union to run for election with the Union Solidarity and Development Party, the junta's proxy party, conjured into existence the previous year. Dunkley was scathing about his partner's excursion into politics. 'TTO is a reptile so he'll only vote one way,' he said, 'like a lizard going to water.'[9]

The election was comprehensively rigged, but not sufficiently so to get 'the reptile' into Parliament. But meanwhile the election coverage of the *Myanmar Times*, perhaps more robust than expected with the Australian team's cameras covering the whole thing, excited the hostility of the regime at an exceptionally sensitive moment. On polling day, Dunkley and Burmese colleagues were watching the activity around a Rangoon polling station when they spotted the tall, lean figure of Aung Thein Lin, the Rangoon city mayor, emerging. Dunkley urged his clearly reluctant Burmese colleagues to interview him. 'The Mayor is here – why wouldn't we want to talk to him?' he said in tones of consternation. 'He's the Mayor, mate, it's a great opportunity . . .'[10]

The two young Burmese approached the regime politician and from a respectful distance said, 'We are from the *Myanmar Times*.'

'We won't take questions,' the Mayor shot back. 'Don't take photographs. Leave now.'

The journalists persisted. 'The editor-in-chief wants to ask a question.'

'It doesn't matter. We are not in a position to answer. Go away!'

'All right,' they said, retreating to their car. 'Thank you.'

This brief exchange captures how remote the rigged 2010 polls, which the USDP won with 80 per cent of the vote, were from the spirit of real democracy; how little the ruling generals had changed when they changed out of their khaki uniforms – and how perilously out of step Ross Dunkley and his colleagues were with the nation's frightened, anxious mood.

*

The 2010 election may have introduced a dubious sort of democracy into Burma, but the military's grip had in fact been reinforced by their party's landslide victory, its power legitimised, and the pressure on the *Myanmar Times* grew worse than ever. The Australian film crew who had followed Dunkley and colleagues around during the campaign were expelled for activities incompatible with their (tourist) visas. Dunkley began to worry.

'TTO fails to win a seat, he's potentially an angry man, he'll look to blame people, he'll say everything's out of control at the *Myanmar Times*, people are getting expelled,' he fretted. '[He'll say that] he'll have to walk in as CEO, and only he can solve the problem. Well I've a very simple answer to that, that is "no", because when there's a bullet pointed it's going to be pointed at you and either I'll fire it or [the regime] will fire it, so you coming in is just another dead sentence . . . so stay away, mate, you're not going to make it.'[11]

But Dunkley's bluster didn't get him far: with both Sonny and his father still in jail, he had no handle on power, even indirectly. The coming weeks brought that home. Several staff were expelled, his own application for a new visa was turned down. Then on 10 February 2011 he was arrested and taken to Rangoon's Insein Prison. And the outcome that he had done all in his power to fight off since the folding of his 'political umbrella' came to pass: Tin Tun Oo took over as chief executive.

Initially Dunkley was told that the reason for his arrest was a visa infringement, but as he was paraded in handcuffs tramping in and out of court – it was the first time news cameras had been allowed near a Burmese courtroom – it emerged that the actual charge was far more serious. It was alleged that he had detained a pregnant sex worker, plied her with drugs, and assaulted her.

Geoffrey Goddard, Dunkley's right-hand man on the paper, told the Australian film-makers:

> Ross said, 'She came on to me straight away when I entered the bar.' She must have had some attributes that appealed to him because he took her home. When they got home he became convinced that something strange was happening so he decided that the intelligent thing to do would be to get her out of the house as soon as possible. So that's what he did. He made no mention of any struggle. A couple of days later he's accused of having assaulted this woman and having held her hostage for three days, which is absolute bullshit.
>
> They took him to court and said that Ross had breached his visa conditions by criminal activity. The woman apparently wants the assault charge withdrawn. Anyone who knows Ross knows he's not a saint by any means, but bashing up women is not on his list of sins.
>
> There's no doubt that the incident with the girl was a set-up. I am not suggesting for a second that Dr TTO was necessarily involved with that set-up, but someone in a position of power was, and it was part of a very deliberate attempt to embarrass Ross and perhaps have him removed from Myanmar.[12]

Then, just as the sight of Dunkley in his white executive shirt and plucky grin shuffling in and out of court in handcuffs was beginning to get repetitive, a god descended from the heavens to rescue him: Dr TTO himself, wreathed in compassionate smiles, ready to bail his partner out. 'He is my friend, my comrade, my colleague,' he told the television cameras in Burmese. 'His [court] case is his personal affair. It is nothing to do with the *Myanmar Times* . . . I have absolutely no involvement in this case. If he is eligible for bail, we are prepared to pay it. There is no grudge between us. We are good friends. Now I am wishing him the best of luck.'[13] And eventually, on 29 March 2011, forty-seven days after he was arrested and one day before President Thein Sein's inauguration, TTO's bail offer was accepted and Dunkley went home. 'I want to thank the judge for being so kind as to give me bail,' Dunkley said as the two men embraced and beamed for the cameras outside court. 'I thank my partner for standing by me at this time.'

The Australian's ordeal was not over yet. After more than twenty more court appearances during the next six months, he was finally acquitted of all charges except that of 'simple hurt' and went back to work, editing the paper. But despite the grinning double act with his hated partner, nothing had changed, no lessons had been learned: TTO remained locked out and the feud continued.

In January 2014, TTO's wife, Khin Moe Moe, went to the newspaper's office and informed the staff that she would take up management duties there at 1 p.m. the following day. Dunkley fired back an emailed memo warning her not to come to the office without his permission. When she nonetheless turned up as promised, she and the Australian 'were involved in a confrontation . . . in front of shocked newsroom staff' as the newspaper dutifully reported.[14] Dunkley yelled at her to get out; she replied, 'I am the owner of this company, you are the employee,' before retreating from the building. She then filed charges alleging 'assault or criminal force to a woman with intent to outrage her modesty'. Dunkley replied with a suit of his own alleging criminal intimidation.

It was all futile. Despite these further shows of bravado, the game was over. As aeroplanes crammed with salivating Western executives descended on Burma, eager to 'go forward and prosper responsibly,' as Sir Thomas Harris had urged them, Dunkley, the brash pioneer and forerunner of them all, quit the paper he had founded and fought so hard for and left the country.

*

When his boss and friend was in prison, Geoffrey Goddard reflected on the sad events and what caused them. 'I think Ross should have read more Kipling,' he said, and quoted the famous lines from his poem 'The Naulahka': '. . . A fool lies here/ Who tried to hustle the East.' 'Ross would have been wiser to devise some modus operandi for working with [TTO] instead of antagonising him constantly. He pushed the envelope too hard. He forgot that he was the outsider in Myanmar.'[15]

That is one of the obvious morals of Dunkley's downfall, and is clearly connected to the man's brash character: one suspects it would have been as hard for him to act more emolliently as it would have been for him to learn Burmese. The other related error, a fundamental one, is that, in his almost child-like desperation to vanquish TTO, he forgot the first lesson for every Westerner who chances his luck east of Suez: the vital importance attached to face. Dunkley may have thought he was merely engaged in an executive power struggle, but in Burmese terms he was publicly humiliating this wealthy, well-connected man every day.

For the Western business person, the hazards of Burma, as exemplified by Dunkley's progress, were terrifying; the rewards firmly located in the realm of the hypothetical. That's why, in the months after Suu Kyi's election to Parliament, thousands of them came to 'look, learn, laugh and leave' as a former diplomat put it – to go home without making any commitment.

For the holidaymaker, however, the leap into Burma was an easier choice, a joyful adventure. Everywhere else in Asia was old hat. Even Cambodia had come in from the cold. Vietnam was a backpacker cliché. Bali was overrun, Thailand all too familiar, and its capital an excellent example of how to ruin a nice old town with money and concrete.

So this was Burma's moment. It was little known compared to the other countries in the region; the word 'exotic' could still be applied to it without irony. It was Buddhist, which still, just about, meant sweet, smiling, good-natured, benevolent. Like Thailand, there were pagodas everywhere but they were of a different shape. Monks, many of them children under ten, left their monasteries every morning to file picturesquely down the streets collecting alms – scenes rarely to be glimpsed in any other Buddhist country. Little nuns in their pink robes did the same.

These were the Burmese: not knowing, not corrupted, not even modern to any discernible extent. Unlike Bangkok, there was no Patpong with its live sex shows and massage parlours, no gruesome Western wrinklies with local totties on their arms, no ladyboys, at least none in evidence, and while this might deter a certain class of traveller, for the majority it was fresh and attractive. Every British high street worth the name has its Thai restaurant, alongside its Chinese and its Indian. But who knew what the Burmese ate? Who had ever read a book by a Burmese, or seen a film, or heard a pop song? These people had been in their own bubble for half a century. And now they were coming out.

As with so much else in the previous twenty years, it was Aung San Suu Kyi who held the key. Back in 1995, General Khin Nyunt had attempted to use Suu's first release from house arrest to lever the nation open a crack, declaring 1996 'Visit Myanmar Year'. Suu wasted no time in pouring cold water on that initiative. 'Make 1996 a year for *not* visiting Burma,' she told the *Independent* tartly. 'Burma will always be here. Visitors should come later.'

This off-the-cuff remark in an interview was a good demonstration of her remarkable influence: her throwaway advice turned into a de facto boycott that lasted fourteen years. But now Suu was finally persona grata in her own country, a Member of Parliament, and free to travel, with a personal assurance from the president that if she went abroad, she would be allowed to return. And as she ended a hiatus lasting twenty-two years, boarding a plane for Thailand in May 2012, the world – with the boycott formally lifted by Suu herself, seconding a remark by U Win Tin – began coming the other way. Between 2010 and 2013 the number of foreign tourist arrivals nearly trebled;[16] in 2012 alone, income from tourism increased by 70 per cent.[17]

As is often the case, the early birds got the worms. In the first three years after Suu's release and Thein Sein's election, Burma was struggling to adjust to the new realities, so the country had all the unique, off-beat crankiness of the old days but with enough of the new efficiencies to sand some of the rough edges off a visit.

Taxis were the beaten-up, recycled Nissans and Mazdas of tradition; they had right-hand drive, as in Japan and Britain and a few other places, but the nation also drove on the right – a dangerous combination when overtaking on winding roads as the driver has to commit his vehicle to the oncoming lane before he can see if traffic is in fact oncoming. Like many of the crazier aspects of life in Burma, the lane change was a Ne Win caprice, announced and implemented overnight and without explanation in 1970, on the orders of the man whose word could not be questioned. It was mad, but it was also one of the things that made Burma stand out from the crowd.

Even after March 2012, when Burma abolished its dual exchange rate racket, it remained a cash economy: it would be another two years before a tsunami of ATMs hit the country. Until then, tourists who omitted to pack enough pristine dollar bills to cover all eventualities were in trouble. But it was trouble you could take in your stride; trouble that, in a homogenised world, when practically everywhere one can think of 'has been zoned commercial' as one happy hedge fund manager put it to me, one almost welcomed; trouble you could write home about and joke about later.

Burma's emergence as a destination of interest, which one could now visit with a clean conscience, also coincided with an extended period of political trauma, protest and deadlock in the neighbouring country which had prospered for decades while Burma stagnated: Thailand.

The reversal of fortunes was remarkable.[18] Week after week Thailand was in turmoil, red shirts and yellow shirts on the streets of the capital locked in bitter dispute which no one seemed able to defuse and few to understand; the nation suddenly dumped, after a half century of dramatic economic progress, in a tight political cul-de-sac. Meanwhile, across their long shared border, Burma, so recently the region's pariah, enjoyed the sort of accolades which had seemed Thailand's by right.

The disparity in living standards remained glaring, but while Thailand's wealth resulted in the capital city's historic charms being buried in concrete canyons, and the countryside growing ever more bland, Burma retained abundant charm along with its quirky driving practices and lousy Internet connections.

Visitors discovered that Burma wasn't all monks and nuns. On the west coast there were beach resorts including the most famous one, Ngapali, with long, pristine beaches and the sort of rough-and-ready appeal that was only a vague memory in Phuket or Koh Samui. And while Bangkok drowned in ferroconcrete, Burma's commercial capital Rangoon, by far the biggest, most dynamic and important city, was also, for an Asian city of 5 million or more people, uniquely unspoiled. With investment finally released from the bonds of isolation and autarky, it was of course at imminent risk of going the way of Bangkok. In the hope of preserving it from that fate, a group of local architects and lovers of the city took up arms to defend it.

Rangoon remained Asia's most colonial capital. The city had been named Yangon, 'End of Strife', by King Alaungpaya when he conquered it in 1755. But Burmese monarchs had always chosen to build their capital cities in the central dry zone, not on the coast like Rangoon, where the heat and humidity and accompanying disease, not to mention the threat from sea-borne invaders, were acute. In this sense the new capital, Naypyidaw, is a return to ancient form. Under the rule of the Burmese kings, in contrast, Yangon was peripheral.

After its annexation by Britain half a century after Alaungpaya's invasion, Rangoon became an archetypal colonial city. The city's two great Buddhist *zedi* or stupas, Shwedagon and Sule, dominated the panorama as they still do today, but in most other respects this was a British town. Like the great British cities of India, its organisation was clear and plainly legible. It was divided into three elements: a cantonment, the army base near the present-day airport; civil lines, the relatively fresh and cool zones, upland and inland, where the foreigners built their comfortable homes; and the bazaar, the tight-packed commercial area downtown, on the shore of the Yangon River, built on a tight Manhattan-style grid. This area was also home to the large Victorian buildings from which the city was run and where the money was counted: the city hall, the banks, the customs house, the general hospital, the Pegu Club and the vast domed and turreted Government Secretariat from which the colony was ruled.

It is these colonial relics, most built of red brick and redolent of certain parts of central London, which came to define the city's character. They were left to crumble and decay during the days of Ne Win's Burma Socialist Programme Party, and now, with new money battering at the city's gates, eager to throw up office towers and re-fashion the city in the mould of Bangkok, their future is increasingly under threat. And the fact that these buildings are so un-Burmese in their origins and appearance worsens the odds on their survival.

Moe Moe Lwin, the architect who heads Yangon Heritage Trust, the organisation created to throw the city's historic urban fabric a lifeline, is well aware of the challenge. 'Urban conservation has never been part of our education,' she told me. 'Many architects say, "What are you doing with those colonial buildings? They have nothing to do with us!" Older people were taught all their lives that everything colonial is bad, and that's hard to change.'

Yet, as the Trust's work of documentation reveals, old Rangoon is far more than colonial domination writ large. Here are the buildings where Burma's currency was invented, where Armenian and Chinese and Baghdadi Jewish immigrants sank roots and threw up extraordinary palaces. It was in the sprawling Government Secretariat building that the father of the Burmese army, Aung San, exercised a modicum of power before independence, as leader of the interim government, and here he was tragically assassinated. Every step of the old downtown is dense with the history of a city of hard-working immigrants. It remains a city of rich diversity today, despite the forced repatriation of tens of thousands of ethnic Indians early in the Ne Win years.

If any of the old buildings channel patriotic Burmese rage about the humiliations of the past it would have to be the old Pegu Club, where the colonial elite met to sink their gin and limes and exchange rancorous gossip about the natives, just like the club bores and soaks in Orwell's *Burmese Days*. Yet shorn of those odious connotations the club, though now badly decayed, appears for what it is, an airily floating teak masterpiece, one of the few colonial buildings whose design and construction acknowledge that it is in the tropics rather than the City of London.

Despite its ramshackle state, the Pegu Club's potential as a heritage palace is beyond doubt. 'It could be converted into a hotel,' Moe Moe Lwin suggested, 'perhaps incorporating a modern hotel building in the compound, which is quite large, and using the old building as a lobby, dining and bar area.'[19] Burma is poised at a delicate moment in history when its past is a closed book, but the future teems with possibilities.

But there is an ideological element to all these discussions, an element of which most foreign newcomers are entirely unaware. To Ross Dunkley it stood to reason, mate, that a foreign owned and edited newspaper was a good thing, a necessary step in dragging Burma into the modern world. To lifelong expatriates like Thant Myint-U, grandson of the Burmese UN General Secretary U Thant and the moving spirit behind the Yangon Heritage Trust, conserving Rangoon's nineteenth-century fabric is a vital way to honour a city of special richness and diversity.

But the gut feeling of many Burmese, educated and otherwise, both rich and penniless, is different. For them, it was the foreigners (Westerners) who had caused all Burma's problems in the first place, destroying the monarchy, shattering the nation's sense of itself. In throwing them all out and closing the country, Ne Win had tried to undo the damage. But now the same thing was happening all over again. Dunkley, the Yangon Heritage Trust, the tourists tramping all over the temples, the new whizz-kids settling in Rangoon, looking to make a buck – they were all part of the same phenomenon. None of it would bring lasting good. And worst of all was their nauseating hypocrisy.

My friend Edward (not his real name), half-Burmese, half-British and a successful businessman, has spent most of his life outside Burma and is one of the most sophisticated Burmese I know. But even he is not immune to these emotions. In March 2015 he forwarded me an invitation he had received from the British Chamber of Commerce in Burma to attend a lecture at the Yangon University of Economics. The subject: why responsible business matters in Myanmar. The speaker: Lord Green, the UK Minister for Trade. When we met up Edward said:

> They send Stephen Green over to lecture us on business ethics. This is the man who earned more than £25 million year after year when he ran HSBC, who was in charge at the bank when the Afghan Taliban used its services to launder $100,000, for which it was fined $1.9 billion, and whose Geneva office was raided last month on charges of allowing money-laundering all over the world. And he comes to Rangoon to lecture us Burmese on ethical business . . .
>
> That's the style. They come over, people like the former British ambassador who runs the Myanmar Centre for Responsible Business, trying to tell us how to do things correctly, when they are up to all sorts of skulduggery themselves, trying to corner the markets just as they have been doing since the Opium Wars.
>
> Why don't they pack up and go home? We don't need their advice! Look how ordinary Burmese responded to Cyclone Nargis, pouring out their own money to charter cars and boats to take aid to the Delta . . .

With all this talk of ethics, all they are trying to do is corner a lion's share of the new Burma business without looking bad to shareholders or the media back home. Behind it, there is this old sense of entitlement: as one retired ambassador said to me long ago – 'Burma is OURS' . . .

My friend's indignation is understandable. Burma had been isolated for the whole of his adult life. Suddenly it is in touch with the world again. The old bans on speaking out have been removed. The arrival of democracy promises to put power, or at least a bit of power, in the hands of the people. The result – among all the good, positive results of reform – has been a steep rise in feelings of xenophobia. And in the only corner of Burma in which large Buddhist and Muslim populations live in close proximity, the outcome of all that was a wave of murderous violence that shocked the world.

8
ALIENATION

BARELY one month after Aung San Suu Kyi and her National League for Democracy colleagues took their seats in Parliament, a twenty-eight-year-old Buddhist woman was reportedly raped and killed by three Muslims on the island of Ramree, in the south of Arakan state, on Burma's west coast. Human Rights Watch reported:

> Details of the crime were circulated in an incendiary pamphlet, and on June 3 a large group of Arakan villagers in Toungop stopped a bus and brutally killed ten Muslims on board. Human Rights Watch confirmed that nearby police and army stood by and watched but did not intervene. In retaliation, on June 8 thousands of Rohingya rioted in Maungdaw town after Friday prayers, killed an unknown number of Arakan, and destroyed considerable Arakan property. Violence between Rohingya and Arakan then swept through Sittwe [the capital of the state] and surrounding areas.[1]

There was nothing unpredictable about the eruption of violence in Arakan. The following year, as communal antagonism spread across Burma like a virus, attacks occurred randomly around the country. But the violence in Arakan was of a different order. It was an outpouring of bitter hostility – not unlike that between Catholics and Unionists in Northern Ireland during 'the Troubles' – between communities which lived in close proximity but with zero integration, amid growing competition for what few jobs and resources were available in this dirt-poor state, the second poorest in Burma.

With the return of democratic elections in 2010, a new and especially incendiary element was added to the mix: competition for power. After fifty years of tyranny, the people of Arakan were no longer merely at the mercy of the junta's whim, closely monitored and tightly controlled. All those bonds were slackened. Now they were allowed to run their own affairs, voting for their own representatives. And suddenly, for the majority Arakan Buddhists, the demographic weight of the rapidly growing Muslim community, who in the capital Sittwe were numerically almost equal to them, changed from being an irritant and a simmering fear to an existential challenge. Who was going to run Sittwe, to run Arakan? In whose name, and for whose benefit? With what consequences?

No doubt about it, this was political violence, covertly organised with the complicity and sometimes the active participation of the authorities, aimed at changing the balance of power in the quickest and crudest way possible – by forcing the enemy to flee. And Muslim communities responded in kind. 'Marauding mobs,' Human Rights Watch reported, 'from both Arakan and Rohingya communities stormed unsuspecting villages and neighbourhoods, brutally killed residents, and destroyed and burned homes, shops and houses of worship. With little to no government security present to stop the violence, people armed themselves with swords, spears, sticks, iron rods, knives . . .'[2]

The upshot – no surprise – was a victory for the majority community: the desired demographic shift was accomplished, as Human Rights Watch documented: as a direct result, some

140,000 Muslims – many of those forced to move did not identify themselves as Rohingya – were settled in temporary camps, miles from their homes. 'The Burmese army's presence in Sittwe eventually stemmed the violence,' Human Rights Watch wrote. 'However, on June 12, Arakan mobs burned down the homes of up to 10,000 Rohingya and non-Rohingya Muslims in the city's largest Muslim neighbourhood while the police and paramilitary Lon Thein forces opened fire on Rohingya with live ammunition.'[3] Before the violence, Human Rights Watch noted, Sittwe's population 'was about half Arakan and half Muslim . . . most Muslims have fled the city or were forcibly relocated . . .'[4]

I flew to Sittwe to try to understand what had happened there. I was expecting a gritty, congested, densely urban place not unlike downtown Rangoon, with alien communities crammed up against each other where tempers could flare and trivial incidents quickly turn into bloody conflicts. I found instead a sleepy, dusty, overgrown village where time appeared to have stopped not long after the British left in 1948. Sittwe has long sandy beaches and a port facing the Bay of Bengal which one might expect to be the Liverpool of Burma, full of ships loading and unloading. Instead – a legacy of General Ne Win's closed-country policy and its long shadow of insularity – it is home to a few antiquated wooden fishing boats and little else. To buy petrol for our scooter we hailed an old woman by the side of the road who sold us a few jugs of it. The Internet is a challenge all over

Burma; in Sittwe it was an impossibility. Perhaps the air of torpor and sloth reflected the fact that the source of tension for the town's Buddhists – the presence of a population of Muslims roughly equal in size – had been purged so thoroughly that there was no longer anything to get excited about: only one small Muslim ghetto remained, guarded by police. On the main road out of town we passed a gleaming golden pagoda. Opposite were the burned-out ruins of one of the many mosques destroyed in the violence.

We drove out of town, past Sittwe University, and in a small house set back from the road met Aung Win, a grey-bearded Rohingya activist, who told us his story.

He was born in downtown Sittwe in 1956. In his youth Arakan's Muslims were still free to move around the country, and he graduated from Rangoon University in 1976, after which he returned to his home town and worked with his father in the town's market. 'Problems occurred between the communities during the years of the military dictatorship – I remember one incident in 1999 – but they would only last a day,' he said. 'The bar on movement began in 1994, but I got around it by paying bribes to the immigration department, so my son and two daughters could go to Rangoon to study.' All three graduated and now work in a friend's company in that city.

Why did he think the violence of 2012 was so much worse than previous incidents? 'In the past the military could get it under control within two or three days. This time the Arakan Nationalist Party and the governmental party were behind the violence – they wanted to show the people, you need the military to control the situation . . . I want to say to President

Thein Sein – I love him dearly, by the way – why did you say we are not citizens of this country? Why are you still keeping our people in camps ten months after the violence, with the rainy season coming?'

One of the camps set up for those who had lost their homes was another mile down the main road, behind a police barrier. Across a few acres of bare earth, 7,000 former residents of Sittwe were living under canvas, with a madrassa and a few other facilities housed in crude shacks. No one had a clue how much longer they would have to stay there, or where their next destination might be. The ethno-religious segregation of the Arakan capital was practically total.

Back in Sittwe in the evening, at an open air tea shop where men of the town sit and chat, we met activists belonging to the Arakan Nationalist Party, which had won forty-five seats in Parliament in the 2010 election. These were the men behind the recent violence – or rather, behind the Buddhist self-defence against Bengali violence, as they preferred to describe it.

For these men, the violence was sparked by Muslims from whom they have always been estranged, who they say have no roots in the city or the larger region, and of whose aims they are deeply suspicious. 'There are no Rohingyas settled in this region,' I was told. 'Muslims came into this region from Chittagong [from across the border in Bangladesh] to work as farm labourers at harvest time, after the First Anglo-Burmese War. Then they returned to Chittagong.'

What happened in June, they told me, was that the Bengalis 'transformed a civil argument into a religious matter. They gathered in a mosque then set our houses on fire and killed our people. Nine Arakan villages were set on fire. Our Arakan people were attacked by them. Later we had to defend ourselves from the attacks. It is our right.'

I was introduced to a large, shambling man of sixty-five, an engineer who did some fortune-telling on the side and who said he was the son of a farmer from Cox's Bazar, on the Bangladesh coast close to the Burmese border. Judging by his blue eyes he may well have had some European blood, too. Like the other activists we met in Sittwe, he declined to give his name. At 10 p.m. he interrupted our conversation to turn on his transistor radio to listen to the BBC World Service Bengali language news.

He took a long historical view of Arakan's communal problems. 'In the fourteenth century, Islamic terrorists came from Turkey and destroyed Nalanda University' – the great Buddhist university in eastern India that had stood for 1,000 years – 'in twenty-four hours . . . Everywhere, Islamic fundamentalism is a problem. In 1994 an armed force of Taliban-trained Bengalis entered Maungdaw' – in northern Arakan state, which today is 97 per cent Muslim – 'and exploded eight time bombs. Their plan was to occupy the state. Yes, we have the military on the Burma–Bangladesh border but they are doing nothing, they are sleeping. We are afraid of the explosive growth of the Bengali population. You in the West have a human rights way of thinking that doesn't work here. Our problem is that we are caught between Islamism and Burmanisation. We are afraid of being Islamised.'

*

It is impossible to grasp the scale and nature of the Rohingya problem without a historical perspective – and a clearer one than that provided by the fortune-telling engineer. Like many other comparable ethno-religious nightmares around the world, it was born of a situation created by colonialists for their own economic and political convenience, who had returned to their homes on the other side of the world before the dire consequences of what they had done had fully developed.

Arakan state was the first part of Burma to be conquered by Britain in the First Anglo-Burmese War of 1824–6. Rather than ruling the country as a separate colony, they tacked it onto the side of the Indian Empire. They promoted farming in Arakan and later in the Irrawaddy Delta, south-east of Rangoon, while Rangoon, which they practically built from scratch, became a thriving commercial and port city. And with the frontier between Burma and India erased, Indians, including both Hindus and Muslims, poured into Burma in search of work.

Within decades Indians had become the largest population in Rangoon, while in Arakan the British granted thousands of acres of arable land to Muslim *zamindars* or landlords on ninety-year leases. 'Bengalis are a frugal race,' explained a report from 1887–88, 'who can pay without difficulty a tax that would weigh very heavily on the Arakanese . . . [They are] not addicted like the Arakanese to gambling, and opium smoking, and their competition is gradually ousting the Arakanese.' This scheme, so satisfactory to the colonial tax-farmers, had two pernicious results, the shadow of which still lies across the state.

The Arakanese, though Buddhists, regard themselves ethnically as distinct from the far more numerous Burmans and have long had antagonistic relations with them. When the Burmans conquered Arakan – before the British came on the scene – many Arakanese fled into what is now Bangladesh, which was already under the relatively benign rule of the British (who had been present in that region since the seventeenth century), to save their skins. With the advent of British rule in Arakan after 1824, these Arakan natives came back – only to find that their ancestral land was now occupied and farmed by Muslim zamindars and their hard-working tenants. In this way the seeds of demographic fear and resentment were planted, nearly two centuries ago.

Another factor aggravated the latent tensions between the indigenous Arakanese Buddhists and the Muslim newcomers. As the historian Dr Aye Chan writes:

> Most of the Bengali immigrants were influenced by the Fara-i-di movement in Bengal that propagated the ideology of the Wahhabis of Arabia, which advocated settling *ikhwan* or brethren in agricultural communities. The peasants . . . besides cultivating the land, should be ready for waging a holy war upon the call by their lords. In the Maungdaw Township alone there were, in the 1910s, fifteen Bengali *zamindars* (landowners) who brought thousands of Chittagonian tenants . . . building mosques with Islamic schools affiliated to them.[5]

The potential for communal discord – with expropriated Arakanese and militant, fundamentalist Muslims living cheek by jowl – was obvious, but it did not much matter to the British who had engineered the situation because the firm hand of colonial military power was always there to keep it in check. What mattered were agricultural productivity and punctual payment of rent. And in any case, the cowed and marginalised Arakanese were moving out, as noted impassively by the British in the *Akyab* [former name for Sittwe] *Gazetteer* of 1917, edited by Deputy Commissioner R.B. Smart:

> That the Arakanese are being pushed out of Arakan before the wave of Chittagonian immigration from the west is only too well known. The Arakanese not having been accustomed to hard manual labour for generations cannot and will not do it now; it has to be brought home to him that if he will not do more for himself he must give way to the thrifty and hard working Chittagonian and his only reply is to move on.[6]

During the seven decades since independence, the Arakanese have been attempting to frame a different reply to merely melting away. Tragically, it often takes the form of arson and murder.

*

The word 'Chittagonian' is not much in use these days, and will leave most readers scratching their heads. But the dispute in which the people once known as the Chittagonians are enmeshed, and which the British unintentionally set in motion nearly two centuries ago, has lost none of its voltage or its ability to cause misery and mayhem among the communities affected.

Today they refer to themselves as Rohingya, and it is the persecution of the Rohingya and the refusal of the Burmese authorities to grant them citizenship that has ignited a

183

worldwide campaign in their support. But as the preferred term used by the Chittagonians to describe themselves, 'Rohingya' is a recent coinage. Scholars are in agreement that it has only come into currency in the past sixty-five years. The Burmese authorities may seem pig-headed in refusing to countenance the use of the word to describe the Muslims of Arakan. But they have their reasons.

'Chittagonian' was the word consistently used by the British to describe the Muslim immigrants who moved from the Chittagong Hill Tracts, in present-day Bangladesh, into Arakan state. An exhaustive search of the archives maintained by the British on Burma matters since the First Anglo-Burmese War of 1824–6 has not located even a single reference to 'Rohingya'.[7] This includes successive censuses which broke native populations down into precise and sometimes tiny ethnic categories.

Historically, the only recorded use of the word occurs in a linguistic note by Francis Buchanan, an explorer, who visited Burma's then capital, Amarapura, near present-day Mandalay, in 1799. One dialect he collected there, he recorded, 'is that spoken by the Mohameddans who have long been settled in Arakan and who call themselves Rooinga, or natives of Arakan.'[8] But despite the word's hoary origins, it was not used of or by the 'Chittagonians', the Muslims who moved into Arakan in strength during British rule. In modern times, according to Dr Aye Chan, 'The word "Rohingya" was first pronounced by Mr Abdul Gaffar, an MP from Buthidaung [in northern Arakan] . . . on 20 August 1951.'[9]

It is clear that by calling themselves Rohingya, the community's leaders are attempting to claim that they are as Burmese as the Arakanese, having been 'long settled in Arakan' as far back as 1799 – and therefore entitled to be counted as one of Burma's national ethnic minorities.

But the claim is both specious and confusing. The descendants of the Muslims who were indeed 'long settled in Arakan' in 1799 long ago adopted other names for their communities.

*

It was the British who had blithely assembled this tinderbox, thinking only of the commercial gains of having hard-working Bengali peasant farmers under the thumb of reliably tax-paying Bengali zamindars. Meanwhile the Arakanese Buddhists still laid claim to the land they had lost and were now back in Arakan, jobless, impoverished, and quietly gambling and opium-smoking themselves out of the national script.

It appears that the British gave no thought to the friction this might cause: the problem, after all, was irrelevant as long as the platoons of soldiers of the Raj (mostly Indian) were on hand to deal firmly with any disorder. The resentful emotions of the Arakanese and the possible jihadi intentions of the thousands of alien Muslim *ikhwan* (brethren) settled on Arakanese land were not an issue for the shareholders back home as long as order was maintained. Even more remote from their thoughts was the question of how those communities might fare living at such close quarters when the British army was no longer around. It is by absent-mindedness of this order – or indifference, to call it by the right name – that most of the world's most intractable problems have been brought into being.

Then in December 1941 the Japanese bombed Pearl Harbor and the following year invaded South East Asia, and the colonial power, in a desperate last-minute attempt to prevent or at least postpone the loss of Burma and defend India, made it all very much worse. They tossed a match into the tinderbox.

The Muslim immigrants settled in Arakan were the clients and natural allies of the British: it was the British who had given them new horizons and a new source of wealth. So it was natural that, just as the retreating British recruited the (largely Christian) Karen and Kachin on Burma's eastern and northern borders to help them resist the Japanese invasion, in the west they should cut a similar deal with the Chittagonians, forming them into a guerrilla force to fight the invaders. Aye Chan writes: 'The V Force, as it is called by the British Army, was formed in 1942 soon after the Japanese operations threatened the British position in India. Its principal role was to undertake guerrilla movements and to act as interpreters.'[10]

But in their haste the British had wildly overestimated the willingness of the Chittagonians to defend British interests – and fatally underestimated the strength of their animus against the indigenous Arakanese Buddhists. According to Aye Chan:

> The volunteers, instead of fighting the Japanese, destroyed Buddhist monasteries and Pagodas and burnt down the houses of the Arakanese villages. They first killed U Kyaw Khine, the deputy commissioner of Akyab District, left behind by the British government to maintain law and order in the frontier area; they then massacred thousands of Arakanese civilians in the towns and villages.[11]

Chan quotes the hand-wringing report of the secretary of the British Governor of Burma in exile, dated 4 February 1943, recording the disasters caused by this reckless V Force initiative:

> I have been told harrowing tales of cruelty and suffering inflicted on the Arakanese villages . . . Most of the villages on the west bank of the Mayu River have been burnt and destroyed by the Chittagonian V forces. The [Japanese] enemy never came to these villages. [The villagers] had the misfortune of being in the way of our advancing [V Force] patrols. Hundreds of villagers are said to be hiding in the hills . . . It will be the Arakanese who are ousted from their ancestral land . . .[12]

The V Force had no interest in protecting let alone perpetuating British rule in Burma: the pious object of these Wahhabi-influenced Muslims, Chan writes, was

> the creation of a Dah-rul-Islam [an Islamic emirate], or at least to their being united with their [Muslim] brethren in the West [i.e. in what was then Bengal, later to become East Pakistan then Bangladesh]. It also aimed at the extirpation of the Arakanese . . . The events during the war contributed to the Chittagonians' fervent sense of alienation from the heterogeneous community of the Arakan.[13]

Anthony Irwin, in his book *Burmese Outpost*, published in 1946, spelled out the consequences of this alienation. 'The Arakan before the war had been occupied over its entire length by both Mussulman and Maugh [an archaic term for

Arakan Buddhists]. Then in 1941 the two sects set to and fought.' The result, Irwin said, was that the state became a no-man's-land in which 'the Maugh took over the southern half of the country and the Mussulman the north. While it lasted it was a pretty bloody affair. My present gun boy, a Mussulman who lived pretty near to Buthidaung [in the north], claimed to have killed two hundred Maughs . . .'[14]

The upshot, when the Japanese were finally defeated and peace returned with the victorious British, was a region ethnically cleansed and polarised as it had never been before in history, with Muslims concentrated in the north and Buddhists in the south. Then the British announced they were quitting. 'As the British Labour Government promised independence for Burma,' writes Chan, 'some Muslims were haunted by the spectre of their future living under infidel rule in the place where the baneful Arakanese were also living.'[15] They petitioned the British to incorporate the three towns where they were overwhelmingly concentrated – Buthidaung, Maungdaw and Rathedaung – into East Pakistan.

It was a reasonable request: after all, East Pakistan, then still known simply as East Bengal, was where their parents or grandparents had come from; and in the partition settlement that preceded the British departure, the Pakistan border with India, both in the East and the West, was determined by the awarding of every state with a majority Muslim community (with the fatal exception of Kashmir) to Pakistan. If the British had done as the Chittagonians wished, it is reasonable to suppose that all the strife that has enveloped Arakan from the first day of independence right up to the present would have been avoided. But neither Britain nor the newborn state of Pakistan was willing.

The result was predictably disastrous.

*

The tragic paradox of empire is that what made dominion possible for the foreigners – divide and rule – made it impossible once independence was gained. The divisions the British created remained after they left, rendering the territory ungovernable.

Frustrated in their wish to merge with Muslim Bengal, their country of origin, two years before Burma's independence Arakan's Muslims began preparing for an uprising. The Muslim Liberation Organisation changed its name to the Mujahid Party, appointed commanding officers and assembled the weapons that had been collected during the war in mosques. Then six months after independence they sent a list of demands to Burma's new government.[16]

It was uncompromising: an Arakan homeland for Burma's Muslims where Urdu would be the 'national language' and with Arakan's Muslims 'accepted as [one of] the nationalities of Burma'.

'When the demands were ignored,' Aye Chan writes, 'the Mujahids destroyed all the Arakanese villages in the northern part of Maungdaw Township [and] some villagers and Buddhist monks were kidnapped for ransom.'[17] In June 1951 they published a Charter of 'Constitutional Demands of the Arakani Muslims', demanding that 'North Arakan should be immediately formed a free Muslim State as equal

189

constituent Member of the Union of Burma like the Shan State, the Karenni State, the Chin Hills and the Kachin Zone . . .'[18] This, too, received no reply from the government. Two months later, in Burma's *Guardian Daily* newspaper, Abdul Gaffar became the first member of North Arakan's Mujahid Party to use the word 'Rohingya' in print – in a studied, even erudite attempt to turn the imagined community of Arakan Muslims into a nationality.

The attempt was fatally successful: the self-defined Rohingya have been isolated, stigmatised, disenfranchised and spurned ever since. None of the peoples on Burma's borders was treated well by the military regime, but none was as badly abused as the Rohingya, who were not only denied the status of 'nationality' which they demanded but, under General Ne Win, were even barred from obtaining citizenship. That remains the state of affairs today: far from ameliorating their conditions, the advent of a sort of democracy has, by enfranchising their historic enemies, the Arakan Buddhists, caused them to be driven ever more pitilessly into their own ghettos, with no hope of relief except by surrendering to the extortions of traffickers and setting off across the Andaman Sea in the hope of finding asylum and work, usually in majority-Muslim Malaysia. As a result they have been, for many years now, the object of a global outpouring of compassionate concern.

But they have been their own worst enemies. By embracing the most fanatical strain of Islam, Wahhabism, and doing their best to drive the native Arakanese out of the northern part of the state and turn it into an Islamic emirate, they ensured that they would for ever after be looked on with fear and suspicion by their Buddhist neighbours. Yet at independence Pakistan rejected their attempt to attach northern Arakan to East Pakistan; and when the Pakistani civil war broke out in 1971, the Rohingya backed the West Pakistanis – ensuring, when the war ended with the victory of East Pakistan and its re-branding as Bangladesh, that they would have scant real friends on that side of the border either. Today Bangladesh treats those who have fled into Bangladesh to escape Burmese persecution just as badly as do the Burmese.

If the Rohingya bear heavy historic responsibility for their desperate situation, Burma's rulers have done much to make it worse. In 1956, during the so-called 'parliamentary period', U Nu, Burma's first prime minister, became the first and only Burmese leader to grant the Rohingyas' wish to be recognised as an ethnic nationality, and he promised to give northern Arakan the status of an autonomous zone, like other areas where ethnic minorities are in the majority. But far from being a historic compromise with the old enemy, an attempt to weld Burma into a genuinely diverse nation, this was merely a cynical manoeuvre to politically marginalise the Arakan Buddhists – thus adding even more fuel to the latter's hatred of both the Rohingya and the Burman establishment. The cynicism became apparent five years later when U Nu made Buddhism Burma's official state religion, to the dismay not only of Muslims but all the other minority religions as well.

The Rohingyas' claim to being an ethnic nationality resident in Burma for centuries was decisively rejected in the Citizenship Act of 1982, in which only the so-called 'big eight' groups settled in the country before the First Anglo-Burmese

War of 1824–6 were recognised as such. Like others who had arrived after 1826 but before independence – including large numbers of Indians and Chinese – General Ne Win offered what he termed 'associate citizenship'. Associate citizens, he said, could not be involved in 'the affairs of the country and the destiny of the State. This is not because we hate them. If we were to allow them to get into positions where they could decide the destiny of the State and if they were to betray us we would be in trouble.'[19]

The old monster had a point. Burma was too young as a nation, too frail, too beset by challenges to its very existence, to go along with the obviously mendacious claims of a Muslim community which had done its best to purge non-Muslims from the area where it lived, having failed to detach the area from Burma altogether. If ever there was an existential threat to a young nation's existence, this was it.

But the 'associate' toehold he offered them was not nothing. It gave those who held that status security of residence and much else. Most Rohingya arrived well before the 1948 cut-off point, so were entitled to this form of citizenship. But they insist on being recognised as an ethnic group, present in the country for centuries, and thus entitled to full citizenship and autonomy, too.

There is no indication that they are going to get it, and to drive the point home Thein Sein's government refused to countenance any official use of the word Rohingya. For example, Burma agreed to participate in an emergency conference on the boat people disaster, held in Bangkok in May 2015, on condition that the 'R' word be barred. Nor is the National League for Democracy shaping up to be any more emollient on the issue. That is the subtext of Suu's refusal to speak up in any substantive way for the Rohingya: the damage to her reputation as a symbol of human rights in the West matters far less to her political prospects than being boxed into a corner on an issue about which most Burmese have very clear negative views.

Even Muslims in the opposition camp are firm on this question. Mya Aye, a Muslim who was a leading democracy campaigner during the 1988 uprising and spent many years in jail as a political prisoner, told me, 'I'm not interested in the Rohingya as such. I'm doing politics, not for Buddhists or Muslims but for human beings. We need to amend the 1982 citizenship law, but I'm very concerned about the risk of Burma becoming a failed state. All citizens need to have an attitude of responsibility and accountability to the state.'[20] Mya Aye's implication is that, with their history of fanaticism, intolerance, irredentism and insurgency, the Rohingya have not demonstrated that they have such an attitude of responsibility.

But what sort of state is brave new 'democratic' Burma becoming?

9

THE ROAD TO NIRVANA

THE entrance lobby of Burma's new Parliament complex in Naypyidaw, up a long flight of marble steps and through high doors, is dominated by an enormous object which, to the eyes of someone raised in the Christian West, resembles nothing so much as a church font, fantastically enlarged to accommodate the baby of a giant. In fact it is not a font but a giant replica of the alms bowl of a bhikku, a Buddhist monk, on an equally oversize stand.

Burma, five years into its new political adventure, remains the only country in Asia where the daily ritual of monks collecting alms is still a common sight. And the huge replica of the bowl in Parliament tells the nation and the world how tightly enmeshed that simple act of collecting alms is with Burmese concepts of state, sovereignty, and legitimate power. These concepts have resonated in Burma for centuries. But can they sustain a modern, democratic state?

*

In backstreet Rangoon, shortly after dawn in the hot weather, a light haze is in the air. Massed crows screech, innumerable sparrows tweet in the trees. The makers of *mohinga* noodles and the fryers of parathas at their tiny stalls, and the market women who will spend the hot day selling fresh fish or green vegetables from the pavement, scrub the street clean and rig up plastic roofs against the sun and unpack their raw materials. Stray dogs, of which Burmese cities have as many as do Indian ones, but which compared with their Indian cousins seem to be well fed (though otherwise treated with indifference), wake, stretch, nose around glumly.

A shabby off-white pickup truck with a canopy over the back, packed with monks in maroon robes, pulls up on the street. The monks clamber out, each carrying a large black lacquer bowl, and they commence walking slowly down the side of the street in single file. The residents of the street have been expecting them: now, as if by some secret signal, every few yards along the street a woman stands in bare feet with a bowl of freshly steamed rice in one hand and a spatula or spoon in the other. As each monk reaches each woman he raises his bowl and she slaps a few spoonfuls of rice into it, then the monk moves on. Neither words nor glances are exchanged, and the line shuffles forward. When they reach the end of the road the monks climb back into the truck and drive round the corner to repeat the drill on another street.

We call it a begging bowl, but they are not begging. On the contrary, in the Buddhist view it is they who are the donors. The food flows one way and the merit, the virtuous consequence of the giving, flows the other. The Burmese word for the merit, the spiritual potency which is in the power of the monks to confer, is *hpoun*. Monks cultivate *hpoun* by having their heads shaved, renouncing the secular life, accepting the ten basic precepts (including chastity) of the monastic life and many other rules that go with it, and dedicating themselves to meditation, study and prayer. In the process they acquire spiritual potency which they are then in a position to give to those who give them the wherewithal of material life – food, robes and so on – thus enabling them to continue meditating, studying and praying. And so it goes on, in a perfect virtuous circle, by which the monks create 'merit fields' that benefit their networks of lay supporters.

We can see this exchange, food for merit, acted out every day on the streets of Rangoon and other Burmese towns and cities. And the enormous alms bowl displayed at the entrance of Parliament is a symbol of how this principle of the unbroken circle goes all the way to the top – to the king. Ingrid Jordt, a former Buddhist nun in Burma who is now an anthropologist, writes:

> For the past 800 years the authority of the Burmese sovereign has been dependent on the Sangha, the Buddhist monastic order whose forswearing of power and renunciation of worldly things is the source of spiritual potency, or hpoun.
> . . . At the top of the political food chain, the Sangha must supply hpoun to the ruler, who lacks legitimacy without it. In order to control the populace, the ruler must have access to the merit fields of the monks.[1]

The country's most senior monks acknowledged the right of the king to rule by accepting his offerings. The king, in return, conferred food, robes, money, Buddha images, monasteries and fine stupas plastered with solid gold on the Sangha. In mutual dependency, the king gained legitimacy and the monks gained political protection for themselves and for their religion. All proceeded in stately and codependent fashion towards the great goal, nirvana.

At least, that was the theory. But as human beings were involved, with all their flaws and failings and impurities and complications, it rarely worked out as cleanly as that. Burmese princes, for example, would often carry out large-scale massacres of their siblings before they could attain the throne and gain the blessings of the Sangha. Likewise venal or cowardly or politically ambitious monks would bestow their moth-eaten *hpoun* on monarchs who plainly did not deserve it, and both sides would flourish in turpitude.

*

'The Buddhist monk grabbed a young Muslim girl and held a knife to her throat,' wrote Jason Szep, a Pulitzer Prize-winning Reuters journalist. '"If you follow us, I'll kill her," the monk taunted police, according to a witness, as a Buddhist mob armed with machetes and swords chased nearly 100 Muslims,' in the central Burmese city of Meiktila in April 2013. '. . . Within hours, up to 25 Muslims had been killed. The Buddhist mob dragged their bloodied bodies up a hill . . . and set the corpses on fire. Some were found butchered in a reedy swamp. A Reuters camera-man saw the charred remains of two children, aged 10 or younger . . .'[2]

All things human tend towards corruption, but the tendency is most startling when it affects institutions and people who loudly proclaim their virtue and spiritual attainment. That's why it was shocking and bewildering to learn that Burmese Buddhist monks were deeply implicated in the violence against Rohingya in 2012, and the expanding circle of attacks against other Burmese Muslims which continued deep into the following year, as instigators, cheerleaders and even participants.

I visited the city of Meiktila a few days after the pogrom of April 2013 and met Ma Khin Aye, a survivor of the attacks who had returned to the charred ruins of her home. In a wilderness of scorched rubble, twisted corrugated iron and smashed pots, she was trying to locate what was left of her life. The jasmine flowers in her hair had wilted and she was trembling with fear. An unmarried woman in her forties, she sold toys in the market. She was afraid to speak in the open so we invited her into our car. 'I have no enemies, I have been living here for a long time,' she told us. 'Our communities have always been friendly: nothing like this has ever happened before. At Thingyan [Burmese New Year] they would invite us into their homes, we would invite them into ours for Eid.' Who started the attacks? 'Some of them were strangers – but when they wanted to find the homes of the "*kalar*" [a hate word for dark-skinned Muslims] it was local people who brought them here.'[3]

Two years after Burma began its trek towards democracy, one year after Aung San Suu Kyi's by-election triumph, Ma Khin Aye lost everything when the anti-Muslim mob – which included Buddhist neighbours with whom she had been on friendly terms for years – set her home on fire along with all the others in the block. Armed with sticks and iron bars they then stood in a line in the street, threatening to murder the terrified residents as they fled. Ma Khin Aye recalled, 'They stood there with sticks, shouting, "Come out, *kalar*, and we will kill you . . ."'

She escaped the flames with her aged mother, who was almost comatose with shock. She managed to get her onto the back of a scooter and took her to hospital. Now, one week later, she had come back to the ruins, rooting through the rubble to see if anything could be salvaged. While she did so, youths were openly looting the neighbourhood of anything of value that remained, loading up with metal buckets, wheel hubs and other saleable scraps. Meiktila had been under army lockdown for a week, but neither soldiers nor police were there to stop them. When we began talking to this victim, a woman from the majority community came up and screamed that we were only interested in one side of the story.

The massacre was triggered when a row over a damaged hair clip broke out in a Muslim-owned pawnbroker's shop in the town. Customers accused the shop owners of cheating and tensions grew. Weeks before, flyers had been distributed which claimed that local Muslims, financed by money from Saudi Arabia, were meeting in local mosques to plot against the Buddhists. That evening a monk on the back of a motorcycle was struck by a sword; the motorbike crashed and the monk was struck a second time then his body was doused in petrol and set on fire. News of the death flew through the market, and the town exploded.

The anti-Muslim violence took at least forty-three lives in Meiktila and left thousands homeless. It raged for days and was only quelled when the president declared an emergency and sent in the army. Unlike the anti-Muslim eruptions in Arakan state in 2012, where hostility has been simmering for decades, the Meiktila attacks came out of nowhere. The army succeeded in restoring order, but the anti-Muslim fanatics merely moved further on, attacking communities in fifteen towns and villages to the south of Meiktila and demolishing mosques and homes.

And then, most ominously of all, the flames arrived in Rangoon: fifteen young students died from smoke inhalation when the madrassa where they were boarding caught fire. The government was quick to say it was an accident, blaming an overheating transformer, but Muslims I spoke to, including a leading politician, claimed it was a deliberate attack, pointing to evidence of petrol burns inside the building. And the following night it almost happened again: five men were apprehended carrying petrol cans into a mosque near the city centre. A group of Buddhist monks spotted them before they could do any damage, and arrested two.

And then, to huge relief, the violence stopped, as mysteriously as it had started.

×

The one certainty about the Meiktila violence is that it was instigated by outsiders. Everyone I spoke to in the town, including members of the opposition NLD and citizens from the majority community who lost their homes, made the same point: it was 'travellers', 'strangers' or 'outsiders' who led the attacks. It's disturbing enough that ordinary citizens were so easily prompted to attack their neighbours' homes. But the opaqueness of the inspiration for the attacks causes darker fears.

One theory is that the riots were simply due to the recent liberation of the Burmese from fifty years of authoritarian rule: destructive urges held in check all these years were being given vent. But spontaneous mass action is practically unthinkable in a society as fearful and tightly controlled as this one: even today, very little that is transgressive happens without some nod of approval from authority.

As Kyaw Zwa Moe, editor of the Irrawaddy news website, pointed out, religious riots also occurred under military rule. 'In past decades, many Burmese people believed rulers of the Socialist and military regimes used religious tension as a political weapon to distract the public from anti-government movements,' he wrote. 'When opposition protests took place, religious riots often occurred as well, and many were convinced this was no simple coincidence. Today, with the Meikhtila violence, people are coming to the same conclusion.'[4]

But it is all extremely murky: there is no smoking gun. 'The theory that the violence was legitimised by powerful figures and that it was timed to go off when Suu Kyi began her overseas travels – that's been the theory for a long time,' a senior Western diplomat told me. 'But I haven't seen good evidence of high-level machinations. Everybody has spun that conspiracy theory. We have looked into it but no one has given us evidence. So I'm leery of it. There's something going on, it's certainly an organised effort at some level, but whether it's from the leadership I'm not convinced.'

But in fact the involvement of monks in the front line of the violence – with no official censure – establishes the complicity of senior figures in Burma's hierarchy of power beyond any possibility of doubt.

The Burmese monarchy is long gone: the last King of Burma was deposed by the British and exiled to the west coast of India in 1885. But the monks remain, in their hundreds of thousands; the rites of merit and patronage are enacted on the streets of Rangoon every day. And nearly seventy years after independence, Burma's rulers aspire to legitimise their rule by the same means that the monarchs used for 800 years.

Only a few years before these bloody events, in 2007, the West watched amazed and awed as hundreds of thousands of Buddhist monks seized the city streets in defiance of the military junta, walking through the monsoon rain in their robes, chanting the sutra of loving-kindness. Undercover video journalists filmed it all, and when the riot police and the army went in to club and shoot the monks, the same brave cameramen recorded every blow and every drop of sanctified blood that was spilt.

For Westerners sympathetic to Buddhism like me there was an extra reason to be impressed, even gratified, by the monks' courage. Other religions might carry out crusades and holy wars, glorify murderous martyrdom, debate which wars were good and which less good, call down blessings on soldiers going into battle. This by contrast was the religion of the Dalai Lama, who said, with reference to the Chinese who had invaded his homeland, 'your enemy can be your best teacher', the religion whose first precept was not to kill any sentient being, whose monks had tried to bring peace in Vietnam. It is the religion whose techniques for calming the mind and cultivating equanimity have been refined and passed down over millennia, and which on that account has gained tens of thousands of adherents in the West.

But in 2013 it was hard to recapture that Saffron Revolution mood. The undercover video journalists who filmed the

Saffron Revolution were now working for the world's Islamic media, and the footage that found its way onto YouTube was more hideous and disturbing than anything filmed in 2007: murdered babies, dozens of blackened corpses laid out neatly on the ground, a terrified figure fleeing then felled by a fierce blow, surrounded by men baying with bloodlust, who douse him in petrol and set him alight; his body twitching and squirming as he died.

Buddhist monks bear a grave responsibility for the carnage. In an article published in Burma's daily press, one of the most revered Buddhist teachers in the country, Sitagu Sayadaw, wrote that he 'deeply denounced these racial . . . conflicts without exceptions . . . Lord Buddha teaches non-violence . . .' The nation's 500,000 monks 'should deploy the weapon of loving-kindness . . . to dismantle the ugly unrest.'[5]

That was the tone we expected to hear from a Buddhist master, even if the comparison of loving-kindness to a weapon was unfortunate. But his message was drowned out by the rants of younger, strident teachers with very different ideas in mind.

Ashin Wirathu, the monk who has become internationally famous thanks to his grotesque moniker 'the Buddhist Bin Laden', is no more than five feet tall and delicately made. He became famous as the inspiration behind the so-called '969' movement which urges Buddhists to shun Muslim-owned shops and businesses.[6]

I met him in his leafy monastery in the south of Mandalay, a monastery, the Ma Soe Yein, which was of importance during the Saffron Revolution. So it is a turbulent, frame-shaking, game-changing sort of place, despite the peace and tranquillity that prevail in its expansive grounds.

We sit in the sunshine and I ask him about the pogroms that have wracked the country. Wirathu, who in 2003 was sentenced to twenty-five years in jail for preaching incendiary sermons (he was released with many other political prisoners in 2010), tells me he does not condone violence against Muslims, let alone advocate it. What he advocates is shunning them: encouraging Buddhist shops and taxis and other businesses to identify themselves as Buddhist, and encouraging the Buddhist public to patronise those businesses and not those belonging to the other community.

That is a long way from dousing individuals in petrol and watching them die. But it is not totally unconnected. Both actions – the passive shunning, the active slaughter – can be placed on a spectrum of responses to the message: that community is alien, and it menaces your safety and prosperity and the very future of your race and your religion. He told me:

> Our goal is a strategic one. We represent Burma's 135 ethnic groups. We are urging members of those ethnic groups not to follow the Muslim religion and not to sell anything to Muslims, and that includes paddy fields and houses. The reason is because we have to protect our religion. If we trade with the Muslims, they become rich: many Muslims have grown rich and have built big houses for themselves, and mosques, and slaughterhouses, which are a problem for Buddhism. Muslims are now dominating the Burmese economy.[7]

By urging Buddhist traders to put stickers in their windows to identify themselves, Wirathu and his fellow zealots hope to reverse the tide.

Listening to Wirathu's chauvinistic homilies as he urges his flock to close their hearts and minds to those who do not share their faith, one has to ask – were we simply taken in by the rhetoric of Buddhism, the calm smiles, the Dalai Lama's radiant humanity? Did we gravely misunderstand the import of that tide of saffron carrying all before it through the streets of Mandalay?

Dr Maung Zarni says yes. Writing in *Tricycle*, an American Buddhist magazine, the veteran Burmese activist and scholar blames the West for its 'rose-tinted Orientalist take on Buddhism', 'an age-old Orientalist, de-contextualized view of what Buddhists are like: lovable, smiley, hospitable people who lead their lives mindfully and have much to offer the non-Buddhist world in the ways of fostering peace.'[8] Instead he takes us back to the history, where in the first decades of the twentieth century, Buddhism became the rallying cry of Burmese nationalists campaigning against the British Raj.

All the early Burmese rebels against British rule were monks, he points out: the root of their anger was that the British had destroyed the monarchy which held the country together. Before the British arrived, the Burmese king and the monks had a symbiotic relationship. As Ingrid Jordt puts it, 'The monks' role was to admonish the king, and the king's role was to purify the Sangha.'[9] The spiritual and the political power were interdependent, each buttressing and legitimising the other. But with the monarch gone, the keystone of that arch was removed, and the society fell apart.

Aung San, the father of Aung San Suu Kyi and the man who engineered Burma's independence, was free of religious motivation, but what Maung Zarni calls 'ethno-religious nationalism' was revived after independence as the frail democracy sought ways to appear legitimate in the eyes of the people. And today, he says, '. . . the same ethno-religious nationalism that once served the Burmese independence movement has provided an environment in which . . . racism can flourish.'[10]

Professor Jordt says the psychological background is that Theravada Buddhism – the strain found in Burma, Sri Lanka and Thailand, and regarded by its followers as 'the pure teachings' of Buddha, as opposed to the supposedly impure developments in the Mahayana branches found in Japan, Korea, Tibet and Vietnam – is thought to be in peril. The Buddha supposedly predicted that his teachings, collectively known as the Dharma, would remain in human memory for five thousand years. Burmese Buddhists, says Jordt, 'feel that their religion is in decline in cosmological terms, and historically under threat . . . They are preoccupied with the fact that it is already past the two thousand five hundred year mid-way mark.'[11] In this context, she goes on,

> the opening of the country to the outside world has always been viewed with dread as the moment for further decline of the religion. I have heard monks talk about military rule and how dictatorship is actually *good* for the religion. Under military rule, people only spend their time doing religious works and spend their holidays on picnics at Shwedagon [Burma's most famous pagoda] rather than watching movies or shopping or other modern late-capitalist consumer activities. Part of the shared collective idea between military and laity and monks is the notion that preserving the religion is of paramount concern for the people.[12]

She goes on,

> One of the main ways that the military has historically kept
> tensions up, and kept attention off their activities, has been
> to drum up fears about how the religion is being threatened
> from outside – promoting xenophobia towards the West . . .
> and most especially through targeting Muslims as the biggest
> threat of all to Buddhism. The cautionary tales, often told by
> monks, about how Muslims essentially eradicated Buddhism
> in India, and the historic accounts of how monasteries and
> Buddhist texts were burned and statues defiled – this is rich
> lore that gets regularly exploited in the collective psyche.[13]

In Jordt's view, both 2007's Saffron Revolution and the
recent atrocities were motivated by the same urge: to protect
Buddhism from abuse and attack. The marching monks
wanted to save it from abuse by the army; the zealot Ashin
Wirathu wants to save it from Islam. The monks' first protest
in 2007 was a small demonstration against a steep rise in
petrol prices (which impacted on the contents of their bowls),
but their movement only began to grow after they were beaten
by police and the authorities refused to apologise. 'This was
a protest about protecting the religion,' says Jordt, 'not about
human rights violations or freeing Aung San Suu Kyi. There
was a component of that, but that is not what the monks were
en masse protesting. They were protesting the treatment of
monks and the threat to the religion. That they would now
be supporting the racist policies of the government is not a
surprise because it is still about the same issue – protecting
the religion.'[14] In September 2007, one group of marching
monks found their way to Suu's home where she was still

in detention and where she greeted them at her gate with tears in her eyes: they went to her with their palms pressed together. The meaning of this encounter was that the monks felt she offered a model of righteous, legitimate, protective sovereignty in contrast to the brutish and sacrilegious hand of the monk-beating military.

*

But with the arrival, in however imperfect a form, of democracy, the nature of the perceived threat to Buddhism has changed. It is no longer the military – who have, in name at least, renounced their claim to sovereignty in favour of elected MPs and an elected president – that menaces the Sangha and its teachings. Now – once again, as often throughout history – enemy number one is Islam, and those who adhere to it. And today the military, the monks' former enemy, is doing all in its power to pull the monks' strings.

Dr Zarni is right: the widespread appreciation of the philosophical insights of the Buddha Dharma, and the growing Western belief in its universal relevance – at a time when fewer and fewer people accept the claims of revealed religion – has blinded us to the fact that in certain key respects Buddhism shares the fatal weakness of both Christianity and Islam: namely that in a country where it is the dominant spiritual influence it becomes intimately linked to the political status quo, with consequences that can make a mockery of its moral tenets.

During the decades of military rule, the monks were often at loggerheads with the army. General Ne Win, for example, tried to sever the link between political authority and the Sangha, with the unintended consequence that the monks became increasingly independent of central control and connected instead to an expanding network of lay meditators, as Ingrid Jordt recorded in a fascinating study.[15] This gave them a degree of political independence from the junta, manifested in their support for Suu and the NLD in the election of 1990, and again in their participation in the protests of 2007.

But the military saw the danger of the monks becoming independent, and in the past ten years they have been doing all in their power to rein them in: putting them under curfew, limiting their ability to move around, requiring official permission for every sermon, planting agents in monasteries to keep account of who paid what to the monasteries, and leaning on major donors to make equivalent large contributions to state construction projects.[16] The overall effect – a paradoxical one in Burma's increasingly free climate of debate since 2010 – has been to make it far harder for independent-minded monks to get away with defying and challenging the government as they did in 2007.

The result is that today the monks are an overwhelmingly conservative force: paranoid about Muslims, hostile to secularisation, nervous about the opening of the country to the outside world; and, in the crucial face-off between the army and the forces of democracy symbolised by Suu, increasingly prone to side with the former.

Part of the reason for that is that Suu's interpretation of Buddhism – central to the development of her political identity and political thought since her return to Burma in

1988 – is itself seen as a suspicious and possibly dangerous foreign import.

Like the tens of thousands of students who took to the streets of Burma's cities in 1988, Suu knew what she wanted: an end to the dictatorship of a military which risked coming 'to be hated by the people', as she told the huge crowd at the Shwedagon Pagoda on 26 August of that year. Its rule should be replaced by multi-party democracy. 'Our purpose,' she shouted from the stage, in her first-ever appearance before a large crowd, 'is to show that the entire people have the keenest desire for a multi-party system of government.' She went on: 'All the people assembled here have without exception come with the unshakeable desire to strive for and win a multi-party democratic system.' And she reminded the crowd of the words her father Aung San had written. '"We must make democracy the popular creed,"' she read out. Democracy was '"the only ideology which is consistent with freedom . . . an ideology that promotes and strengthens peace".' In conclusion, she declared, 'Free and fair elections [must be] arranged as quickly as possible.'[17]

These were the fighting words that transformed Suu overnight from an obscure housewife with a famous name to the leadership of the biggest mass movement in Burma's history. There is no doubt that she spoke for the vast majority of her listeners that day. But when she spoke of democracy and the crowd roared their approval, were they talking about the same thing?

Suu knew plenty about the theory and practice of democracy in Britain from her twenty-three years living there. And although, as a Burmese citizen, she didn't have the vote, she had firm political views: when canvassers came to the door of the family home in Oxford at election time, her husband Michael would tell them to come back when she was home, because it was she who would tell him who to support.[18]

Suu left Burma in 1959, as the nation's fragile 'parliamentary era' was close to collapse. She was only thirteen. She spent the rest of her adolescent years in New Delhi, where her mother, Daw Khin Kyi, was the Burmese ambassador; at the age of twenty she moved to England to take a degree at St Hugh's College, Oxford. In all those years she kept up her Burmese, and she started writing a biography of her father. But until 1988, when her mother's sudden illness prompted her to rush back to nurse her, her only encounters with the country were on brief visits. U Win Tin confessed to anxiety about her debut performance at Shwedagon; and part of that was down to the fact that she was in many respects a foreigner.

So although Suu devoted much time in Oxford and elsewhere to thinking about her country and its development, these were home thoughts from abroad. And much of her thinking was coloured by her teenage years in India. In an essay of hers published after her return to Burma in 1988, in which she compared and contrasted the intellectual life of the two former colonies, she drew attention to the way that leading figures in the Indian Renaissance had acknowledged the barbaric practices, such as sati, which had become ingrained in the culture, and concluded that India had lessons to learn from outsiders. She quotes Ranmohun Roy, known as the father of the Bengal Renaissance, who wrote, 'The present system of religion adhered to by the Hindus is not well calculated to promote their political interests . . . It is, I think, necessary that some changes should take place in their religion at least for the sake of their political advantage and social comfort.'[19]

The contrast with the Burmese experience was marked. Burma had for centuries been badly ruled, Suu wrote, but the corruption and indolence of the rulers had little impact on the ordinary people because 'Burmese society, imbued with the spirit of Buddhism . . . was remarkably free from social injustices. It had no rigid caste or class stratification. Women enjoyed rights and privileges which a Victorian lady might well have envied. The practice of the ubiquitous monastery providing at least a basic education for local children had resulted in a high percentage of literacy.'[20] She quoted an early British administrator in Burma, Fielding Hall, who wrote: 'The land laws, the self-government, the social condition of the people were admirable.'[21]

But complacency about the equilibrium of Burmese society did not survive independence. The wild oscillations of the independent nation, lurching from a frail democracy into a vicious military dictatorship, proved it. Social reform was urgently called for. As a guide to what needed to be done, Suu quoted the words of J.S. Furnivall, the Victorian Englishman who founded the Burma Research Society. 'The Burma that we hope to assist in building,' Furnivall wrote, 'is like some old pagoda recently unearthed and in course of restoration. [It is] necessary to clear away cartloads of rubbish . . . I for one firmly believe that if the Burma of the future is to be a lasting fabric, it must be built up on the old foundations.'[22]

Suu commented, 'In such views can be seen the seeds of a renaissance: the urge to create a vital link between the past, the present and the future, the wish to clear away "cartloads of rubbish" so that old foundations might become fit to hold up a new and lasting fabric. But it was a renaissance that did not really come to fruition.'[23]

Now – returning in 1988, swept up in the popular revolution – it was time to make a second attempt. Because while the Burmese at large may, in the old days, have lived their lives little affected by the follies and failings of their remote masters, that was no longer the case in modern times, when the baleful influence of tyranny was felt right down at the grassroots.

Coming back to Burma from a country with a long-established secular democracy, she was clear about what was wrong with her homeland. 'It is not power that corrupts but fear,' she wrote, in an essay published in 1991 to coincide with her being awarded, in absentia, the Sakharov Prize for Freedom of Thought, her first major award. 'Fear of losing power corrupts those who wield it and fear of the scourge of power corrupts those who are subject to it.' The 'chief cause' of Burma's democracy movement, she wrote, was 'the humiliation of a way of life disfigured by corruption and fear'. The totalitarian regime 'deprived the present of meaningfulness and held out no hope for the future.'[24]

And the cure? A revolution of the spirit, she wrote, 'born of an intellectual conviction of the need for change in those mental attitudes and values which shape the course of a nation's development . . . A people who would build a nation in which strong, democratic institutions are firmly established as a guarantee against state-induced power must first learn to liberate their own minds from apathy and fear.'[25] And what were the prerequisites for liberation of this sort? '. . . A historical sense that despite all setbacks the condition of man is set on an ultimate course for both spiritual and material advancement,' she wrote. 'It is his capacity for self-improvement and self-redemption which most distinguishes man from the mere brute . . . It is man's vision of a world fit for rational, civilised humanity which leads him to dare and to suffer to build societies free from want and fear.'[26]

It was a ringing but vague manifesto, one which, combined with the persecution she so stoically endured for twenty years, hoisted her into the pantheon of our heroes. Naturally enough, it was a manifesto rooted in her life in the West, in her experience of its democratic institutions, her long exposure to the humanitarian values on which those institutions were founded: the ideal of 'a world fit for rational, civilised humanity',[27] in which material and spiritual improvement proceeded in lockstep. This was her road map, her sketch of the route Burma must take from fear-ridden tyranny to a nation of 'strong, democratic institutions', ridding itself of 'desire, ill will, ignorance and fear'. It was a vision in which the Buddhist principles with which she grew up were not denied but subsumed in a formula which did no violence to the Enlightenment-derived world view of the Sakharov Prize judges.

But now, on the cusp of crowning her long struggle with electoral success, there are those who say that the journey has not followed the route Suu intended. The people do not understand where she wants to take them. And now that the common enemy of military tyranny has been shaken off, those who do understand would prefer to go in a quite different direction.

Professor Jordt writes:

The Burmese democracy movement has always been first and foremost an anti-regime movement and Suu Kyi has long been the best-positioned opponent of the regime. But she herself takes a secularist approach to Buddhism. Her presentation of the faith as a 'revolution of the spirit' towards Western humanist principles has never been fully accepted by even her most ardent supporters inside Burma.

This secularised vision – a far cry from the Burmese ideal of a Buddhist state – was tolerated and overlooked by Burmans who recognised her ability to represent the cause of Burma to the international community. But now she is caught in a bind.

Standing up for human rights means siding with the Muslims and not supporting the place of Buddhism in the nation. Siding with the Buddhists undermines her credibility as a human rights superstar. She has chosen to remain silent – and drawn criticism from every corner.[28]

Instead it is people like Wirathu who take centre stage. Endorsing President Thein Sein for a second presidential term as the candidate best capable of defending the religion, he said of Suu, 'She doesn't know about Burma and if she became the President, the governance would be in chaos. Racial and religious conflict would deteriorate.'[29]

True or not, these are charges to which Suu – as she took her seat in the elected multi-party Parliament she had campaigned so hard and long for – struggled to find an answer.

10
THE ENIGMA OF SUU

WHAT are heroes for? Why do we need them?

As long as Aung San Suu Kyi was under house arrest, the point of her was easily grasped. She was Burma's bulwark against the total victory of the illegal military junta, a symbol of the regime's inability to convert total power into mass compliance. As she was unable to communicate publicly, little was demanded of her except resistance, consistent resistance: she must not bow, must not concede, must not give up and go away or change her mind. She must be not so much a human being as a rock. For more than twenty years, more than fifteen of them incarcerated at home, Suu played the role to perfection.

It was no fault of hers that her admiring public, which really knew little about her beyond her beauty and her defiance, filled the gaping holes in their knowledge with fond imaginings. This brave and beautiful woman had not only those essential qualities of heroism – bravery and beauty – but all the other ones too: she was a wise leader, a mistress of strategy, a person of compassion and patience in her private life, resourceful and astute in her dealings with her adversaries, good at judging her followers and preferring the able without alienating those less gifted. She must be as wise as an owl, crafty as a fox, strong as an ox, with the morality of a saint and the gentleness of a dove. She must also be of the same opinion on all matters as those who idolised her – for how could one idolise a person with whom one disagreed?

A list like this makes it obvious that such a person cannot exist. In particular, the image of the person, as fragile and inflammable as a poster bearing her image, cannot survive contact with power, which is like putting a lighted match in contact with paper. Nelson Mandela oversaw South Africa's peaceful transition to democracy but had a chaotic personal life, accepted favours from the wealthy, and did a deal with the Afrikaner establishment that many of those who had idolised him hated. Martin Luther King was a womaniser whose family have feuded over his name and legacy ever since his death. Mahatma Gandhi's limitations and quirks fill numerous books, and his legacy survives because he was never allowed to put his cranky ideas into practice. And so on.

We need these people. We need their sacrifice. And after that? Perhaps the awkward fact is that we need them to die, as Suu's father Aung San died, in their prime, before they can expose too much of their human frailty. To die as John F. Kennedy died, with his looks and his myth intact.

But Aung San Suu Kyi lives, her whole life pointed like an arrow at achieving the goals for which she suffered the loss of her freedom, the destruction of her family and the end of all the mundane comforts and pleasures she had enjoyed before. And since the end of her house arrest in November 2010 she has become an object lesson in the slipperiness of the concept of heroism, and the folly of hero-worship.

*

The date is 17 April 2013. Suu is on the stage of the Ishihara Hall in the University of Tokyo, where she has been invited to give a lecture on the subject of 'Democracy and Expectations on Young Leaders of the World'. She is resplendent in canary yellow, her habitual longyi paired with a tailored silk jacket, with a string of what may be pearls at her neck and a silk scarf. She is sixty-seven but looks twenty years younger.

After a brief introduction by the vice chancellor in clumsy English, she takes the floor and tells the packed hall that she did not choose the subject of the lecture but that sometimes obedience is necessary. It's a rather captious, ungracious opening that puts her hosts in the wrong and makes her appear their unwilling tool. If the subject is worth addressing, why quibble about who proposed it? If it's not worth addressing, shouldn't she have either imposed one of her choice or refused the invitation? Her grudging acceptance of the topic is the more surprising because, given the great age of all the senior leaders of the NLD other than herself, bringing on talented and ambitious young party members would appear to be an important priority for the party leader.

But for Suu and her party, ambition is a problem: she makes that very clear. This is a theme she has given much thought to. Those reckless or conceited enough to think they might walk in her footsteps need a good bout of self-examination about their motives. After being released from house arrest in 2010, she says, 'Questions were asked about the leadership of my party, the NLD, and there was a large cry for younger leaders to be brought in, and young people started talking about getting influential positions, meaningful positions, in the party.' She was not having any of that.

When I was released I made it quite clear that one should not think in terms of position but in terms of responsibility. I said that I was not interested in giving particular positions to anybody, young or old. I would think of it as giving people a responsibility, giving them a chance to take up certain responsibilities. And this is how I would like young leaders to look upon their tasks in life . . . It is not a question of becoming a leader, it is a question of assuming responsibility.[1]

A question occurs to me, sitting near the back of the hall on the left-hand side: are the two motivations, for position and responsibility, not complementary? Were you yourself and your colleagues not possessed of both in those far-off revolutionary days of 1988?

'Once you have assumed a responsibility,' she continues severely, 'you have to stick with it. Very often, my colleagues and I have asked how we were able to carry on through decades of oppression. Why was it that we decided not to leave our chosen path? . . . For me it was not possible to give up a responsibility that I had assumed out of my own free will.'[2]

So that is the problem for those people, young or old, who would like to work in responsible, influential positions in 'her' party: will they stick with it? Who's to know? Will they not crumble and collapse at the first signs of hostility or intimidation? Suu and her party co-founders stuck with it: they have the mental scars to prove it. But what about these thrusting young people?

Of course the only way to find out is to take a chance on them. But that is something which Suu and her party have found enormously difficult to do: hence the glaring lack of any promising successors to her, the scary void in the party ranks of people of some age and experience, people who should be the party's core.

There are two reasons for this: one is the belief, deeply rooted in Burma as in some other Asian societies, that young people should be respectfully subordinate to their elders. But reinforcing that cultural tendency rather than mitigating it, there is also Suu's suspicion – to invert Groucho Marx's famous maxim – that anybody who wants to belong to her club doesn't deserve to. The fact of aspiring to lead is a priori proof that they are not of the right moral calibre. That's because they have not given proof that they are of that calibre. What is the proof that you have that stuff, the right stuff of righteousness? Well, you must be willing to sacrifice.

There then follows an interesting though contradictory discussion of the notion of sacrifice. First she disavows it, as applying to herself. She says:

> I would like to talk about the word 'sacrifice'. People talk a lot about the word sacrifice. I find it personally rather embarrassing when people talk about the sacrifices I have made. Because I do not think I have made any sacrifices. I chose the path I wanted to follow and I walked that path out of my own free will. There was no sacrifice involved. When people follow a path they have chosen then talk about the sacrifices they have made, I want to say, what sacrifices? You chose this path because you wanted it, you believed in it. It is as though you were forced to give up something because other people made you do it . . . If you follow the path of your own choice you are not giving up anything for anybody else. You

are fulfilling your own destiny out of your own free will, so you do not have the right to demand anything in return, not even gratitude.[3]

Suu's grown-up sons, Alexander and Kim, do not seem to have followed her career, post-detention, all that closely. One hopes that is still the case now. One hopes they do not have to hear their mother telling the world that turning her back on her family – choosing politics over her husband and children – was no sacrifice.

And yet, having discarded the 'embarrassing' notion that choosing years of detention over the chance of being reunited with her family involved a sacrifice of some kind, she returns to this problematic word. 'In the old days,' she says, 'when the Greeks made their live animal sacrifices to the gods for a particular boon to be granted, they always said that for that boon to be granted, for that sacrifice to be successful, the animal's sacrifice must be willing.'[4]

Of course the notion that a sacrificial animal might be 'willing' to die is the purest anthropomorphism. But, having strongly rejected the notion that she had sacrificed anything of value, she now embraces that primitive idea. 'Behind that savage practice was a tremendous understanding of the meaning of sacrifice,' she says. '[The Greeks] said that unless the sacrificed animal was willing, the boon would not be granted. Sacrifice is something you make out of your own free will and you do not have the right to demand anything in return.'[5]

So there she was, being led through the gates of 54 University Avenue into indefinite house arrest – the sacrificial animal, 'that heifer lowing at the skies,/ And all her silken flanks with garlands drest . . .' She rehabilitates this 'embarrassing' sacrifice idea, applying it to herself: she gave herself willingly to those fires of solitude that burned so long.

But sacrifice can apply to other people as well as oneself. How is one to contemplate let alone describe the suffering of those – her children – who were sacrificed to her career without having any choice in the matter?

Suu has often faced the charge of being hard-hearted. If true it could be forgiven, considering the great stakes for which she has played and is still playing. But wrapped up in this Tokyo meditation of hers on sacrifice and free will one detects something worse – a ravenous egotism that perhaps the years of isolation only made worse.

*

Who exactly was this woman the world had lavished honours on for so many years? What made her tick?

For many months after her release, criticism of Suu was rare, and when it came it was as mild and tentative as it had been when she was a prisoner. That was partly because she was world famous yet almost unknown. But over the months, as she started travelling and speaking and then entered Parliament and got down to work, slowly she came into focus. We began to see through the startling beauty and the years of imprisonment to the person within.

It was remarked that she seemed to have a strong sense of entitlement. As an undergraduate at Oxford she had left her student friends, as ignorant of matters Burmese as everyone else, in no doubt as to the importance of her father, and of the value she attached to his legacy and to being the daughter of her nation's founding figure. From her earliest years these were things of pride and importance to her, but for a very long time she didn't know what to do with them, and had no inkling of where they might lead her. But she sensed that they could mean something tremendous, and before she married Michael Aris she elicited his understanding and consent in the event that some day, in some way, her Burmese destiny might call her.

In the meantime, as she flipped and flopped through the various options that life, post-Oxford, presented, the knowledge of who she was gave her a certain queenly rigidity. She always looked perfect, and usually perfectly Burmese. She was morally upright to the point of priggishness. When one of her permissive contemporaries at St Hugh's asked if she didn't want to sleep with someone, she replied, 'No! I'll never go to bed with anyone except my husband,' which raised 'a storm of mostly derisive laughter'.[6] Girlish gaucheness mutated into precocious upper-class hauteur: her Burmese bloodline got some Oxbridge polish, so that when, during a stint working in a lowly capacity for the UN in New York, she was hauled over the coals by the Burmese embassy on a passport issue, her dignity and elaborate courtesy left the embassy bureaucrats floundering.

The queenliness might have made her insufferable, buttressed as it was by perfectionism that bordered on the fanatical: her Christmas cards were always the first to be sent out, the cake that she baked for her son's birthday (in the shape of a tank) was immaculate,[7] and at the children's birthday parties, where the games were straight out of the textbook, no deviation from the rules was permitted. But these off-putting tendencies were counterbalanced by the slightly comical fact that her own life appeared as messy and incoherent as the next person's: she had obtained only a sorry third-class degree from St Hugh's, had dropped out of graduate school in New York for no clear reason, had struggled without great success to become an author and/or a scholar. She was a demanding, devoted mother and a supportive wife to her poorly paid husband Aris, a Tibet scholar at Oxford with his head in the Himalayan clouds. She made a start on writing a biography of her father, and dreamed vaguely of doing something back in Burma sometime, which might involve setting up libraries.

And politics? Unlike Benazir Bhutto, whom she preceded at Oxford and who became president of the Oxford Union, Suu had taken no part in the university's political life. We can take it on trust that she had strong political opinions, because she was in the habit of telling Michael which way to vote, but she left no record to indicate what they were. But we can be pretty sure – given all her declarations since – that they were closely linked to her views on the importance of duty and responsibility. So for example, when a close friend at Oxford called her attention to the struggle of the Greenham Common women besieging the US military base in the English countryside in protest at the installation of cruise missiles with nuclear warheads, her response was that these women would be better advised to go home to their families and their duties as wives and mothers.

This reaction suggests that she had something of a tin ear for politics, which is a little surprising. The daughter of Burma's most successful politician and of Daw Khin Kyi, Burma's first ever female ambassador who was also a fierce opponent of Ne Win and his regime, she spent all her childhood and adolescent years surrounded by the passions of post-colonial politics. Her uncle was the leader of the Burmese communist party, which was quickly embroiled in an insurgency against the Union government. The military regime's decision to appoint her mother ambassador to India was a polite way of sending this doughty enemy into exile. In New Delhi the prime minister, Jawaharlal Nehru, who had been a friend and comrade of Aung San before independence, took them under his wing and installed them in the fine Lutyens bungalow that later became the headquarters of his party, the Indian National Congress. Suu's guardians when she arrived in England were a distinguished diplomatic family. At Oxford she read politics, philosophy and economics, the aspiring politician's degree par excellence, and there and at the UN in New York she was in the midst of a budding international political and diplomatic elite. A number of her friends at Oxford and beyond went on to become diplomatic high-flyers.

But she didn't seem to get it, any of it. At university she devoted her spare time not to student politics but to theatre and learning to how to punt. She disliked her course, which explains why she tried without success to change to English. When she and Michael were visiting her mother in Rangoon in 1974, after the Ne Win regime had suppressed protests about the price of rice, she was called in by officials and asked whether she planned to get involved in anti-government activities. She told them sincerely that she did not.

Ten years later, one of her commissions as a journeyman author was a little volume for children entitled *Let's Visit Burma*. Her comments on recent events in her country went as follows: 'Burma under army rule became a socialist republic, guided by the Burma Socialist Programme Party. No other political party is permitted. This and other measures limiting the political liberties of the people are aimed at creating a stable government and a unified country. But unity can only come with the co-operation of the people.' The closest she came to swingeing criticism was, 'The economy has not been well managed, and Burma today is not a prosperous nation. However, with its wealth of natural resources, there is always hope for the future . . .'[8]

Reading such stuff, the regime censors no doubt advised their masters that, regarding Aung San Suu Kyi, they could sleep easy in their beds. That anodyne volume was published in 1985, when Suu turned forty. As it happens, this was also the year of her political awakening.

With her younger son Kim she travelled to Japan on a scholarship to study Burma's independence movement, and while there she met some Burmese students. According to Noriko Ohtsu, a Japanese friend of hers from Oxford, 'Their attitude to her was totally different from other people [she had met], because of the respect in which they held her father.'[9] Suu had long been obsessed by her father, and as she confessed in an early television interview, 'When I was young I could never separate my country from my father . . . even now it is difficult for me to separate the idea of my father from the concept of my country.'[10] But the students she met at International House in Kyoto made the link for her between filial piety and political actuality. Her father was not just hers. He belonged to her nation, including these young people, born twenty years after he died – for whom his mission and his achievement were of commanding political importance.

. . . Or so we may suppose. Nothing much came of these encounters, at least nothing concrete. Suu went on to write two academic essays which go much deeper than anything she had written before into the political and cultural challenges her country faced. But these were scholarly pieces, with no practical implications for political action.

Then in 1988, after witnessing months of anti-regime turmoil on the streets of the capital without showing any interest in participating, she finally succumbed to the appeals of intellectuals like U Win Tin, who understood – as the Burmese students she met in Kyoto understood – the political voltage inherent in her name. She agreed to speak out. On 26 August outside the Shwedagon Pagoda in Rangoon she made the speech that catapulted her to leadership. And a movement, a mission, a vocation and a new epoch in Burma's contemporary story were under way.

Like all her previous attempts at putting political ideas into words, this speech, too, revolved around her father. And her target being Ne Win, Aung San's former comrade and his successor as head of the Burmese army, the combination of subject matter, speaker and speech were dynamite. The fact that, apart from paying reverence to her father and his works, she had never given public expression to a political idea was of no relevance.

*

More than most fields of endeavour, politics is Darwinian. In a democracy, nobody attains even the lowliest elected rank without applying themselves. Even to become a candidate for a fringe party in a municipal election, with scant hope of success, takes effort and determination and study. To rise higher requires an unusual combination of attributes: gregariousness, skill at picking useful and hard-working associates, an ability to see both immediate and longer-term goals, a willingness to give and take and do intelligent deals in the interest of party harmony, flair for organisation, tactical astuteness, capacity for hard work, a thick skin. Good looks and eloquence are helpful but not sufficient, and some politicians go a long way with neither.

Suu had to jump through none of these hoops to reach the top. As a politician she was born fully formed at the vertiginous summit of the most dangerous and powerful popular challenge Burma's junta had ever faced. She needed great courage, which she demonstrated over and over again, she needed eloquence, which she plucked from nowhere; and above all she needed a sense of destiny: the sense that she, her father and her country were in some semi-mystical sense one, and that her challenge was to make that unity real. The military regime betrayed her father's legacy. Her father committed himself to making Burma a multi-party democracy. Before entering democratic politics he removed his uniform and became a civilian again. She would follow faithfully in his footsteps.

There followed the most convulsive eleven months in Suu's life, during which some eight thousand protesters were shot dead in the streets, she and her new colleagues created the

NLD, she travelled the length of the country addressing huge crowds in defiance of the regime – then in July 1989 her colleagues were imprisoned and she was put under indefinite house arrest.

With the exception of brief interludes between stretches of detention, that was the end of her political life for the next twenty years. When she re-emerged on 3 November 2010, she was as close to being a political virgin as any world-famous political leader has ever been.

*

As the biographer of Aung San Suu Kyi, I am often asked about my relationship with her. Was the biography authorised? Do I have a direct line to her? How many times have I met her?

My first meeting with Suu was in May 2002, a few days after what turned out to be her penultimate release from house arrest, amid great excitement about the much-anticipated announcement of political reform – hopes that were cruelly dashed the following year. We had a friendly, straightforward and constructive interview upstairs in the NLD's headquarters, at the start of which she asked me to give my regards to 'all my friends at the *Independent*', the London paper I worked for. My former colleague Terry McCarthy had formed a close friendship with her in 1988, during the uprising.

In 2003 she disappeared from view again and was not seen for another seven years. By this time I was deeply engrossed in writing *The Lady and the Peacock*, and very much wanted to interview her again. I had met everybody I could think of who knew her well, and had received warm and generous help from her British in-laws, but none of this was a substitute for talking to her in person. As she was incommunicado throughout those years I had had no chance to ask her the sort of factual questions any biographer would want to ask of a living subject. I sent her a draft of the manuscript, hoping that she would read it – not because I wanted her approval of the contents but because I wanted to avoid making mistakes. Of course I dared to hope she might also like the book.

There was no response from her office, and my plan to get a place in the queue to interview her immediately after her release was thwarted when I was expelled from Burma a few days before the general election. However, I contrived to get back to Rangoon in March 2011, and in the weeks before that I tried in every way I could to set up an appointment to see her: requests to her relatives and close friends, to the British Embassy, to campaigning organisations and charities which were in contact with her, as well as emails directly to her office. No one was able to promise anything, though they all said they would try. No word of any sort came back from her office. I decided, as I had in 2002, simply to go in and try my luck.

Although it had been shut up during her years of detention, NLD headquarters, the 'cowshed', as she has described it, looked much as it had done nine years before: like a rustic enclave in the middle of the city, with incongruous educational trimmings. Her office was up a steep flight of stairs on the left, near the entrance. At the top, two or three elderly party members behind desks in the hallway acted as Suu's last line of defence. I explained who I was and what I hoped to do. The scowling old man at the desk said that no email had been received and it was impossible to make an appointment because she was busy. In fact she would be busy all week – as she was forbidden to travel outside the city, party delegates were coming to Rangoon to see her. Nothing was possible all that week. Nor could I make an appointment for the following week. She was busy.

In growing desperation – I had come to Burma for no other purpose than to interview her – I once again lobbied the embassy, the NGOs, the personal friends. I sent new emails to the people who were allegedly in charge of her schedule. I began to realise that I was at serious risk of going home with nothing at all. But by great good fortune Suu's British sister-in-law Lucinda, the elder sister of her late husband Michael, was in Rangoon for the first time in her life, and she twisted Suu's arm until she finally agreed to a brief encounter, with a photograph to be taken by my son Mario. It was not an interview, I was told, but an opportunity for a photograph, and only granted at Lucinda's express request.

On 21 March 2011 we made it up the stairs, past the – now grimly smiling – gatekeeper and into her room, which compared with the rest of the office was like a small, cosy boudoir. I reminded her who I was, of our previous meeting, of her friendship with the *Independent*. I handed her a list of factual queries. She told me bluntly that she 'would never agree to an interview for a biography as it is a way of seeming to give authority to the biography, and we get so many of these requests'. My list of queries lay unattended on her desk. As the interview I desired had been so flatly refused, we passed the remaining minutes in idle chat. Was my son really a photographer? (Perhaps she suspected the camera had no film in it.) Yes, in fact he had a degree in the subject. Really? Was it possible to take a university degree in photography? Well yes, it was, and he had done so . . . And so on. Meanwhile, as Mario set up his tripod and got down to work the gatekeeper by his side muttered, 'Photo, photo, photo, quick, quick, quick . . .' Within twenty minutes it was all over and we were going back down the stairs. This was my own experience, trivial but slightly bruising, of how Suu interacted, post-release, with the outside world.

She had no inhibitions about hurting people's feelings and rejecting their requests. No harm in that: famous people who are much in demand reject people's requests all the time, even when they come from influential media who are known to be sympathetic. But Suu's approach was almost recklessly brusque, and the unpleasant impact was compounded by the chaos in her office. I would have swallowed her rejection far more easily if it had come in a response to at least one of my emailed requests, or if one of the intermediaries I had been leaning on had delivered it to me. Instead, because of the disarray with her staff, I had to go all the way to Rangoon, wait a week and climb those stairs to her little office, merely to be told in person to buzz off. This was not the honesty she prized so much but callous disregard: a close relative of egotism. And it was nothing new: Suu was notorious, even before her entry into politics, for her cavalier approach to other people's feelings, in the interest of telling the truth. Of course there are ways of softening the blow. But in Suu's view these are forms of dishonesty.

Her Japanese friend Noriko Ohtsu told me a story to illustrate this from their Oxford days. Suu had said to her, in the presence of Suu's husband Michael, 'Noriko, as you well know, some British food is really awful. When we get invited out to eat and the food is bad, I don't say it's delicious. I'm a person who doesn't tell lies. But if they ask Michael, he always says, "Thanks for the delicious meal . . ."'[11]

Rather than 'telling lies', one might call Michael's approach social grace, courtesy, concern for others' feelings. For an Oxford housewife, it probably doesn't matter what you call it: your friends will either drift away in irritation or accept that your bluntness is part of the package. But it is not a trait that could survive one week in practical politics, in any country, at any level: the rankest political beginner learns the art of the social smile, it is the first lesson in survival. But it is a lesson that Suu, entering politics right at the top, never had to digest.

She inflicts bruises like this on people she meets every day of the week. Many other journalists who have approached her for an interview have similar tales. They don't get into print because the story is much bigger than personal rudeness, and no one likes to advertise their personal hurt. And during her interludes of freedom since 1989, the great majority of media people who sought Suu out wished her well. Likewise her peers in international politics and diplomacy kept their personal dismay to themselves, or confined it to quiet mutterings to their staff. But slowly this began to change.

In June 2013, Japan's Prime Minister Shinzo Abe came to Burma. Japan is not only a country with which Suu has strong personal and family ties, but is also a very important donor of aid. It has historical links to Burma, both positive and negative, which rival Britain's. It is also a country with a high regard for courtesy – but this was not something Suu felt she had to pay attention to in her one-on-one with the man who had just announced $500 million in new loans and the write-off of $1.74 billion of Burma's debt. '[Mr Abe's] meeting with Miss Suu Kyi went badly,' the *Economist* reported.[12] 'She seemed uninterested, the Japanese felt, and lectured them irrelevantly on health issues. A recent party of foreign businessmen was similarly unimpressed, bewildered at her argument that Myanmar needs horticulture more than garment factories . . .' 'Miss Suu Kyi,' the article (which was headlined 'The Halo Slips') concluded, '. . . may be misinformed, misguided, even high-handed. But nobody questions her fundamental integrity.' But the days were coming to an end when criticism of her could be dismissed, as a supporter of hers in Rangoon dismissed it in the same article, as 'bad press fed by the other side'. Whether it was her idea of honesty, or simply indifference to the administrative chaos of which she was the tranquil, untroubled centre, she seemed to have no compunction about treating many of those who sought her out with gay contempt.

We make quite an eminent little club, we who have been given short shrift by the Lady. The president of Mongolia, Tsakhiagiin Elbegdorj, paid an official visit to Burma in November 2013 in the course of which he met both President Thein Sein and Aung San Suu Kyi. But arranging the meeting with Suu proved a challenge. Letters and emails went unanswered, phone calls from his office to her office were met with a blank response. In exasperation the president phoned her office himself. 'I am the president of Mongolia,' he told the functionary at the other end. He was told to 'please send in your CV'.[13]

The former president of the Maldives, Mohamed Nasheed, now serving a thirteen-year jail sentence after being overthrown in a military coup, received similarly offhand treatment when he tried to set up a meeting with Suu.

The billionaire investment guru George Soros has for many years been a mainstay of opposition to military rule in Burma. Through his Open Society Foundation he has consistently funded some of the most important organisations working for Burma's democratic transformation. After the election of President Thein Sein, he was permitted to visit the country. He obtained one meeting with Suu, but arranging a second took months of lobbying. In advance of her visit to the United States in September 2012 he offered her the use of his homes there. The offers were not accepted. She finally agreed to meet him during her stay on the West Coast. According to an informant the meeting 'did not go well'.

The Dalai Lama and Suu have plenty in common besides the Nobel Peace Prize. Both are stout defenders of the interests of their people in the teeth of dictatorship, both are devout Buddhists although of different schools. But when he wrote to Suu in September 2012 to vent his concern at the explosions of violence in Arakan state, there was no response. 'We wrote a letter to Suu Kyi regarding the violence but we got no reply,' he said. 'There is no channel for us to approach.'[14]

Joan Lestor, the veteran Labour MP who died in 1998, once gave this advice to a young colleague in the party: 'Always be nice to people on the way up, because you are going to need them on the way down.' Suu's problem is that she was never on the way up. She started at the top.

11
IN THE LINE OF FIRE

THE above list of snubs and faux pas, which is only a sample, begs the question, why did no one on Suu's staff find a way to put things right? There was nothing to be gained by sending the Japanese prime minister away in a bad mood, or telling the president of Mongolia to send in his CV. Suu might choose to regard the language of diplomacy as telling lies, but was there no bright spark in the back office who saw that this sort of thing harmed her standing, and who could quietly make amends?

The short answer is that for a long time there was no such person. If her manners were recklessly rough, her staff was absurdly small. The director of one organisation committed to the cause of a free, democratic Burma, who at her request met her twice in 2012, at an interval of six months, said, 'At this second meeting she didn't bring up any of the topics we had discussed at the first one.'[1] That was because she managed without a secretary, never mind a secretariat. Nobody was taking minutes.

This lack of organisational capacity came to international attention when she took her first trip abroad, flying to Bangkok in May 2012. The trip was announced a few days in advance, but no one from her office had bothered to inform the Thai Foreign Ministry. After her arrival, a spokesman for the ministry said, 'We'll have to play it by ear, I guess.'[2]

On that trip Suu planned to visit one of the refugee camps near the Burmese border, set up to accommodate some of the thousands of Karen and other Burmese who had fled the war zone. But Tak province, where the camps are located, is a restricted area and permission to visit must be obtained in advance. The governor of the province, Suriya Prasatbuntitya, told the *New York Times*, 'We are only learning about her arrival from the media, not from her team. I guess we'll have to get details of her schedule on her own – and be prepared.'[3]

Another person kept in the dark was President Thein Sein, who had long planned to visit Thailand during the same period, and address the same conference, organised by the World Economic Forum, at which Suu had been booked to speak. On the conference schedule, announced the previous week, Suu was given top billing. Thein Sein cancelled without explanation.

'Miss Suu Kyi's style,' the *New York Times* commented, 'might be described as spontaneous.'[4] The same approach can be found in her meetings with foreign heads of government: it's just her, accompanied since late 2012 by her now inseparable personal assistant, the chunky and bespectacled Dr Tin Mar Aung. There is a photograph of Suu at a meeting in Delhi in November 2014 with Narendra Modi, the Indian prime minister. Mr Modi is accompanied by ten men in suits, plus an interpreter. Suu is accompanied by her female aide, Dr Tin Mar Aung. The satirical blog Burma Tha Din Network, which posted the photo, captioned it, 'Aung San Suu Kyi and her policy team meet with the Indian Prime Minister and his policy team.'[5] This wasn't satire, it was the bizarre truth.

Quietly and diplomatically, some of her foreign friends tried to steer her in a more methodical direction. 'When she came to London in June 2012 to meet David Cameron, William Hague and so on,' an insider told me, 'it would have been normal to take her directly from the street into the meeting with Hague. Instead she was led to the meeting room on a circuitous route through the Foreign Office which took her through the offices of private secretaries, permanent advisers and so on' – making her see with her own eyes the dozens of experts on whom the Foreign Secretary depended before opening his mouth. It was an attempt to bring home to her the extent to which the British government depends on expert council – and to nudge her into doing likewise.

The attempt was in vain. Instead of expanding her support staff, she shrank it. In theory the NLD was there to back her up: a different leader would have tapped the ranks of its young volunteers for their energy and brains. But although the party headquarters in Rangoon was back to its old pre-detention rhythm, with English classes, a lending library and the selling of posters, T-shirts and other Suu and Aung San memorabilia proceeding in tandem with the slicing of vegetables for the daily communal curry, Suu spent less and less time there. She worked from home, or, when Parliament was sitting, from the modest suburban house she was provided with in Naypyidaw. The upstairs room in NLD Central where I had met her in March 2011, and from which I had been so smartly evicted, stood empty most of the time. The grizzled old members of the nomenklatura at the top of the stairs, the 'uncles' as they were known, had been stripped of their gatekeeper role; they were replaced by the ubiquitous figure of Dr Tin Mar Aung, who made sure that only persons of the rank of Foreign Minister or above got past her door.

For more than fifteen years of enforced detention, Suu had been entirely alone, except for a couple of live-in servants. Now that she was free to do as she wished, and in demand around the world as never before, it seemed that solitude was the only condition that suited her; with the solitary addition of a single trusted person whose role was to keep the rest of the world at bay.

Her increasing detachment from her party became evident during her visit to England in June 2012. While she and her small retinue moved seamlessly from Westminster Hall to the Speaker's Chambers to the covered courtyard of the Foreign Office nearby, her party delegation was nowhere to be seen. 'They were disappointed about how little time they had with her in England,' I was told. 'They were not invited to the big events with her but were left to their own devices. They were put up in hotels at the expense of the UK government, but Suu Kyi told them firmly not to use the hotel minibars or the laundry. So these party grandees spent their evenings in London in their hotel rooms, washing their smalls . . .'

Clearly, this was how she liked it. If she learned about the world's criticisms of her style, the disorganisation in her office, her alleged high-handedness, if she understood the message that William Hague's people were trying to impart, it certainly didn't show and she didn't allow it to change her behaviour. The world would have to take her or leave her on her own terms.

But the game she was engaged in was different from the one she had played in 1989. Back then there was the give-and-take,

the comradeship and hopes and fears that she shared with
the fellow founders of her party, a tight group of whom had
travelled the country with her, frequently in great discomfort.
Today those of the founding generation who are still alive are
elderly, and if the regime hadn't succeeded in killing them all,
it had killed off the ties that bound them together, merely by
the attrition of the years. Rugged self-sufficiency had enabled
Suu to get through the years of solitude, and it was what she
fell back on now. But it wasn't enough.

*

The Internet was in its infancy when Suu disappeared
behind the walls of 54 University Avenue. It was one of the
many ways the world had changed in those years. When she
emerged in 2010 she had never used a mobile phone, never
accessed the Web. It was a battleground she knew little of. So
the dis-inhibiting effect of the new digital world must have
come as a shock.

'Aung San Suu Kyi is the worst person in Burma,' a
Thailand-based blogger called Roland Watson wrote on
his personal ranting platform, www.dictatorwatch.org, in
October 2012. He went on, 'What a shocking statement! How
could I say such a thing about The Lady, Mother Suu, Aunty
Suu, the revered Nobel laureate, and the leader of all peace-
loving Burmese?'

Why was Suu the worst? he asked rhetorically. Why not
the soldiers gang-raping village women in Kachin state,
the 'Rakhine madmen, who . . . want to kill every single
[Rohingya]'? The reason was because

she is . . . directly responsible for the carnage because she is the only person in Burma who has the ability to stop it, or at a minimum to reduce its scale.

Suu is the only person with real moral authority over the Burmans . . . were she to call loudly and repeatedly for the attacks to end, including for the Rohingya to be protected and for the Burma Army to withdraw from Kachin areas, the violence would subside . . .

Watson's post had the splenetic, let-it-all-hang-out trademarks of communications in the brave new world of the Internet. Suu wasn't 'indirectly' responsible for the 'carnage' but 'directly', which could only be true if she had actually committed rape, murder, etc. 'Many, many' Rakhines were mad and genocidal. 'Many' soldiers were committing gang-rape. But all this horror would end if Suu only spoke up. 'She should ask to speak on national television, and make just such an announcement. If refused permission, she should make a statement to foreign media.'

This was the fantasy activism of Twitter and Facebook, where the louder and more unhinged the rhetoric the more clicks, the more likes and unlikes, the greater the (momentary) attention, and to hell with the nuances, to hell with the actual facts of the subject at hand.

What was also new was that Suu was in the line of fire for this stuff. This was shockingly novel. She had never asked to be canonised, to be hauled onto some kind of holy pedestal: it had all happened when she was unable to express an opinion on the matter. She hates attention directed at her person – hence her blanket rejection of biographers' queries including mine, hence also the interesting fact that, although she struck up a warm and enduring friendship with Michelle Yeoh, the Malaysian actress who played her in *The Lady*, the Suu biopic directed by Luc Besson, she has never (I was reliably informed) seen the film.

Celebrity was neither her wish nor her intention. It had happened to her nonetheless. And now she was paying the price – nationally and internationally – for not being someone she had never claimed to be, for failing to live up to an image she had never aspired to. But she had no right to complain. As she said repeatedly in the years after her release, she was not an icon but a politician. And now she was getting the critical battering that politicians in a democracy get.

Attached to Roland Watson's choleric blogpost is a YouTube video originally posted by the Democratic Voice of Burma, the dissident news organisation formerly based in Norway before being permitted to relocate to Rangoon. Suu is seen in the back seat of a luxurious SUV: her chin resting on her forearm, she stares blankly out of the window in the direction of a crowd. The date is 13 March 2013. As usual, numerous cameras are snapping her but gone are the luminous smiles, the waves, the sense of her easy rapport with the people. On the sound track there is a strange unhappy hubbub, a hundred unhappy female voices raised. The camera pans: a crowd of village women are staring in Suu's direction and wailing, crying, venting their anger. Some of them are shaking with sobs. Now we see one of them close up, crying freely and raging while she wipes her eyes with the heel of her palm. 'It's like she's just sitting aside,' she is saying, according to the subtitles. 'All the love we have for you, now it's nothing . . . You're supposed to protect the people, the monks . . . We had so much hopes on her . . . But now her report is like a death sentence for the people . . . Daw Suu! Don't come here, Daw Suu . . . You said you wouldn't trick the people . . .'[6]

The events that provoked this short but stunning video illustrate how everything had changed. In May 2003, Suu found herself in the town of Monywa, 130 kilometres west of Mandalay. Released from detention the previous year amid high hopes of a political breakthrough with the junta, she had used her freedom to go back on the road, reprising the mass meetings of 1988 and 1989. In Monywa, speaking from a balcony in the town centre, she reminded the large crowd of her father's visit to the town in 1947, and recalled her own visit in 1988 when the town was 'extraordinarily firm' in its support for the NLD and its hostility to the junta. She warned that 'bullying' crowds belonging to the army's proxy party were trying 'to destroy our work', but said she drew strength from the fact that 'the people have been supporting us in massive numbers. I believe they support us because they can't stand bullying and injustice.'[7]

It was later that day, north of Monywa, that the junta launched its most determined effort to eliminate Suu: a large, well-armed mob attacked her convoy, killing dozens of NLD members. Suu and the other passengers in her car were lucky to escape without injury.

Nine years on, in 2012, Suu remained a headache for the generals and ex-generals who still ran the country – but under the wily leadership of President Thein Sein they now had subtler ways to deal with her than paying a mob to mug her. A few miles west of Monywa, across the Chindwin River, the fertile rolling hills are seamed with copper. The metal has been mined here in big and small operations for centuries, but in 2010 a Chinese firm and one owned by the Burmese military signed a deal to jointly develop a large mine at a place called Letpadaung. Farmers with land in the way were booted off unceremoniously, as was the norm all over Burma, with token compensation. As the mine expanded, those who continued to farm in the area found the water turning toxic, birds and bees disappearing[8] and their health deteriorating – a copper mine is a bad neighbour for farmers.

So in June 2012, reinforced by students and activists from the '88 Generation movement, the shock troops of Burmese dissidence, they began to protest. The previous year, large-scale opposition to a huge, half-completed Chinese dam at Myitsone in Kachin state – opposition that Suu had endorsed – had prompted the president to order its construction to be suspended. Perhaps the Letpadaung farmers could achieve a comparable success. The protest brought the mine's operations temporarily to a halt.

When the protesters returned to do battle again in November, they were resolute. 'Our mountain, do not invade,' read the banners. A farmer called Ko Myint Tin, who claimed he had been tricked out of his twenty-four acres of farmland by the mining company, said, 'We are ready to give up our lives to get our land back.'[9] The protesters succeeded in closing the mine down for eleven days, but that was too much for the authorities. In a dawn assault, the army attacked them with tear gas, water cannon and white phosphorous smoke bombs, injuring dozens, many of them monks.

Visiting Monywa soon afterwards, Suu told a large crowd in the town centre that people had the right to ask why the authorities had reacted so harshly to the non-violent protest, and demanded an apology.[10] The apology duly arrived – with a sting in the tail. The government announced an investigation into the dispute at the copper mine, with Suu as its chair.

There were cogent reasons for the appointment. It was the NLD which had brought the Letpadaung crackdown issue before Parliament. As of August, Suu was also chair of the Lower House's Committee for the Rule of Law and Tranquillity. From one perspective, the Letpadaung clashes were a matter of the rule of law.

Like entering Parliament, this was another step forward for Suu – another step in her evolution from human rights icon to working politician. It was also – as she might have been told were she open to being advised – a way of walking straight into another Thein Sein trap. The president had no doubt studied the text of Suu's comments during her visit to the area and seen that, despite the demand for an apology and the criticism of the means used to shut down the protest, she had not condemned the protesters' forcible eviction, nor had she called for the mine's development to be stopped.

Relations between Suu and the president, which Suu had hoped would develop into a Burmese answer to the partnership of Nelson Mandela and F.W. de Klerk,[11] had deteriorated soon after the April by-elections. But the shrewd ex-general understood how she ticked: she was *majime*, to use the evocative Japanese adjective: as at her children's birthday parties forty years before, she believed in doing her duty regardless of what other calculations might dictate. Doing one's duty, behaving responsibly, was an imperative, and trumped everything else, including the sort of reckless political imagination exhibited by her father, who did not hesitate to swear continuing fealty to the Japanese army during the war, when he had already decided to switch to the British side.

The commission of inquiry did its work. There are photos of Suu in a hard hat with binoculars at the mine site. Then in March 2013 it delivered its report. Despite the injuries incurred by the protesters, especially monks, the report's criticism of police was mild: it argued that the officers did not understand the use of smoke bombs, and recommended that they receive riot control training. It accepted that environmental controls on the mine were inadequate, and that it would not create more jobs for local people. But it did not demand any significant changes, and concluded that, as Associated Press reported, 'honouring the mining contract outweighed villagers' demands that the operation be halted'.[12]

Predictably, the report was met with outrage and indignation by protesters against the mine: they had banked on Suu taking their side and pressing their cause. Two days later she returned to Letpadaung to meet them. This is another step that it is hard to imagine a conventional politician taking, unless he or she had arranged matters very carefully in advance. This was the visit on which she was filmed staring fixedly at the crowd – AP says it numbered 700 – while furious villagers raged and wept in frustration and disillusionment. It was the first anti-Suu protest Burma had ever seen.

Later the same day she met some of the villagers. She told them, 'If we stopped [the mine] completely, where would we get the money to heal the current environmental destruction? The shutdown of the mine is not beneficial for locals. If we break the agreement made with another country, the countries of the world will suppose that Myanmar is financially unreliable.'[13]

These were valid points, yet there is something sadly invertebrate about the conclusions her commission reached. Suu showed courage in coming face to face with the angry villagers; but it would have been more impressive if she had summoned similar reserves of courage to confront the Chinese, whose indifference to the environmental damage their operations cause, at Letpadaung as in many other places around the world, was notorious. They were on the back foot after the suspension of the Myitsone dam; a robust, well-researched report calling on them to provide adequate environmental safeguards, repair the damage they had already done and improve compensation deals might well have been accepted. If they had rejected it, their true colours, and those of their Burmese military business partners, would have been garishly displayed. Either way, Suu would have emerged with both domestic and international credit, having managed the transition from activist and icon to practical politician with elan. Instead – to the Letpadaung protesters and to many of her supporters elsewhere – she looked like a patsy, or worse, a person actively in cahoots with her former gaolers.

AP reported: '[Suu] told villagers that if they wanted to protest the report's findings, they should do so at her home, not at the mining company.'[14] She was fortunate that they did not accept the invitation.

*

The world was beginning to see beyond the beautiful and saintly image of Aung San Suu Kyi to the living person she was, and it was not happy about what it saw. The subject around which this realisation crystallised was her response to the Rohingya crisis.

As I described in Chapter 1, Suu did not attempt to ignore the violence that broke out between Muslim and Buddhist communities in Arakan state. On the contrary, she called attention to it in her speeches in Oslo and London in June 2012, only weeks after the violence started. The previous month, at home in Burma, she had appealed to the majority community to be considerate to Muslims, and had been attacked for saying so.[15] But her failure to take sides clearly, to condemn both the ongoing violence by the Buddhists and the political context of Rohingya statelessness in which it had occurred, made her the lightning rod for fierce criticism abroad which did more than anything else to erode her international stature. As early as July 2012, she was singled out on the Opinion pages of the *New York Times* for 'ducking' questions about the Rohingya, and the attacks by human rights activists and Islamic media such as Al Jazeera got steadily harsher the longer she failed to provide satisfaction.

Why was she unable, despite these increasingly acerbic demands, to formulate a decent response to this appalling crisis, in which more than a million Burmese Muslims were treated as if they did not exist and had no rights?

Some believe it is simply a matter of prejudice: that, as a Burman Buddhist, she shares the same bigoted views as many of her fellow citizens, perhaps reinforced by regular exposure to the opinions of her constant companion, Dr Tin Mar Aung, an Arakanese Buddhist who it is said – I have seen no evidence of this – is herself strongly anti-Rohingya. One snippet of gossip supports this explanation: after a particularly bruising interview with Mishal Husain of the BBC, Suu was heard to mutter angrily, 'No one told me I was going to be interviewed by a Muslim.'[16]

It is always hard to prove a negative. The comment about Mishal Husain, rather than reflecting anti-Muslim sentiment pure and simple, is more likely to be the product of a not-unfounded sense on Suu's part that aggressive and chauvinistic voices within the international Muslim community – voices with no organic connection to the Rohingya community either in Burma or abroad – have deliberately fuelled a hate campaign against her.[17] That may well be her suspicion, and she may well be right. But it doesn't mean she is personally prejudiced against Muslims, and there is plenty of circumstantial evidence that she is not.

She spent more than twenty years in multicultural Britain, at a social and intellectual level where crude prejudice is hard to sustain. Her first serious boyfriend at Oxford was a Pakistani, who went on to become a high-flying diplomat for his country. In 1988, the man who did more than anyone to persuade her to take the plunge into politics was Maung Thaw Ka, a Burmese Muslim who was also a journalist, translator and best-selling writer and who later died a terrible death in jail as a political prisoner. Although a practising Buddhist – serious about her meditation practice, which she adopted during her first years in detention – Suu's intellectual formation was quintessentially Western and secular.

As I described in Chapter 9, those views, expressed in some of her most important essays, were starkly at odds with the Buddhist ethno-nationalism of many ordinary Burmese, which harks back nostalgically to an imaginary Golden Age of Buddhism-fostering kings and merit-making Buddhist subjects. Suu's vision was closer to that of Indian thinkers like Tagore, Gandhi and Nehru, emphasising generosity and amplitude and tolerance. 'It is not power that corrupts but fear,' she wrote in her most famous essay, already quoted above. 'The quintessential revolution is that of the spirit, born of an intellectual conviction of the need for change in those mental attitudes and values which shape the course of a nation's development.'[18] Hers was a progressive, humanistic, forward-looking message. And there is no evidence to suggest she retreated from those views. And yet – she remained tongue-tied. Why?

The claim has been frequently made that she kept quiet to avoid alienating her Buddhist vote bank out of cynical political calculation. Dr Maung Zarni, for example, the Burmese dissident-turned-academic, said, 'Politically, Aung San Suu Kyi has absolutely nothing to gain from opening her mouth on this . . . She's a politician, and her eyes are fixed on the prize, which is the 2015 Buddhist majority vote.'[19]

This is a claim that would make eminent sense for any other aspiring political leader with a support base among Burmese Buddhists. But not, in my opinion, for Suu: calculation of this crude sort is not in her character. This, after all, is the woman who told her Tokyo audience, 'One should not think in terms of position but in terms of responsibility . . .'[20] This was the demand she made – unrealistic, sanctimonious, idealistic, however one describes it – of her party's youthful members, and she demanded it equally of herself. For Suu the end could never justify the means: virtue is engraved on her heart. Even those dismissive of her other qualities do not question her integrity. For a person who aspires to lead her country, that is in fact saying a lot. There was, however, political calculation of a different sort behind her silence.

Suu was determined to become president of Burma. I first heard her make this declaration at a press conference in Tokyo in April 2013. She has made it numerous times since. Repetition does not lessen the strangeness of it. She is just one of the founder members of her party. As the name says, it is a democratic party, in name and aspiration. No one doubts that Suu is and has been, since the party's foundation, by far the most popular figure in it. One sensed that she retained this popularity throughout the wilderness years, and her margin of victory in the 2015 general election confirmed it.

But there is something discordant and incongruous about anybody, however popular, claiming, as a member of a democratic party, the presidency of a democratic country as of right. She is entitled to say she would like it, that she aspires to it, that she hopes to be worthy of it. There should always be such caveats. But there never are. Suu wants to be president: *punto e basta*. That's why – in order for her to be eligible to be president – the priority for amending the constitution was not eliminating the 25 per cent of military MPs, not erasing the army's right to appoint three key ministers, not cutting back the powers of the military council – but removing clause 59(f) which bars a person with a foreign spouse or children from being a presidential candidate. That was the priority for Suu, and her party meekly fell into line behind her. The ravenous egotism that sometimes manifests from within that elegant form was once again on display.

Suu is bent on becoming president because that is the only thing that will make sense of the sacrifice of her life. Merely being another politician will never do at all. She is bent on becoming president, and thus on a par with all the heads of government with whom she is on such familiar terms. She looks forward to the day when she will be inaugurated. In her imagination she is already more than halfway there. She cannot do anything to prejudice that ambition, nor to limit her scope when she finally attains it. That is why – to take one example – she cannot bring herself to condemn the Chinese at the Letpadaung copper mine: as president she will have to deal with the Chinese leadership at the highest level, and so in the meantime she does not want to do anything to imperil that relationship.

Likewise with the Rohingya. As president, she will be the leader of her country, including all those who live in it. That includes Arakanese Buddhists, however bloody and intolerant. It will also include large numbers of Rohingya. As president-in-waiting she will do nothing to appear partisan on this problem. She will wring her hands over the suffering, lament the violence and destruction; but even on questions as basic and bloody-obvious as citizenship she will resolutely keep as many options open as possible until the glittering prize is achieved. That is the best explanation for her failure to pick up even the most explicit cues on this question.

In May 2015 I interviewed U Nyan Win, the NLD spokesman, at the party headquarters, who told me, 'The

Rohingya problem needs to be solved by the law. The law needs to be amended. After one or two generations they should have the right to be citizens.' My article in the *Independent* quoting U Nyan Win was promptly picked up by the Burmese media, and two days later in Parliament I took the opportunity to ask Suu if she shared his views. She told me 'I don't know what his views are, so I can't answer the question.'

Suu's calculation appears to be that she will do nothing that might prejudice her ability to rule as president. And the tragedy is that, in the process of securing her future power, she refuses every possibility of using the power she has right now, as the de facto leader of the opposition, the head of Burma's most important democratic party and a political figure of world stature, to make good and useful changes.

Roland Watson, on his electronic soapbox at dictatorwatch. org, claims without evidence that Suu could heal her nation's ills at a stroke, merely by condemning them. That is obviously wrong, a wild exaggeration. Yet by speaking up simply as her spokesman had done – by demanding for the Rohingya the simplest, basic necessity of human life, citizenship – she could have changed Burma's debate on this question, and without incurring political damage. Yet she shrank from doing so.

As at the Letpadaung copper mine, where she funked the opportunity to tell uncomfortable truths to the Chinese, this woman of dauntless political courage shrank, bizarrely, from the opportunity to commit herself, and thereby change the political weather. For all her proven bravery, she thus laid bare an unsuspected and disastrous streak of timidity. At its root were her complex and ambivalent feelings about the Burmese army and the generals who commanded it.

12

THE LADY AND THE GENERALS

Suu Kyi's life has been entwined with the Burmese army, the Tatmadaw, since her infancy. As we have seen, her father Aung San, 'Bogyoke', 'the General', founded the army under Japanese patronage, and his fledgling force accompanied the Japanese invasion in 1942. He returned to civilian life when he entered politics, but in popular imagination and Suu's dim memories of him – he died when she was only two – he is always in his general's uniform.

Even after his death, soldiers were a constant and benign presence in her home, as they came to pay respects to the widow of the great man and play with his children. She was left in no doubt that her father was a patriotic hero and that the army was his great legacy. And his achievement, playing a key role in wresting his country out of the grip first of the British, then the Japanese, and negotiating independence, was the guiding inspiration of her life. A friend from her first school recalled, 'Suu was always speaking about her father and always saying how she . . . has to follow her father's line.'[1] At first she meant it literally. 'When I was ten or eleven,' she said after her first spell of house arrest, 'I wanted to enter the army . . . I wanted to be a general . . . because I thought this was the best way to serve my country, just like my father had done.'[2] Before puberty she came as close to that as was possible for a young girl: her friends remember her as a tomboy, and she joined the Girl Guide troop her mother had founded.

She has never shied away from admitting her attachment to the army. Listeners in the UK were taken aback to hear her declare, during her appearance on the BBC radio programme *Desert Island Discs*, 'I was taught that my father was the father of the army and that all soldiers were his sons – and therefore part of my family.'[3] How could she speak of the Tatmadaw in such a way after the military regime had taken away her freedom, destroyed her family life and locked her up in her home for fifteen years? Clearly, this attachment was rooted so deeply in her mind as to be beyond the reach of experience, knowledge and mental pain to budge. She acknowledged as much in an interview soon after her release. 'I was brought up to be fond of the military,' she told David Pilling of the *Financial Times*, 'to believe that everybody in military uniform was, in some way or other, my father's son. This is not something you can just get rid of.'[4] It has left its stamp on her whole life, carrying over into her bearing, her rigidity, her constant stress on duty, responsibility and self-discipline. I noticed it the first time I met her: 'she steps briskly into the office,' I wrote in 2002, 'arm swinging like a soldier . . .'[5]

The army, Aung San's army, has dominated Burma's life for all but the first thirteen years of independence,[6] more than three-quarters of its short life. In that time, as the only privileged body in the country, with its own schools, hospitals, sports facilities, housing compounds and much else, the military became a proud, distinct, elevated caste within society. It had more in common with the British officer class than with the common people. Army officers are better educated, better fed, taller and healthier than any other group in the country. Because General Ne Win was so intolerant of dissent, several of the founding figures in the NLD were former officers who had been purged, including U Tin Oo, former commander-in-chief, who as a very junior soldier had served Aung San himself, and who is still Suu's most loyal and unquestioning party colleague.

And yet . . . the army is her enemy and the enemy of her party. General Ne Win betrayed her father's legacy. Aung San removed his uniform before running for Parliament: civilian rule was an unshakeable principle for him, but Ne Win put the army in power and bankrupted Burma in the process. In 1988, after she emerged to lead the democracy movement, the army she loved slaughtered 8,000 unarmed protesters in the streets.

How could she reconcile her deep attachment to the army with its appalling behaviour? How could she fight to overthrow an institution that was closer to her heart than anything else in life?

*

In their endless war against ethnic peoples on the borders, the crimes committed by the Burmese army have been closely documented by brave investigators and collected in many chilling reports. As I have written earlier the army's methods include the use of rape as a weapon of war, the shelling of defenceless villages, the large-scale stealing of land, the use of civilians as human landmine detectors and porters, and many, many cases of summary, extrajudicial killing. UN special human rights rapporteurs tried with scant success to jolt the regime's conscience by publishing details of these crimes.

Nothing worked until 2009 when President Omar al-Bashir of Sudan, formerly a brigadier in the Sudanese army, was indicted by the International Criminal Court (ICC) in The Hague for his alleged crimes – not dissimilar to those which the Burmese army was accused of – in Darfur.

At the time of writing President al-Bashir has yet to be arrested, but this was the first time a serving head of state had been indicted by the court. Despite failings which have been widely discussed, and despite the fact that the United States, for example, refuses to recognise it, the court, and allied tribunals such as the one set up to examine crimes committed in ex-Yugoslavia during the wars of the 1990s, have achieved important results. Slobodan Milošević, the Serbian strongman, died in The Hague during his trial; the trials of former Bosnian Serb leaders Ratko Mladić and Radovan Karadžić are still under way. As a means for the international community to break through the encrusted impunity of some of the worst rogues on the planet, the ICC was a unique success: the greatest step forward ever taken towards the elusive and perhaps fantastic dream of world government.

So it is not surprising that influential voices lobbied loudly for Burma's generals to get the Omar al-Bashir treatment. In March 2010, eight months before Suu's release from detention, the British government joined their number. Sir Mark Lyall Grant, the UK's ambassador to the UN, said Britain supported a recommendation by the UN special rapporteur on human rights in Burma that the ICC should open a war crimes investigation.

If the outrageous behaviour of the Tatmadaw gets less attention than the Sudanese army in Darfur it is probably because these are the longest-running civil wars in history: as a result they have lost their novelty appeal for the international media. But merely because the Burmese military have been using the same barbaric tactics for nearly sixty-five years does not make them any less abhorrent. According to Harvard Law School, whose International Human Rights Clinic carried out a detailed examination of a Tatmadaw offensive against the Karen National Liberation Army (KNLA), on Burma's eastern border, in 2005 to 2006, the evidence of war crimes committed by the army was overwhelming. The authors wrote:

> Based on evidence gathered during its investigation the Clinic has concluded that Myanmar Army personnel from Southern Command and Light Infantry Division 66 committed crimes against humanity and war crimes, as defined by Articles 7 and 8 respectively, of the Rome Statute of the International Criminal Court. Moreover, the Clinic has found that officers from Southern Command and LID 66 could – pending further investigation – be held legally responsible for these crimes under two theories of liability: individual criminal responsibility . . . and command responsibility.[7]

The crimes in question, committed while the army was forcing villagers out of areas controlled by the ethnic enemy (whom the villagers provided with food and shelter), include murder and execution without due process, torture, rape, enslavement, pillage and forcible transfer. The findings were published in 2009. The following March, Tomás Ojea Quintana, the UN's Special Rapporteur, drove the point home when he spoke of 'a pattern of gross and systematic violation of human rights'[8] of Burmese civilians, the result, he said, of long-standing state policy. Referring to the elections scheduled for later in the year, Anna Roberts of Burma Campaign UK said, 'The generals in Burma will never allow justice and democracy . . . Rather than engaging with the fake elections, the international community should focus on putting the generals in jail, where they belong.'[9]

Some observers think it was the combined effect of the al-Bashir indictment, the Harvard investigation and the growing UN Security Council consensus that persuaded Burma's generals to buy time and a modicum of goodwill by holding elections and releasing Suu as scheduled, then carrying out the raft of reforms leading up to the by-elections which put Suu and her colleagues in Parliament.[10]

But in fact there was no indictment, and no further steps were taken towards launching one. All high-level discussion of the possibility fell silent. The reason was simple, according to insiders: Suu, released from detention and able to give her view, would have none of it. She killed the proposal stone dead. And given her status and her unique access to senior foreign diplomats and politicians, her opposition was enough to remove it from the international agenda.[11]

As the authors of the Harvard Memorandum write in their preface, 'Countries in transition face profound and difficult questions about how to address past abuses . . . While the Memorandum concludes that international crimes have been committed, international criminal law is not the only means of addressing Myanmar's legacy of abuse.' Fear of being dragged to The Hague may well have persuaded the generals to improve their image. But the converse may also be true: once the risk of indictment had faded, thanks to Suu's intervention, the urgency of further reform dwindled away. After half a year of frenetic change, the process ground to a halt. Suu would not hear of an ICC indictment, and the generals knew it. The panic was over.

When Suu entered Parliament it was a moment of joy and emancipation for her people and her supporters worldwide. But this was an unusual sort of democratic forum. The majority of MPs belonged to the Union Solidarity and Development Party, created by the regime in advance of the 2010 elections and correctly seen as the military's political wing; many of them had won their seats corruptly. Aside from them, one quarter of MPs were serving soldiers: they had not been elected, and represented no constituency except the military which appointed them. To ensure there could be no doubt about their loyalty, they came to the chamber in uniform. The ministers of Home Affairs, Defence and Border Affairs likewise wore uniforms and were direct military appointees. The Speakers of both houses, though they wore civilian clothes, were former generals, like the president himself.

For Suu, entering a parliament so densely peopled with soldiers and ex-soldiers must have been like Daniel going into the lion's den. Or perhaps, given her unshakeably fond feelings for the military, it was more like going home.

*

Naypyidaw, Burma's new capital, 400 kilometres north of Rangoon, entered the world's consciousness abruptly in 2005 when government ministries were moved there overnight. You can drive for miles along its eight-lane highways without finding anything that resembles a city, except for some whimsical modern hotels, garishly illuminated at night, housing estates for bureaucrats, and the occasional hypermarket.

Getting anywhere in the city involves driving. To visit the military museum you have to travel 30 kilometres from the middle of town to the edge of the north-eastern hills. The museum is colossal, its galleries complemented by grounds dotted with Spitfires and Second World War tanks. When I visited, the officer who showed us around – he had decided we must be arms dealers until I disabused him of the idea – said it was staffed by 500 serving soldiers.

The next day I asked U Ye Htut, President Thein Sein's spokesman – a man, one diplomat told me, who had evidently made a close study of the works of Alastair Campbell, Tony Blair's former spin doctor – why they had decided to put the museum so far away from the centre of town. Simple, he said: it is also the location of the main regional army base (or 'cantonment' as they call it, in the jargon of the British Raj) and the army didn't want to put it too close to Parliament. 'In the past, the military was 100 per cent in control of the country,' he reminded me. 'Today it is only 25 per cent in control' – a reference to the quarter of MPs who are serving army officers. 'In future with trust they might reduce it further. This is the exit strategy of the military – a slow exit. We want to avoid chaos and bloodshed: to create a political space, create trust and move forwards.' Those 30 kilometres of empty road were symbolic of the expanding political space between the military and the 'discipline-flourishing democracy' they have brought into being. It is an attractive idea, the sort of notion one would expect from a spin doctor. But is it true?

Suu, who had hoped that her relationship with the president would become a real working partnership, became disillusioned with him soon after entering Parliament. The reform process got stuck. A second round of by-elections was scheduled, then cancelled, reportedly because they would have been too expensive[12] – a disastrous explanation in a democracy as new and fragile as Burma's. Thein Sein had agreed with Suu that the constitution should be amended, but broke his word to her that he would help to make it happen. And so on.

But she was not friendless in the lion's den. The biggest lion in the pride became her new best friend. Needless to say, he was a soldier – perhaps the most valiant of the lot.

Thura Shwe Mann is not a name that trips off the tongue but the world is going to learn it in years to come. Like President Thein Sein, he was a general before becoming a *baung-bi-chut*, a 'man out of trousers', replacing his Western-style uniform with the traditional skirt-like longyi. Like Thein Sein he was a protégé of former Senior General Than Shwe, with certain differences: he is bigger, taller, stronger-looking, more youthful and virile; no glasses, no pacemaker. Unlike the president, no one would consider him a fossilised has-been, or debate whether (as people debated over Thein Sein) in his younger days he would have been a front-line officer or a desk man. His title – the prefix 'Thura' – says it all: 'Brave Hero', awarded for valour in battle. Born two years after the president, he looks fifteen years younger.

The two men were rivals to become president in 2011, and Shwe Mann was considered the likelier candidate, not only because of the attributes mentioned above but also because he was senior in the hierarchy. He was passed over for reasons we can guess at. Cunning Than Shwe may have considered that Thein Sein, an unimpressive, bookish-looking bald fellow, who as prime minister had got to know his ASEAN peers on diplomatic junkets, was a better bet as the innocuous face of democratic transition. It is hard to imagine Thein Sein ordering his men to mortar a village, shoot fleeing villagers or murder the porters. In the case of Shwe Mann it is not so hard. And that 'brave hero' tag might have invited unwelcome investigation from the nosey international community.

Whatever the reasons, Thein Sein beat him to the top job, and Shwe Mann responded by mutating into an efficient, conscientious Speaker of Parliament's Lower House, which – as in some other parliaments – is a far more powerful job than its counterpart in the UK's House of Commons. As Speaker, Shwe Mann sets the political agenda, choosing which bills to advance and which to retard, which speakers to call on and which to ignore. He was the single most important figure in turning the Naypyidaw Parliament into a far livelier body than the Chinese-style rubber-stamp parliament it was expected to become, challenging the government on a range of issues including land reform, the environment, government expenditure and pensions.[13]

A crucial clash between Parliament and president occurred early on, and saw the first blossoming of the unlikely alliance between Suu and Brave Hero. A weapon in the president's armoury is the Constitutional Court: he appoints the judges, ex-generals and academics who staff it and who are the nation's top authority on constitutional issues. In March 2012, these eminences had ruled that parliamentary committees did not have the right to summon ministers or overrule the government because they were not 'national-level' organisations. Parliament objected strongly: as one MP put it, 'If they have power above Parliament, there will be no one who can control the government. We are worried that there will be no checks and balances on the government and [it] may act [in a similar way] to the last military regime.'[14]

It was a well-founded fear. Parliament was in its rights to throw down the challenge, and when Shwe Mann smoothed Suu's path to becoming chair of the Rule of Law and Tranquillity Committee in August 2012, the issue gained momentum. On 6 September Parliament flexed its muscles decisively, voting to impeach all nine justices; they resigned the same day. This was a demonstration that Parliament had the self confidence to defy the president, that it understood its constitutional significance, and took seriously Suu's favourite mantra of the importance of the rule of law.

On Shwe Mann's part, it showed that he was happy to throw obstacles in the path of the president, the rival who had bested him, especially if this was pleasing to Suu. As time passed, their parliamentary partnership flourished and it became clear that it had a strategic as well as a tactical dimension. This one could run and run.

A firm alliance – given the necessary mutual trust – could benefit them both. Neither has chosen to speak out publicly on an electoral pact of some kind, let alone a joint ticket, and Suu has been particularly reticent on the subject. But her growing admiration for Shwe Mann – in contrast to her increasing impatience and dissatisfaction with the president – are common currency. And the Brave Hero's on-the-record words about the Lady verge on the effusive. 'Daw Aung San Suu Kyi has much goodwill and she wants to develop the country,' he said at one point. 'We have a good relationship, we are colleagues,' he told another forum. 'We share the same ambition – to serve the nation and the people.' And again: 'I am ready to co-operate with Daw Aung San Suu Kyi today, tomorrow and in the future as well.'[15]

Both Suu and Shwe Mann have repeatedly and publicly said that they are interested in becoming president. But their prospects of doing so are quite different. The NLD has always been expected to do very well in a free and fair general election, as it did in the by-elections of 2012. But even if it swept the board, its MPs would not be able to vote Suu onto the presidential throne because she is barred from the presidency on account of her foreign sons.

Shwe Mann has no such difficulty. In many ways he is the obvious choice to succeed Thein Sein. But there was no guarantee that the USDP, of which he is a senior leader, would do well if the next election were held freely and fairly: as we have seen, on the two previous occasions in which the Burmese people had the opportunity to give their verdict on rule by a proxy party of the army – in 1990 and in the by-elections of 2012 – the result was an overwhelming thumbs-down. The same was expected to happen in 2015, in which case Shwe Mann's presidential aspirations could be shipwrecked by his party's poor showing in parliament.

Burma's president, whose term runs for five years, like

Parliament's, is voted into office by the newly elected MPs. The idea that the NLD could vote a senior ex-general into the presidency seems the stuff of madness, given the party's history of persecution at the army's hands – like America's eighteenth-century revolutionaries voting to bring back British colonial rule, like turkeys voting for Christmas. But it was not beyond the bounds of possibility. Only Suu could make it happen. Only Suu could want it to happen.

In the case of Shwe Mann, the irony is even more pronounced. Twenty years before, he had played a decisive role in trying to wipe the NLD off the face of the earth.

In Burma's only free and fair general election of the past sixty years, the one held in 1990, the NLD won 392 of the seats they contested,[16] more than 80 per cent of the total. The ethnic parties which they were allied with won 65 seats, so in total this was 94 per cent of the seats. The National Unity Party, the re-badged rump of Ne Win's Burma Socialist Programme Party, which, as the only permitted party, had ruled from 1962 to 1988, won only 10 seats.

Once the scale of their victory became clear, the NLD gave the junta, in those days known as SLORC, the State Law and Order Restoration Council, a deadline of four months to hand over power. Three weeks before the deadline, SLORC struck pre-emptively, arresting as many of the party's members as they could lay hands on including its acting leader, U Kyi Maung. The MPs-elect who eluded the crackdown fled east, to the Thai border, where the Karen National Union had been fighting for Karen freedom for forty-five years.

Styling themselves the National Coalition Government of the Union of Burma (NCGUB), the MPs set up their headquarters in a jungle camp called Manerplaw,[17] which by the time I visited it in 1991 was home to a rainbow alliance of rebel groups: students, monks and insurgents as well as the freely and fairly elected representatives of the Burmese people.

The sign over the entrance to Manerplaw read 'GIVE US LIBERTY OR GIVE US DEATH'. It was a place both of despair and of hope: despair, because one generation of ethnic rebels had already gone to their graves without seeing their dreams of liberty come any closer to realisation, and their children could hope for little better; despair, because every person who stayed in Manerplaw, intensely hot and humid when I visited, ended up suffering from malaria; hope, because against all odds this rebel redoubt witnessed an amazing blossoming of the human spirit, as young protesters from the Burmese cities found common cause with the ethnic soldiers and villagers Burma's army had been trying for so long to liquidate.

Symbolic of the brave spirit of the place was the so-called Federal University, composed of two classrooms in huts on a hillock where volunteer teachers from England and Canada taught English, economics, history, music and other subjects to refugee students from all over the country. The ministers in the National Coalition Government were installed in a solid teak house in the camp. Their prime minister, Dr Sein Win, a cousin of Suu, and Foreign Minister Peter Limbin, shuttled between this remote rebel stronghold, accessed from Thailand over the Salween and Moei rivers, and places like Geneva and Washington where Western governments rewarded them with warm sympathy if not diplomatic recognition.

Rangoon sank deeper into the torpor and paranoia of the SLORC dictatorship. Senior General Than Shwe, newly installed as the regime strongman, put his former patron General Ne Win under house arrest and his children in jail, kept Suu locked in her home with barely enough to eat and practised zero tolerance against the forces of democracy. Meanwhile Manerplaw was becoming a hotspot of intellectual ferment, the one corner of the country where the light of idealism continued to burn brightly. It was at Manerplaw that ideas about non-violent struggle – ideas later to exert a profound influence on the 'colour' revolutionaries of post-Soviet eastern Europe – first came into focus when Gene Sharp, the American theoretician of non-violent struggle, turned up in the camp and had long discussions with the rebels,[18] out of which emerged his celebrated handbook *From Dictatorship to Democracy: A Conceptual Framework for Liberation*.

But Manerplaw was very vulnerable, and SLORC was determined to smash it. Every day for the ten days preceding my visit, Tatmadaw units had shelled nearby Karen villages and bombed them from the air; and several times a day Burmese warplanes flew reconnaissance missions over Manerplaw itself. As one of the few strongholds still in Karen hands, it was increasingly in the line of fire.

It was in the same year, 1991, that Shwe Mann, who was born in Kanyutkwin, Pegu division, and who graduated from the Defence Services Academy in 1969, joined Light Infantry Division 66 – one of the two military units which were the focus of the Harvard report on war crimes described earlier in this chapter – in its assault on Manerplaw.[19] The Karen

Independence Army put up strong resistance and the camp held out for another three years. But the army continued to soften it up from the air, then in late 1994 threw newly purchased Chinese armoured personnel carriers into the ground offensive: they broke through defensive positions in the south and crossed the Salween River in the north-west, and on 26 January 1995 the Karen rebels abandoned Manerplaw.[20] With that, the last vestige of democracy on Burmese soil was destroyed.

This triumph was the making of Shwe Mann: he was decorated with the title 'brave hero' for his role in the action, promoted to the rank of brigadier and brought back to Rangoon. As the saying goes, you cannot make an omelette without breaking eggs: a diplomatic cable from the then American chargé d'affaires, Shari Villarosa, to Washington, published by Wikileaks, which described Shwe Mann as Than Shwe's 'preferred successor' and 'right-hand man', noted that 'like most Burmese field commanders, [he] utilised forced civilian porters, including women and children, on a massive scale against Karen insurgents.'[21]

Now, twenty years on, the Brave Hero is again softening up the NLD, preparing for the decisive assault. A general may take off his uniform, but he doesn't stop fighting.

13

IN ARCADIA

Twenty years after the Brave Hero's triumph at Manerplaw, he was back on Burma's eastern border, playing a cameo role in another small war against another ethnic minority. At the base hospital of the army's North Eastern Command, the Speaker of the Lower House of Parliament toured the wards in white shirt and black longyi, greeting and commiserating with soldiers injured in the fighting against a force that styled itself the Myanmar National Democratic Alliance (MNDA) and which had come out of nowhere in February 2015 to shatter the government's hopes of sealing a nationwide ceasefire before the general election scheduled for November.

Thura Shwe Mann walked through the shabby base hospital, a relic of the Raj, its wards housed in wooden pitch-roofed huts, with the cameras of Myanmar state television in tow. It is only in the past five years that the army has begun to advertise its losses. The Tatmadaw has been fighting on different fronts ever since independence, all the time keeping its losses under wraps. That has now changed, and the newspapers and news bulletins of TV Myanmar have begun carrying information about soldiers lost and wounded in combat. The result – accidental or calculated – was that, for the first time in many decades, the army became somewhat popular.[1] Citizens discussed on social media the deaths of the army's brave young men as evidence of their sacrifice for the country. Some openness about the army's vulnerability brought a degree of popular endorsement for the role it had always claimed: as the only force able to prevent Burma from disintegrating.

But there was something not right about this claim. If the army were to succeed, some day the fighting would cease: peace would descend on Burma and the troops would return home to a hero's welcome and civilian life. Yet somehow this never happened. The wars go on and on. When a ceasefire brings one small war to a pause, another splutters back into life.

Such was the case at Kokang, 650 kilometres as the crow flies north of Manerplaw, on the border with China. This is Shan state, where the Shan people, closer in culture and language to the Thais than the Burmans, predominate. But there are many other minorities in this hilly region. One of them is the Kokang, who are ethnically Han Chinese, and speak Mandarin. But during British days, the colonialists categorised them as one of Burma's 'minority nationalities', and, like all the other 134 nationalities classified in this manner, the Kokang cling to the status and the security that this provides, such as it is. It is their guarantee of a toehold of legitimacy in Burma, a nation state with which in other respects, historically, linguistically, culturally, genetically, they have little in common. (It is the guarantee which, on the other side of the country, the Muslim Rohingya demand but the government refuses to give, on the implicit grounds that they had no such status in colonial times.)

Peace does not prevail in Burma. Practically all its borders remain more or less in a state of ferment. A nationwide peace settlement eludes the government. Cynics might say this suits the army very well: it never outlives its usefulness, and has a perennial justification for gobbling one-quarter or more of Burma's gross domestic product.[2] And the cynics may well be right.

George Orwell's first job was as a policeman in colonial Burma. The experience left him with an abiding hatred of colonialism, and was the making of him as a writer. Many of the darker aspects of Burma under the military are uncannily prefigured in *Nineteen Eighty-Four*, including the perpetual war on the borders. The perpetual war, he wrote, 'is unreal [but] it is not meaningless. It . . . helps to preserve the special mental atmosphere that the hierarchical society needs . . . The object of the war is to keep the structure of society intact . . .'[3]

The Brave Hero brings messages of gratitude and good cheer to those who have been wounded. As a politician he is also milking Burma's state of perpetual war for all it is worth. By chance I was on hand to witness his errand of mercy at the military hospital.

*

It was May 2015 and my assistant Han Thar and I had finished our work in Naypyidaw. I had prowled through Parliament, buttonholing NLD MPs, lobbing a question she would not answer to Suu as she walked into the chamber, chatting to Dr Tin Mar Aung, Suu's assistant, and trying to understand why none of my requests for an interview with Suu had received a reply ('We get so many . . .'). From the window of the press box I had watched the Brave Hero, stone-faced and dignified in his *gaung baung* turban, presiding over a glacial debate in Parliament's Lower House.

Our next planned stop was Lashio, the largest town in northern Shan state, and the closest to the Kokang war zone that one could get to by aeroplane. The area of the fighting was closed to foreigners arriving from the Burmese side – a couple of foreign journalists trying to enter it had been deported – but I wanted to get as close as I could. But there were no flights to Lashio from Naypyidaw. The only way we could get there was to return to Rangoon by overnight coach, the way we had come, snatch a couple of hours' sleep in a hotel near the airport then catch the red-eye flight north in the morning, checking in at 6.30 a.m.

As we flew north we got a lesson in how Burma's other half lives. The flight attendant informed us that the plane would be making an unscheduled stop – at Naypyidaw, which we had left by bus seven hours before. On landing we were all herded to the back of the aircraft, leaving the front half free for a party of VIPs: the Brave Hero, half-a-dozen uniformed soldiers and a retinue of bodyguards and civilian officials, with a scrum of Burmese journalists bringing up the rear.

It was galling to learn that our tiring journey south had been unnecessary, though as plebeians we would not have been allowed to board at Naypyidaw even if we had somehow found out about this special flight. But Han Thar, one of the most intrepid, quick-witted fixers I have worked with anywhere, was excited. Several of the journalists were friends of his. With a little help from them and some fancy footwork at Lashio airport we would be able to attach ourselves to this elite group and see what transpired.

My instinct was to walk up the plane and buttonhole Brave Hero where he sat. After all, many of the great and good have taken advantage of the limbo of the air to chew the fat with journalists, notably Pope Francis. But Han Thar would not let me. The consequences, he said, were unpredictable. And as he is the bravest of men, I let him be my guide.

At Lashio we followed Shwe Mann and his entourage as they left the plane. A double line of young Shan girls in native costume greeted him and his party as they walked down the red carpet. We dodged around this group and dashed for the taxi that Han Thar had already booked. Inside the car he changed out of his sweatshirt and shorts into a white shirt and trousers. After a few minutes a line of smart SUVs rolled slowly out of the airport and our taxi attached itself to the back.

At the hospital of the military base, adjacent to the airport, we blended in with the television crew, shadowing the gravely smiling eminence of the general-turned-politician as he passed from one ward to the next, being introduced to the casualties of war, listening to their stories and complimenting and encouraging them. It occurred to me that the little tour fulfilled several functions. Taking place six months before the election – the date had yet to be announced but it was already expected to be in early November – it drew the public's attention to the army's patriotic sacrifices. It showed the caring, compassionate side of the second most powerful politician in the country. It was a subliminal campaign advertisement for him and his ruling Union Solidarity and Development Party. And it reminded anybody who might have forgotten that, despite his civvies, Shwe Mann, like the unlucky young men he was meeting, had dedicated his life to defending his country, and knew all about the terrors of battle.

But as I was the only paleface on the premises, there was a limit to how much I could blend in. A member of his team spotted us, cornered Han Thar and asked him what we were doing and what right we had being in such close proximity to the Brave Hero. This fellow's manner was civil, but he took down all my assistant's particulars then moved on to me. Once he had done with us, Han Thar could not move fast enough: we were out of the hospital, back in the taxi and on our way out of the base in less than a minute. Burmese journalists, he explained, had been jailed for lesser infringements. Authority in this country is still arbitrary, and does not mind demonstrating the fact. Shwe Mann may have rebranded himself as a democrat but everyone knows the reality.

With the cover offered by his new ally Aung San Suu Kyi, Thura Shwe Mann is extending his influence into the realm of democratic politics. But his power, like that of other top army officers, already stretches well beyond military affairs into the larger economy. As the then US chargé d'affaires, Shari Villarosa, noted in 2007 in the cable published by Wikileaks quoted in the last chapter,

[Shwe Mann and his wife Khin Lay Thet] have three sons who are included with their parents in the EU's visa and financial sanctions lists.

Son: Aung Thet Mann. He owns a company named Ayeya Shwe Wa . . .

After the arrest of [former ruling general] Khin Nyunt, Shwe Mann famously said, 'Nobody is above the law.' While he may not be as notoriously corrupt as some of his colleagues, Shwe Mann has solid connections to regime business cronies

Suu at a school opening in Natmauk, her father's birthplace.

U Win Tin, the conscience of the NLD, who died in 2014.

Gentle Rangoon punk 'Einstein' is a sign of Burma's changing society.

Thura Shwe Mann, Speaker of parliament's lower house and ex-general, inspecting troops.

Shwe Mann meeting a soldier injured in fighting in Kokang, eastern Burma.

Dawt Pen and Ni Kil, survivors of the 1943 Japanese occupation of their village in Chin state.

Early morning bus in the muddy main street of Hakha, Chin state's biggest town.

Han Naung Wai, peace negotiator and son of Burma's first president.

Young village boys learning English in Chin state.

Suu answers questions at a press conference in the garden of her Rangoon home, days before the election.

NLD campaign lorry spreading the word in Rangoon.

Below: Suu's huge rally in Rangoon proved her enduring popularity.

Old guard 1: U Tin Oo, emeritus chairman of NLD in his late eighties, campaigned vigorously.

Old guard 2: U Win Thein, co-founder of NLD, was on a short list of possible candidates for president.

Old guard 3: U Nyan Win, the party's veteran spokesman, at NLD's head office.

Young blood: Zayar Thaw, former hip-hop music star, now an NLD MP.

Khun Tun Oo, leader of the Shan NLD, an ally of Suu and a big winner in the 2015 election.

Independent candidate U Myo Khin, who challenged the NLD, outside a polling station.

San Tin Kyaw outside a polling station with friend on election day, when he hoped to represent his Muslim community.

November 2015: eager voters formed queues outside polling stations before dawn.

Many voters were optimistic about the result.

Aung Thein (far right): 'I'm so happy because I am free to vote'.

2 December 2015: all smiles after her landslide election victory, Aung San Suu Kyi shakes hands with President Thein Sein.

. . . He . . . is allegedly involved in fertiliser, brokerage, and fish export businesses. In addition, his sons are reported to use their father's connections to advance their business interests . . .[4]

That is very abstract. What it means in practice is explained in a blog by Hla Oo, 'a Burmese exile', as he describes himself, 'aimlessly wandering in this imperfect world'.

In an entry dated 4 May 2014, Hla Oo quotes Shwe Mann defending his reputation at a press conference. '"My sons do not exploit my status as a general and Speaker of Parliament," the Speaker says. "I always force them to advance in business on their own merit, not on what their father is. I am confident in stating that fact and I dare anyone to show that I have ever given them opportunity in any army-related business by using my position as an army general."'[5]

In reply Hla Oo posts his translation of an open letter by Phoe Thar Aung, a rice farmer who found himself in the power of Shwe Mann and one of his sons. 'I and all the rice farmers in Irrawaddy Division would like him to come back to Irrawaddy Delta and say that to our faces,' the farmer writes. 'In our Delta region there are so many farmers whose lives have been completely ruined by our Dear Speaker Shwe Mann's son Aung Thet Mann's company Ayeyar-Shwewar. My family was one of those thousands of ruined farmers.'[6]

The farmer writes that in 1997 – two years after the fall of Manerplaw – Shwe Mann became the army's divisional commander in Irrawaddy Division. As such he had power far beyond military matters. For example, he was able to give his son's company the local monopoly in fertiliser distribution.

Phoe Thar Aung claims that Aung Thet Mann and his powerful father

forced all the rice farmers in [the Irrawaddy] Delta to buy cheap imported chemical fertiliser only from their [company] Ayeyar-Shwewar.

. . . All rice farmers . . . were forced to take their chemical fertiliser as a loan at the beginning of harvest season without telling us the exorbitant prices [they would] eventually charge. Some of us who were clever enough knew what could happen when our rice-paddy was harvested. So we were reluctant to take their fertiliser and get into their debt. Historically most of us poor rice farmers do not use chemical fertilisers at all as we traditionally used natural fertilisers like cow manure. Even if some of us needed chemical fertiliser we could buy it cheaply from Chinese and Indian shops in any nearby town. There was absolutely no need to take out a fertiliser loan from Ayeyar-Shwewar, especially if you didn't know how much it would eventually cost at the end of the harvest.

But a divisional commander like General Shwe Mann is very powerful and ruthlessly brutal like those Chinese warlords we read about in old books. The township and village bosses also told us that we just had to take it and that was that. Bags and bags of chemical fertiliser from China on our doorsteps. We just had to sign for them at the government's village offices . . . The amount was allotted according to how many acres of paddy land we had and worked. That's it, simple.

The serious trouble started – as some of us had expected – only when the paddy was harvested. The Ayeyar-Shwewar agents supported by the village administrators came and took away whatever quantity of rice paddy they demanded and recorded it unjustly in their loan books. Of course the price of the fertiliser was exorbitantly exaggerated while the price for our rice was unjustly pushed down, so much so that in many cases the rice farmer had no rice left in his barn for his and his family's own consumption, let alone to sell at the market as a fair return for his year-long hard labour.

Some families had to stop sending their children to school as they could no longer afford the expense. Some even had to send their under-age kids to nearby towns to work in the restaurants and shops as the families were starving. Not just the rice farmers but other fertiliser businesses also went down as General Shwe Mann's family tightly controlled the chemical fertiliser distribution in the whole Irrawaddy Delta. That year General Shwe Mann and his sons became enormously rich overnight while many farmers like us were losing their land holdings because of their fertiliser debts to Ayeyar-Shwewar . . .[7]

Phoe Thar Aung is a victim of the way army power in Burma, lacking any pushback from civil let alone democratic authority, has for the past sixty-plus years done precisely what it wants – getting obscenely rich in the process. But there is nothing unique to Burma about this sort of abuse: arbitrary state power was exercised in this way in much of the world for thousands of years before the emergence of democracy.

It is instructive that Shwe Mann and his son made their fortunes by gouging the rice farmers. For many centuries across much of Asia, that was the classic route to wealth and power. If, before the modern age, you were to set about designing an efficient, productive and docile state in this part of the world from scratch, wet paddy is what you would start from.

As the ruler, you require a large, hard-working and productive population firmly settled in one place, where they can be reliably counted and taxed and recruited to defend the state when required. You need productive land to feed the farmers themselves as well as the rulers and to provide a sufficient surplus to pay for the fripperies of authority: palaces, villas and the like, as well as the wherewithal of a serviceable army. The anthropologist James C. Scott writes:

> Virtually everywhere, wet rice, along with the other major grains, is the foundation of early state making . . . The tax collector can survey the crop in the field as it ripens and can calculate in advance the probable yield. Most important of all, if the army and/or the tax collector arrive on the scene when the crop is ripe, they can confiscate as much of the crop as they wish . . . Grain is also relatively easy to transport, has a fairly high value per unit of weight and volume, and stores for relatively long periods.[8]

These are the reasons why, as Scott writes, 'virtually all of the premodern state cores in Southeast Asia are to be found in ecological settings that were favourable to irrigated rice cultivation.'[9] Shwe Mann and his son may not have known it, but by bludgeoning the farmers of the Irrawaddy Division into mass fertiliser-debt they were following in an ancient tradition.

The states created from a basis of paddy cultivation became some of the strongest and most enduring in the world, including Han China and Japan. With the surplus generated by the crop, one by one the rudiments of civilisation were brought into being: solid houses, well-made roads and watercourses, schools and universities and all the arts and crafts that they fostered. Only in such a well-ordered little world could an organised religion like Buddhism come into being, sink roots, build temples and shrines and flourish.

But at the root of this civilised world is the subjection and exploitation which Phoe Thar Aung and the other farmers of the Irrawaddy Delta experienced at the hands of Shwe Mann and his son less than twenty years ago. Coercion, reification, being reduced to a rice-harvesting cipher and the defenceless subject of arbitrary authority, vulnerable to scalping by ruthless tax farmers or losing your sons to the lord's recruiting sergeants: this is the dark other side of the gleaming coin of civilisation. And – at least in the days before democracy – you couldn't have one without the other.

But that deal – serfdom in exchange for security – is one that millions of people in the Burmese uplands have done their best throughout history to escape.

*

Chin state is the poorest in Burma.[10] It is one of the wildest and least-known corners of South East Asia. High in the mountains between Burma and India, it is home to the eponymous Chin, wild mountain men who for centuries hung their huts with their enemies' heads, sacrificed animals to evil spirits, worshipped a Supreme Being called, rather wonderfully, Khawzing, and raided lowland Burman villages to steal babies to be raised as slaves.

For centuries the Chin shared the country that came to be known as Burma with the dominant Burmans in the plains, as well as with dozens of other minorities that made their homes in the mountains fringing the lowlands. They are one of the so-called 'Big Eight' 'national races',[11] along with the Kachin, the Shan, the Kayah, the Karen, the Mon and the Arakan, who lend their names to Burma's seven states, with the eighth and by far the largest and most dominant group, the Bamar or Burmans, living in the nation's other seven divisions.

The Chins' legends reveal that they were in no doubt about their humble status in the Burmese scheme of things, brought about by lowland cunning. All the world's races, goes their creation story, were born from 101 eggs; the Chin were born from the last egg of all, and as a result were the most beloved of their parents. But by the time they emerged, all the desirable parts of the world had already been apportioned out; all that was left for them was the mountains. Additionally, the Burmese man who was supposed to be their guardian cheated them out of the possession of elephants – a Burmese symbol of royalty. And when the time came for lessons in reading and writing, he cheated them again by showing them only the blank side of the slate, so they never learned a single letter.

Today the Chin have left their primitive past long behind, and thanks to Christian missionaries they are also literate. But in the process they have been deposited in a kind of ethnic limbo: Christians in an overwhelmingly Buddhist land, Burmese citizens who feel neither Burmese nor anything else. A century ago they were unrivalled hunters in the dense forests through which they wandered; today the hills are denuded, the tigers and bears and deer are long gone; hunters with locally made guns still march out into what remains of the woods, but the odd wild pig is the best they can hope to bring home. And the plight of the Chin is that of those hunters writ large: locked in a land that is as much their prison as their paradise.

*

One fine, hot day in February 2014, the photographer Chris Steele-Perkins and I left Mandalay at four in the morning, heading west and climbing up into the Sagaing Hills, leaving in our wake the great tail of temples, monasteries, convents and gold-plated stupas that bejewel the heartland of Buddhist Burma. The fine four-lane road shrank to two lanes as we passed mountains of slag left by copper refineries to right and left, then shrank further to one and a half as our four-wheel-drive Nissan, the right sort of car for this terrain, clambered higher and higher into the mountains. And we drove and we drove and we drove.

We passed road-building gangs, women scarfed and cowled breaking big stones into smaller ones under the eyes of a young gangmaster; we came through villages that were no more than a couple of dozen flimsy wooden houses, clinging to the narrow verge on either side of the ribbon of road, a clapboard church with its cross protruding above the roofs on a higher slope. In one of those teetering hamlets we stopped to greet a convoy of Toyotas and Jeeps with luggage piled on the roofs and flags of the now pacified and legal Chin National Liberation Front – two hornbills on a branch on a blue- and red-striped background – strapped to the bumper.

Night fell and still we climbed; a cough I had been nursing since London was getting worse and the temperature was dropping. Finally at 7 p.m., after fifteen hours on the road, the driver told us we had arrived in Hakha, Chin state's largest town. We were at more than six thousand feet; we had left tropical Mandalay, nearly at sea level, where during the first weeks of February the sun blazed down more fiercely every day as summer began tuning up, far behind; now it was a couple of degrees above freezing and pouring with rain. We stumbled from the car into the Grace Hotel, where we learned we were booked into an annexe with no heating or hot water. I had a panicky feeling that I was going to get pneumonia and die here, that my bones would be buried in the soil of Chin.

Chin state is one of the last corners of Burma to be opened to foreigners, and we were among the first non-Burmese to reach here, as the shy smiles and curious glances we received everywhere made plain. Given the rigours of the journey and the spartan character of the hotel – and the fact that this large state, nearly 14,000 square miles in area, considerably larger than Belgium, has no airport – I would hesitate to predict that large numbers will be following us.

At the hotel as the rain teemed down we met our fixers, two young men called Sang and Mang, who took us twenty paces up a steep hill sluicing with rainwater to a cosy eating house where we ate fried rice and a rich dish of fish-head soup washed down with Myanmar Beer. I began to revive, and fears of imminent death receded. The hotel did indeed have no heating – and no electricity after 10 p.m., when the generator shut down – but the duvets were thick and plentiful and I rose in the morning to face another day. And I found myself in a town unlike any in the world – and quite unlike anything I had ever seen in Burma.

The steep main street was lined with clapboard buildings painted lurid shades of yellow, pink and sky-blue. If you were to see a monochrome photograph of the same scene, you would not be surprised to be told that it had been shot on the frontier of the American Wild West, circa 1860. I did not see any bars with swinging doors, nor any horses tied up outside them, and even cowboy hats were in short supply; had these details been present, the illusion would have been complete.

We were among the first foreigners to travel to Burma's Chin state in more than half a century. And yet there is a strong sense that we have got here too late. What we see – this American frontier town – covers up what this land once was, erasing it so completely that we can only guess what it was like before. And to make it even more confusing, this cowboy town is populated by a short, stocky, coffee-coloured race who might be mistaken for Native Americans.

In lowland Burma, everywhere you go the past is with you. The city of Pagan may be only a shadow of the metropolis it once was, but the thousand pagodas tell their story of medieval wealth and Buddhist zeal. The Shwedagon Pagoda in Rangoon is encrusted with modern additions – escalators, souvenir shops, even an ATM – but at its heart is a pilgrimage site that has stood there for a thousand years.

But the biggest town in Chin state is like a stage set for a production of *Annie Get Your Gun*. If they were to haul up the backdrop and pack away the flats, what would remain?

*

The founding parents of modern Hakha were Arthur and Laura Carson, American Baptist missionaries from the Midwest who had already evangelised for years down in the

Burmese lowlands. Now in 1899 they were ready for a more serious challenge: among the Chins of the hills who had never encountered the Bible.

They began their journey up the Irrawaddy River in a steamer, the *Karanee*, which 'towed two flats, one on either side, each of which was loaded with *ngapi* (putrid fish) which is largely used as food by the people of this country,' Mrs Carson wrote in her memoirs.[12] 'The night was hot and the fumes from the fish made me very sick all night so that I could not sleep.'

After a six-week journey through jungles full of tiger and wildcat and up steep narrow paths where trains of pack cattle almost shouldered them over the edge into the abyss, they finally arrived in Hakha, 'a military post where are stationed sixty Sepoys with three English officers'.

Why here? Laura Carson recorded:

> Chin villages abound on the neighbouring hillsides. Many thousands of people are accessible from this place, not one of whom is a Christian and not one can read or write in any language. Their only religion is the sacrificing of animals to evil spirits; it is also their only system of medicine. To these poor people we hope to introduce the everlasting, uplifting influence of the Gospel of Christ and teach them the Way of Salvation.

But on that first day and night Laura Carson quailed at the scale of the challenge. They had arrived, as she wrote, 'beyond the pale of civilisation', among wild tribesmen whose huts had been decorated with the heads of their (human) victims and whose main pastime was raiding Burman villages in the plains. After a succession of small wars, the British forced them to give up these barbaric customs, but they remained who they were – a people whose story had, from its murky beginnings, been lived a very long way from anything that resembled civilisation.

'On the evening of our arrival,' she wrote, 'I looked about in vain for the cleaner, less repulsive, higher class people. My heart sank, for I could not tell the chiefs from the coolies. *All* were dirty and filthy beyond description.' The British assistant superintendent – the ranking colonial official in the town – was out of station but invited them to stay in his home. It was not what Laura had hoped: it was a

> little two-roomed stone and mud hut, with no floor and the ground under our feet worn into hills and valleys . . . I began spreading quilts on the bumpy dirty floor for our bed. Finally, sitting there Turk fashion on the hard ground, I broke out with, 'Arthur, I can't do it! I simply *can't* do it! . . . I can't stay on and live out my life in this awful place, among these loathsome people.' And I wept bitterly.

But the next day something occurred which changed her mind. She was paying off the coolies who had brought them up into the hills when it happened.

> One girl about eighteen was unusually attractive. I had tried . . . to make friends with her on the way up . . . Her perfect figure was clad in a skirt not more than eighteen inches long – that was all. With a beaming face she came to me to say goodbye, patting my face with a very grimy hand and smiling into my eyes . . . I realised that Drummond was right when he said, Love is the greatest thing in the world. It is. I

saw beyond the grime and filth on that perfectly formed and almost nude body. I saw the need of the soul . . . What could not a consecrated Christian woman do for her and those of her kind if she would? What a matchless opportunity had been given me!

Seven years later, in 1906, the Carsons made their first convert. Two years after that – shortly before expiring from appendicitis – Arthur Carson baptised number one hundred. This pioneering, inexhaustible couple had learned the language, written it down in the Roman alphabet, taught their converts to read and write, and had translated several books of the Bible, including the Gospel according to Matthew and the Acts of the Apostles, into Chin, and had them published.

They had brought influential young chiefs over to their side, proved native fears about evil spirits and cursed fields to be bunkum, and, with the discreet assistance of officers of the British Raj, had shown the most promising young Chin that this alien faith could work wonders: could raise them in the eyes of the people who now commanded their land, and allow them to hold their heads high in the presence of the lowland Burmans who had always despised them. Today, thanks to the seeds planted a century ago by Arthur and Laura Carson, Chin state is overwhelmingly Christian.

And as a result, all that earlier reality – the culture of a people who over centuries had fashioned a way of life free from the impositions and profiteering of the plains – is completely inaccessible. It is as if it had never existed. In the process of becoming 'civilised', the Chin have lost something precious: the sense of who they are. By turning them into wannabe whites, with their clapboard houses and homely churches, their sweaters and jackets and trousers, they have alienated them from everything that made them what they once were.

*

'Burma is a long and narrow valley land,' the blogger Hla Oo writes in his self-published novel *Song for Irrawaddy*,

> well over one thousand miles long from north to south and three hundred miles wide from east to west, of the mighty Irrawaddy.
>
> It is surrounded by rugged high mountain ranges and plateaus along the border areas where the ethnic races of Shans, Kachins, Kayins and Chins live, while the dominant Bamar [Burman] race mainly live in the Irrawaddy Valley and the Delta.[13]

Never in history was there a 'Burma' as it exists today. Instead there were, for one thousand years and more, city-states founded variously by the Mon, Burman, Arakanese and Shan races, each based on the reliable wealth generated by the culture of the rice paddy, each in turn challenging the power of the other until the Burmans emerged as top dog. Upland groups like the Chin and many dozens more lived their lives as far removed from the expansionary, predatory plainsmen as they could manage; the price they paid, witness the Chin before the arrival of the Carsons, was the absence of what the people of the plains called civilisation. In their way, however, they were free. As James Scott puts it, they had mastered 'the art of not being governed'.[14]

The arrival of the British, first to punish the Burmans for intruding into British Bengal, later to create a bulwark between French-ruled Indochina and British India, eventually changed everything. Starting with the conquest of Lower Burma in 1824–6, the colonialists dealt with the plains as they had dealt with comparable low-lying, rice-growing regions of central India in present-day Bangladesh, West Bengal and Bihar: imposing European notions of property and taxation (from which the foreigners derived their profits), installing and empowering landlords, tax farmers, money-lenders and shopkeepers from the subcontinent, and in the name of rapid economic development essentially turning the country upside down.

With the uplands, however, their approach was very different. There was little profit to be made in areas like Chin, so the main task was to keep an eye on them, installing a small military force like the one Mrs Carson encountered in Hakha, and perhaps a political resident; weaning them from their 'barbaric' customs, discreetly facilitating the work of the missions but otherwise leaving them alone, to be ruled, to the extent that they were ruled at all, by those who had always ruled them.

The Burmese clamour for independence in the 1920s and 1930s was a phenomenon of the plains and of the plainsmen whose lives and culture the foreigners had profoundly disturbed. Up in the hills the Chin and the rest, now largely Christianised,[15] were not oppressed in the same way by the foreigners, and there was no comparable striving for freedom.

The land now called Burma was thus already polarised between the hills and the plains, and that polarisation gained a political and military dimension after the Japanese invasion of 1942. Retreating from the heartland, the British secured the loyalty of some of the Christianised ethnic groups, notably the Karen and the Kachin, whom they armed and gave the task of being a resistance force behind enemy lines. As I described in Chapter 8, the Bengali mujahideen, who now call themselves Rohingya, took advantage of this situation to attack not the Japanese but their Arakanese Buddhist neighbours. Elsewhere along the border the other minorities were less imprudent. But everywhere the plainsmen and hill tribes found themselves on opposite sides of a new political divide.

With the return of peace, and the agreement of Clement Attlee's Labour government to the demands of the Burmese for independence, this polarisation became a grave problem. 'Burma' in 1945 was not a nation-state. The Burman majority led by Aung San demanded freedom from Britain as soon as possible. The Attlee government, on the verge of quitting India, was equally keen to dump its other South Asian burdens. But while 'Burma' was no more than a redundant colonial construct shattered by the war, setting it free as it was, with the Burmans claiming sovereign rights over hill tribes which had spent their entire histories resisting such domination, was a recipe for disaster.

The Burmans could not obtain independence without reaching an agreement with the hill tribes. The hill tribes, who would have preferred to revert to the status quo ante, the light touch of British rule, were made to understand that this was not an option. The Karen, whose lands had been ravaged by both Japanese and Burmese troops during the war, refused to contemplate a union with the Burmans. 'How could anyone expect the Karen people to trust the Burmans after what happened during the war – the . . . slaughter of so many Karen people and the robbing of so many Karen villages?'[16] one of their leaders, Saw Tha Din, demanded during a Karen Goodwill Mission to London in 1946. Their answer was to declare independence unilaterally and dig in for a war with Burma that was to last for the rest of the century and beyond.

The other main minorities, however, were more compliant. With the British leaning heavily on both sides, the Burmans under Aung San met the leaders of the Shan, the Kachin and the Chin in the town of Panglong, in southern Shan state, in February 1947 and signed the agreement of the same name – 'believing', as they put it in the agreement, 'that freedom will [thus] be more speedily achieved'. The agreement committed the Frontier Areas (as they were described) to 'immediate co-operation' with the Burmese government, on condition that they retain 'full autonomy in internal administration'.[17]

Aung San showed political boldness and imagination in forcing through an agreement that many on both sides disliked. Without Panglong, Burmese independence would have been a far messier affair. But the resolution that was sketched out in the agreement barely survived the packing away of the independence bunting.

Aung San boosters like to say that Panglong fell apart because he was assassinated before he could take his nation into independence. But no genius could have forged a lasting political settlement on such a flimsy basis. This perfunctory, nine-clause deal, clinched at blinding speed, was classic

Mountbatten–Attlee fudge, from the same box of tricks as the Partition of India, and with consequences that in the long run were equally dire. Both were devices to liberate bankrupt Britain from its imperial burdens at top speed and with a facade of decency. In both cases the facade was too fragile to endure. Within months of independence, Burma was already falling apart. Notionally belonging to the new Union of Burma, the central heartland and areas like Chin state remained worlds apart.

*

The last American missionary left Chin in 1966, four years after the coup d'état that brought General Ne Win to power. Everything in Burma that was 'foreign', in Ne Win's view, had to go, from the Ford Foundation to the American Baptists who ministered to the Chin. He threw out all the foreigners and locked his country up inside its borders. The nation which at independence had been seen as the best hope in South East Asia – fancied far higher than Thailand, for example – began its slow slide backwards, under the cranky rubric of Ne Win's 'Burmese Way of Socialism'. By 1988, it was on a par, economically speaking, with the more wretched countries of sub-Saharan Africa.

The Ne Win years had not been too bad for Chin state: like the rest of the country it had stagnated, but unlike Karen state in the east of the country it had not been regarded as dangerously disloyal. There were rebellions, there was a Chin Liberation Front, but it was all low-key stuff compared to much of the rest of Burma, which was in a state of more or less continuous civil war. But with the expulsion of the foreign missionaries, the Chin lost touch with the wellspring of their new faith. Now they were doubly estranged from all that surrounded them, from everything that they were.

Then came 1988, Burma's year of revolution, which saw the emergence of Suu and the foundation of the NLD. The uprisings of that year, sparked by the regime's reckless decision to demonetise much of the currency, were replicated in these hills. They were followed by the same harsh retribution as elsewhere: the heavy hand of SLORC – the State Law and Order Restoration Council – descended. All declared opponents of the regime were put in jail. Those who could flee to the outside world did so, many crossing the border into India. Following decades of isolation, Chin's decline was compounded by a flood of the young, able-bodied and ambitious into exile.

'About 40 per cent of the people left after 1988,' our fixer, Sang Hnin Lian, told me. 'They went to Malaysia, the US, Australia, Germany, Denmark, Norway. They found work and sent remittances back. Now [since the onset of reforms in 2011] people have started to come back. But not many.' The exodus left Chin state's intellectual and cultural poverty more pronounced than ever.

So far Burma's new democratic dispensation has done little to improve things here. This huge state still lacks a university as well as an airport, and has mains electricity for only a few hours a day. The 2008 constitution brought regional parliaments into being as well as the Union (national) one in Naypyidaw, but members of the Chin National Party whom I met claimed Chin state's Parliament was merely a talking shop: real power is held by the chief minister, appointed by Naypyidaw, who rules by a cabinet of ministers whom he picks, who may or may not be local people. The 'full autonomy in internal administration' promised at Panglong is still a long way off. In the meantime the Burmanisation process by which the ethnic minorities are forcibly assimilated with the majority in the lowlands has only been relaxed a fraction: the longstanding ban on studying Chin literature in Chin language has been removed in theory, but it is only permitted up to Grade Two. Teachers who want to teach it have to do so in their own time, without extra pay.

Yet despite all its problems and deprivations, Chin state's great distance from the big city, both physical and mental, does have some benefits.

Sang and Mang brought us on scooters to the village of Nabual, a couple of miles from Hakha along a rough single-track road; 'warmly welcome to NABUAL' the sign read in English, in tender expectation, finally fulfilled, of someone able to understand it.

And once we are in the village, suddenly Chin's limbo doesn't seem too bad a place to be. The loudest noise in this village of fifty houses is the shuttle of a small wooden loom being whacked against the wood of the frame by a pretty teenage girl in her long Chin skirt. Her knees are tucked under her as she weaves away on her sunny balcony, while a tiny kitten washes its face. It takes one month to make the material for a skirt, she says.

The simple wooden village school has three classes and eighteen pupils. Five of them are studying English, chanting the rhyme chalked up on the board:

School is over, oh what fun!
Lessons finished, play begun
Who'll run faster, you or I?
Who'll laugh louder, let us try!

Stop right here, one wants to say: this is all the development you need. In this village clinging to a steep hillside the tranquillity is profound: there are a few scooters but no cars let alone lorries; the rough ribbon of road is barely motorable. The state provides a fitful, meagre supply of electricity, but its meagreness doesn't matter much: in Laura Carson's day the Chin used to, in her words, 'go to bed with the chickens' for fear of the evil spirits abroad at night. Today the superstitions may have receded but the habit remains.

The modern world has not yet twisted the Chin way of life out of shape. There are a few telephones, and coverage enough to justify ownership of that new status symbol, a smartphone. But there are no buildings made of anything but wood, and none higher than two storeys. On small plots adjoining their homes the villagers grow yams, beans, bananas and sugar cane. One man here weaves the handsome cane baskets the Chin use for their shopping.

We are introduced to the old ladies of the village, Dawt Pen, seventy-six, and Ni Kil, seventy-eight. Bare-footed, brown as nuts and deeply wrinkled, dressed in old sweaters and longyis, they are tiny even by the diminutive standards of the Chin. I ask them if they remember the Second World War. They certainly do. 'The Japanese came to the village; they shot and cooked and ate our pigs and cows,' Dawt Pen says. 'There were aeroplanes, too – it was terrifying. We ran into the country with our parents to hide from them. We got so hungry.'

That was in 1943. Two years later the pendulum swung back the other way, and the British who had first rampaged through in the 1890s were back again. Peace returned. Independence brought few changes. General Aung San was assassinated, and his promise of federalism came to nothing. Unexploded Japanese bombs were dug up, defused and beaten into bells for the churches. Chin state slipped back into the obscurity that seems its natural state: '. . . The world forgetting, by the world forgot . . .'[18]

In Nabual the small plum trees are in blossom, the cocks are crowing in the middle of the afternoon, the cats and dogs, loved and well treated as is rarely the case in Asia, seem as contented as the chickens and the people. In the tranquil spring sunshine the rest of the world seems a very long way away.

14
PEACE IN OUR TIME

Aung Naing Oo has experienced his country at its worst, at its best, at its most despairing. Now, as one of the executors of an audacious attempt by the Burmese government to bring the world's longest civil war to an end, he has come home.

Born and raised in Pegu, sixty-five miles north of Rangoon, in 1988 he graduated from Rangoon University in English and began a postgraduate degree there, financing himself by teaching privately. Like tens of thousands of other students in Burma's then capital, he was swept up in the anti-government protests that began in March after the government declared higher-value banknotes worthless, bankrupting millions of Burmese overnight.

The protests steadily increased in size, culminating in the general strike of 8 August – 8–8–88 as it became known – when huge demonstrations were staged in towns and cities all over the country, in defiance of the government's declaration of martial law five days before. Throughout the hours of daylight the authorities did nothing to impede them, and the mood was closer to a carnival than a riot. But trucks full of armed soldiers had been moved into position near City Hall, and close to midnight, without warning, the army went into action.

Aung Naing Oo saw it happen. Many years later he recalled:

The military had blocked off a bridge connecting Rangoon and the suburb where I lived. There were military trucks on the bridge and they shot the people, unarmed people, indiscriminately. I was only fifty feet from the front of the demonstration, I saw with my own eyes how people were killed and it was indiscriminate. It was mayhem, and the shooting took a long time. Every time people rose up, they shot, and a lot of people were killed. I don't know how many people were killed. Everybody was angry. They were so angry that they tried to push, they came out with any weapon they could get and tried to attack the military.

It was really, really brutal, and I had to leave Rangoon, and I went back to where I belonged and I started demonstrations with my friends in the rural areas, trying to spread the message of democracy.[1]

After the massacres, the regime installed a civilian-led government promising the multi-party elections the protesters had demanded – but the massive demonstrations continued, and on 18 September the military struck back, killing thousands more in the streets, deposing the government and installing the military junta which, under different names, was to rule Burma with an iron fist for the next twenty-two years.

The scale of the killing told the students that the game was up. 'After the coup,' Aung Naing Oo says, 'I joined the exodus of some 10,000 Burmese students and people from all walks of life.' He fled for the jungle near Manerplaw, on the Thai border. 'Like thousands of other students and professionals, I joined the All Burma Students' Democratic Front [ABSDF – the largest student group resisting military rule] in the jungle. At the time we firmly believed that the armed struggle was the only option left for us to bring democracy to our homeland. We were determined to confront the Myanmar military.'[2]

He wrote decades later:

Life in the jungle was tough. Malaria left no one untouched. Food was always in short supply. There was constant fear of Myanmar military attack, and few weapons to go around . . . Yet in spite of the endless hardships and the countless bouts of malaria, we were happy and free, willing to sacrifice for the greater good of the nation. We had youthfulness, zeal, and an honourable and idealistic purpose: to bring freedom and democracy to our country . . . We organised students into various camps, drafted a constitution and legal system and tried to demonstrate that we were capable of launching a revolution. In Thay Baw Boe camp, where I was the camp secretary, we established the 'Jungle University' and adopted the slogan 'Revolution is our school – our university'.[3]

But as the jungle years dragged by, the mirage of democracy grew no closer. Instead his own organisation succumbed to what he calls 'the demon that all other political organisations in Myanmar have confronted: factionalism'. The organisation split down the middle, and its members turned on each other. In Kachin, in the far north of the country, thirty-five members of ABSDF were either executed summarily or tortured to death by their comrades in an attempt to crack down on dissidents and suspected spies. After years of revolutionary struggle, the rebels found themselves replicating the brutal methods of the enemy.

Aung Naing Oo was appalled, and his ideas began to change. 'I abhorred [the killings] and spoke out against them,' he said. 'By 1996 I, like many others, had begun to realise that [it was] only through political, not armed, struggle that we would achieve our goal.'[4] When in 1998, despite the organisation's efforts to reform, another illegal killing occurred, he snapped: he left the jungle and the organisation as suddenly as he had arrived.

His new path took him to Chiang Mai in northern Thailand, where he taught at the city's university, then via a short spell at university in Australia to the John F. Kennedy School of Government at Harvard, where he studied conflict, civil war and negotiation. In 2007, during the new eruption of mass protest that came to be called the Saffron Revolution, he emerged as a distinctive voice: a veteran of Burmese protest who denounced Western sanctions as self-defeating, who was outraged by the way the junta was repeating bloody history on the Rangoon streets – but who looked forward, with remarkable prescience, to an imminent change in the national mood.

'There's so much anger, so much anger,' he said then. 'The Burmese have suffered so much. So I think this thing will not simply die down. I think it will go on. I think this will lead to some sort of resolution. Even if the military doesn't give up now, they will have to do something, make some concessions.'[5]

What might those concessions be? he was asked.

'Trying to speed up the road map process, to write the constitution quicker [with] elections in one or two years' time . . .'

Did he foresee the military junta giving up power?

'Oh, they're not going to surrender power. [With] the elections and the constitution, the military [will have] a lot of say, a lot of controls. If this constitution is implemented, Burmese people will have 5 to 10 per cent of freedom.'[6]

Looking back from eight years on, many Burmese would ruefully agree that 5 or 10 per cent of freedom is roughly what they got. It's not much. But it's much better than nothing. And it might, with effort and determination and the spirit, so elusive in this country, of compromise, lead to more – to peace, for example. After all, these views come from a man who spent more than ten years in the jungle fighting for all-out revolution – for all or nothing. His words cannot be lightly dismissed.

In September 2007, as soldiers and riot police began mopping-up operations after the crushing of the monk-led revolt, he insisted:

This is a time for dialogue. I mean, this is a time to end military isolation. Military isolation has caused so much misery in this country. The military has isolated itself. The international community has isolated the military, and the military has made tons of blunders . . . The Burmese people have paid with their lives, with their sweat, with their blood, dearly. In the long run, sanctions are not the answer. The answer is to try to end the military isolation, try to bring the military to the dialogue table.[7]

Six years later, he was sitting at that table.

*

On a stormy monsoon day in 2015, during an interval in yet another round of peace talks, I met Aung Naing Oo at a grand, decaying hotel on Inya Lake in Rangoon. Tall, trim, handsomely greying in the Richard Gere manner, he shows no outward signs of having spent the best years of his life in jungle warfare.

> PP: *How did you get involved in these peace negotiations?*
> ANO: *Three or four months after Thein Sein came to power in March 2011, he offered peace talks to the ethnic groups. No one was sure about it. The head peace negotiator went to Thailand to talk to the ethnic groups – I was living in Thailand again, I hadn't been back to Burma since 1988.*

Aung Naing Oo was recruited as a figure with wide credibility among the ethnic groups, a passionate believer in peace, and a man with training in the required skills at the highest level.

> ANO: *From then on the peace process developed into something much more concrete. After initial talks in the Golden Triangle, in November 2011, the government signed its first ceasefire agreement with the Shan and then two months later they signed the ceasefire with the Karen National Union.*

This was the moment when outside observers realised that something new was happening. It was the first significant move towards peace that the Karen leadership had taken since independence sixty-three years before.

> ANO: *These groups said, they are not asking us to give up our weapons, let's do it. The government was keen to deliver peace – and we proved that we could deliver it if we got a chance.*

PP: *Years ago, General Khin Nyunt signed ceasefires with various groups. What happened to those?*

ANO: *Some of them still held. Some of the smaller groups had surrendered, some like the Kachin had gone back to fighting. Khin Nyunt and the military agreed thirty-eight ceasefires with thirty-eight different groups. So many different groups – it seems like every little ethnic group has its own army, its militia. Some of the bigger groups have splinter groups and they fight among themselves, alliances are formed and broken up and formed again and broken up again . . . this happens all the time, it's part and parcel of the whole pattern.*

The chief difference between those ceasefires and this peace process is that, when the military signed a ceasefire, they maintained all along that they were not the political government, they would not negotiate political settlements. This government not only offers a ceasefire but also political negotiations. This is the key difference. A difference not only of ambition but a recognition that you need to organise a political dialogue to resolve the country's issues politically. It's an ambitious plan, ambitious thinking: maybe it will take ten years to complete it.

A major step forward was taken on 31 March 2015, when delegations representing sixteen armed groups signed the draft of Burma's first-ever nationwide ceasefire agreement. The world took little notice: these small wars had gone largely unreported, and so did this first major step towards ending them all with a general settlement. Some were quick to scorn the deal as a triumph of public relations.

'Much ado about nothing,' wrote veteran commentator Bertil Lintner from his vantage point in Chiang Mai. 'While the foreign peacemakers [the Swiss and Norwegians who had played facilitating roles] were congratulating themselves in Naypyidaw and Rangoon the reality on the ground remained depressingly familiar.'[8] Lintner pointed out the blindingly obvious: the draft deal had been signed while fighting on two fronts, in Kachin and Kokang, continued unabated.

Khun Htun Oo, a leading politician from Shan state, was equally sceptical. He had been sentenced to ninety-three years in prison for high treason in 2005 and only freed in a mass release of political prisoners in January 2012. Over green tea in his elegant home in Rangoon, he told me that the draft agreement was meaningless: peace would not arrive until the Burmans and the minorities reach a political settlement. 'Until we sit down at the table and talk, there is no way out. We've been telling [the government] that for more than sixty years now. The process will be slow. And there is no consensus.'[9]

With a constitution in force that gave the military control of four key ministries, including border affairs, and allowed them to clamp army rule on the country again any time they wanted, no real progress was possible, he insisted. And that militaristic constitution was the work of the same president who was trying to force the pace on the ceasefire. 'You can't hurry much because the main purpose of holding arms and fighting is because of this constitution,' he said. 'Before it was only three or four groups fighting; now there are nearly twenty groups. And all on account of the constitution.'

But despite all the doubts and caveats, the signing of the document gave more cause to cheer than sneer. Something profound had shifted. Expatriates like Aung Naing Oo were quicker to recognise it than those whose whole lives had been defined by armed struggle. Another enthusiast was an aristocrat from Shan state, Han Naung Wai, who had also lived outside Burma. Perhaps their positive attitude is down to the fact that, as outsiders, they have a greater stake in change.

'It's incredible what the government has done,'[10] Han Naung Wai enthused to me. Like Aung Naing Oo, he had spent his adult life wandering the world, far from Burma, never permanently settled, always dreaming of returning to Burma some day. But his early years had promised a very different life.

His father, Sao Shwe Thaik, the ruling *saopha* or prince of one of the larger Shan states, was Burma's first president at independence in 1948. The appointment of an 'ethnic' to this top symbolic post was a way for the new nation to show that it was serious about diversity. Han Naung Wai was born in the year of independence, and passed his earliest years in the presidential palace.

Fourteen years later, in 1962, the peace of the family home in Rangoon was shattered by machine-gun fire as General Ne Win's troops surged in. Han Naung Wai's brother grabbed a tribal spear and went to the door to challenge them but was shot dead – the only casualty in this otherwise bloodless takeover. The family's expulsion was the first act of the coup d'état. Their father died in prison later that year. 'From being one of Burma's top families, now no one wanted to talk to us,'[11] he told me. The family fled into exile in Thailand.

His mother, who had been an exotic presence at Queen Elizabeth II's coronation, reinvented herself as a warrior queen, uniting the Shan states' northern and southern armies into a single force to fight the Burmese takeover of the state.

But like Aung Naing Oo, her son made a life for himself abroad: going into business first in Canada then later back in South East Asia. In September 2011, the president's chief ceasefire negotiator, another ex-general called U Aung Min, met him in Bangkok and persuaded him to become involved in the peace process.

Back in Rangoon now, embroiled in endless discussions with ethnic guerrillas and their political comrades, he has put aside any residual bitterness he may feel towards the Burmese army. 'I never thought I'd say this, given that he is an ex-general,' he said, 'but I think it would be good if President Thein Sein had a second term. It's true that he's not very strong compared to some of his colleagues. But he listens to lots of people.'[12]

With the son of Burma's first president hailing the achievement of the present one, history is coming full circle. In his inaugural speech as president, Han Naung Wai's father declared, 'For a long time the principal races of Burma . . . have tended to look upon themselves as separate national units. Of late, a nobler vision, the vision of a Union of Burma, has moved our hearts, and we stand united today as one nation.'[13] It was a brave but fragile claim: in 1948, all that held the vision together were the nine paltry clauses of the Panglong Agreement. Almost at once the Union fell apart at the seams.

By contrast, President Thein Sein's draft ceasefire took hundreds of meetings to conclude and consists of 106 provisions under 33 headings in 7 chapters. The president showed up at the Myanmar Peace Centre, where the negotiations had taken place, for the signing. With uncharacteristic emotion he said,

'I was so happy I could not even sleep last night after watching the heartfelt speeches by the ethnic leaders.'[14]

With a note of pride, Aung Naing Oo says of the agreement, 'It has been billed as the world's longest and wordiest ceasefire deal.' Of course that is no guarantee it will hold. More important is the vision that drives it: one that unites repentant guerrillas like himself, nostalgic expatriates like the first president's son, and the enigmatic ex-general in the presidential office. Aung Naing Oo calls it 'a political road map for the future'.[15] The signing of the draft was the first step down that long, winding, essential road – a road that, as Suu had said in Oxford in 2012, 'is not even there yet . . . We have to make the road ourselves, inch by painful inch.'[16]

*

The first time I saw punks in Rangoon was in March 2013,[17] almost a year after Suu's election to Parliament. Four or five of them came ambling down the slope of what was at the time the city centre's only flyover. They carried themselves with the narcissistic insolence, the systematic slovenliness, of the Camden and Lower East Side originals. But while our eyes in the West have been tutored through mods and rockers, Teddy boys and beatniks and hippies, in Burma the shock of the look, the spiky hair and slashed T-shirts and safety pins, was so extreme – for me as much as for the local people struck dumb, mouths gaping – that they were like an hallucination, a recrudescence of evil spirits in the middle of the modern town.

Burma's traditional human zoo has a distinctive but narrow stylistic vocabulary: monks in maroon robes, nuns in pink, the women and the older men in longyis, the younger ones in jeans. As in most other Asian countries, there is little in the way of visual eccentricity, and the default attitude of youth is respect and conformity. In that context, the impact of the punk look was explosive.

The first impression is that the style is a simple rip-off: *hommage*, if you like, thirty-five years out of time. But when I took a closer look at Einstein MC King Skunk, as he likes to be known, I saw it was not that simple. I was introduced to him at a punk gig at a rooftop beer hall in Rangoon's Mingalar Market, where bands with names like Chaos in Burma, Hooligan Army and Rebel Rant roared and thrashed their way through self-penned, three-chord musical shitstorms. My friend Daniele Tamagni, the prize-winning Milanese photographer who is a connoisseur of African and Cuban dandyism, had dug this fellow out; unlike the originals in Piccadilly Circus and Camden Lock, he did not give me the finger and tell me to eff off when I pulled out my notebook. We sat on the edge of the roof and he told me his story.

In Britain and the United States, the original punk revolution was a deliberately crude and ugly riposte to the effeminate and flowery excesses of hippiedom. The two styles were at war. But Einstein has found a way of mixing them up. From his head rises the statutory punk Mohican, dyed blond, and he also has blond, vaguely Hasidic ringlets hanging down in front of his ears. His lips and ears are studded and his leather jacket bristles like a porcupine, but John Lennon holds the patent for his granny-like round-framed shades, and he rides an old sit-up-and-beg bicycle painted in psychedelic tones.

The clincher is the gorgeous pink daisy that spills out of a brass vase fixed to the handlebars. No English punk would be seen dead with such a decorative accessory.

'I was born in Rangoon in 1993,' he told me. 'My father is an ex-seaman and my mother works in a supermarket, my brother is an engineer with a government job.' He did well at school: 'I got high marks in maths, chemistry, physics and biology. After that I attended the University of Medicine here in Rangoon.'

The punk look may shock, but there is a bacchanalian aspect to Burmese life that resonates easily with its provocation and exhibitionism: 'ladyboy' dancers who share traditional stages with almost life-size puppets, the mediums, known as *nat kadaws*, who become possessed by *nats* or spirits at *nat pwe* or ghost ceremonies, the annual Thingyan New Year water festival when the whole country goes crazy and everybody douses each other with water.

It was a Thingyan event that introduced Einstein to the world of punk. There is a covered market in downtown Rangoon, known in colonial days as Scott Market and now as Bogyoke Market, in honour of Aung San, which is unlike any other in the country, a magnet for local artists and craftsmen as well as tourists and money changers. It is across the road from Rangoon's only ladyboy colony. Every year, one day before the general water-pelting of Thingyan begins, ladyboys, foreign punks and other marginal types stage their own raucous, sopping-wet event in the market. And in 2008, when he was fifteen, Einstein, real name Satt Mhu Shein, who lived nearby, went to see what was going on. There he saw his first punks. And his life has not been the same since.

He found them fascinating. 'I wanted to know who they were, why they dressed and behaved like this, everything,' he told me. 'I could speak English enough and the foreigners there gave me books about punk and I read all the books and I changed my life.'

At medical college he was on his way to a lucrative and prestigious career as a doctor, but the behaviour of his fellow students alienated him. 'Many of them were rich, they came to university driving their own cars, while the poor ones like me did not get enough money from our parents to survive. The rich people were the sons of senior generals and they tried to pass the exams by bribing their professors, while the poor people with good grades dropped out.' Two years' exposure to the antics of this young elite was enough for him. He quit, and soon Satt Mhu Shein had mutated into Einstein MC King Skunk. 'At Middle School, my friends called me Einstein, because I was smart,' he said. 'MC stands for Medical College, "King" because I was the king of medical school. As for "Skunk" – who knows?' Thus was born his cumbersome new name.

He still lives with his parents, and survives by teaching schoolchildren at an informal crammer in his aunt's home. He has little of the angry nihilism of the typical Western punk. As for his lifestyle, Einstein claims to be clean, and I detected no evidence to the contrary. 'I know the effects of drugs because I studied them at medical school,' he says. 'I don't take drugs and I tell other punks not to take them. I drink a little beer at parties.' But he has his share of anti-establishment opinions. Some Rangoon punks make money selling punk accessories; he despises them, he says, because they are 'capitalists'. 'I'm anti-religious and anti-education, even though I have an education, I hate racism, I had a mission to become a doctor and I studied at medical college for two years so I am a man!'

Punk began to emerge in Burma around the time of the Saffron Revolution of 2007. That uprising was a watershed moment for the democracy movement and, despite the vicious way it was brought to an end, it lent courage to dissenters of every sort, the punks among them. Nonetheless they risked persecution until late 2011, when President Thein Sein began releasing political prisoners and retiring the machinery of surveillance and control that had sustained military rule for half a century. Today, Burma's punks no longer have to skulk. But this remains in many ways a highly conservative society and Einstein's look is guaranteed to have an effect, which of course is at least half the point.

In one of Daniele's photographs, his blond Mohican forms a visual counterpoint to the golden pagoda of Shwedagon, Burma's most famous and revered Buddhist monument. But at the time the picture was taken, the police took exception to the composition. 'They arrested me for having the picture taken there. But Buddha didn't say anything about hair, so why arrest me?' Of course the indignation of straight society is the fuel that keeps punk going; if Burma moves too far in the direction of permissiveness it's doubtful how long these colourful freaks will feel like maintaining their rebellious poses.

Einstein first played bass in a band when he was eighteen; at tonight's gig he expected to be the vocalist with Hooligan Army, '. . . but it's not sure, it depends how things turn out. In my songs I attack the rich people. I also sing spontaneous lyrics of my own. One of my songs is half in Burmese and half in English; it's called "Fuck Off".'

He's learned the patter all right, but Einstein, one feels, wouldn't say 'fuck off' to a goose. Burma's gentle punks are reinventing the genre. PUNKS NOT DEAD as the T-shirts say. Even in Rangoon they survive.

*

But other beneficiaries of the great reforming moment of 2011 to 2012 have been less fortunate. The prison door suddenly swung open. They stumbled out into the light. But before they could take more than half-a-dozen steps, the heavy breath of authority – as arbitrary as ever – was again hot on their necks. Take the case of Burma's journalists.

In 2012, private publishers were given free rein to produce daily newspapers for the first time in sixty years. Within a few months the regime's quirky, tightly controlled English language daily, the *New Light of Myanmar*, was joined by fourteen competitors. The press scrutiny board was closed down. Freedom was at hand.

But freedom did not bring with it the right to prosper, as the publishers soon discovered. In no time this crowd of fresh, raw titles was chasing a market drastically thinned, as in the rest of the world, by the near-simultaneous arrival of cheap smartphones and the rolling out of reliable 3G networks. As a result, many of the new papers struggle to survive. The *New Light of Myanmar* may be one of the world's stodgiest reads, but it has a monopoly on official announcements, has privileged distribution networks and its price is heavily subsidised. Recently it went all-colour and changed its name to the *Global*

New Light of Myanmar. It is as dull and whimsical as ever, but it continues to prosper, as do its state-owned Burmese language siblings. Their continued dominance in an age of partial democracy mirrors that of the army.

'When we came into journalism,' the editor of the *Voice*, one of the new dailies, told me in 2014, 'our dream was to publish daily papers. Now we do that – but the papers don't make money: it is the weekly magazines that keep the dailies going, and now their circulations are going down, too. State-owned newspapers dominate the market: they prepared carefully before the government granted licences to privately owned papers. They have printing presses all over the country, and they put other papers in trouble by suddenly lowering their ad rates.'[18]

And the ending of routine pre-publication censorship did not free editors from state surveillance. In fact it made publication more nerve-wracking: there was no longer a sanctioning filter between the media and the courts, which remained as much a tool of the powerful and wealthy as in the bad old days.

Does a Burmese army base in Magwe, on the banks of the Irrawaddy in central Burma, house a secret factory producing chemical weapons, with the involvement of former generals, Chinese technicians and the base's commander-in-chief? That was the claim of three reporters working for the *Unity Journal*, a vernacular paper. The government declared the story to be 'baseless'. But instead of merely issuing a detailed rebuttal, or better still giving reporters a tour of the facility to prove their point, it sued them. The suit came right from the top, from the office of Burma's great reforming president himself, and charged the three reporters and their editor with breaching the Burma State Secrets Act – a classic piece of repressive colonial legislation, enacted in 1923. In July 2014, all four were sentenced to ten years' hard labour.

This was only the most glaring case of the state using its power of intimidation to replace censorship with self-censorship, to curb the urge of journalists to dig for uncomfortable truths. President Thein Sein was not shy about admitting it. '[If] media freedom threatens national security instead of helping the nation,' he said, 'I want to warn all that we will take effective action under existing laws.'[19] The Irrawaddy website commented: 'Press freedom in Burma is still far from assured.'[20]

And if journalists had imagined that the loosening of the state's grip was a licence to engage in free debate, another high profile case underlined the limits on what one could write in print without facing jail.

*

In October 2014, a charismatic political commentator who was also the NLD's information officer told the audience at a Burmese language literary festival outside Mandalay some home truths about Buddhism and the Ma Ba Tha organisation, which is the mouthpiece of Burma's most rabidly nationalist monks.

In his sardonic, gravelly voice, Htin Lin Oo told the audience, '[The Ma Ba Tha] claim to teach the Dharma, Buddha's teachings, but they do vile things: they yell and shout and preach lies and prejudice to the people, and I am absolutely disgusted by them.' He went on, 'One thing for sure is that the Lord Buddha was not Burmese, or Shan, or Kachin, or Karen, or Arakanese – he wasn't from one of Burma's ethnic groups. Brothers and sisters, are you aware of this? So if you want to be an extreme nationalist, and if you love to maintain your race that much, don't believe in Buddhism.'[21]

The speech was an outspoken retort to the jingoistic Buddhists who since 2011 have tried to whip up the paranoia of ordinary Burmese Buddhists, specifically in connection with Muslims. Htin Lin Oo was providing a corrective – saying what many in the outside world, including Buddhist teachers and scholars, have been saying for years now: that ethno-nationalistic Buddhism is a travesty of what Buddha taught.

It is a message which, perhaps in less strident terms, one could imagine the Dalai Lama giving. But this simple message is one that is very dangerous to convey in Burma today. Htin Lin Oo quickly learned that when he was arrested and charged under Article 295a, which prohibits 'deliberate and malicious acts intended to outrage religious feelings', and Article 298, which forbids 'uttering words . . . with deliberate intent to wound religious feelings'. He was held in custody for the next six months. Activists from Ma Ba Tha piled on the pressure, crowding around the court for every hearing of the case. On 2 June 2015 he was sentenced to two years' hard labour.

Outside court that day, he was defiant. 'What I said was in the interest of love and peace between different communities with different faiths,' he said. 'I received two years' imprisonment for that, but I won, because I can reveal the people behind all these haters. As a result of my case, the whole country now knows who is the black hand behind the scenes.'[22]

The case and the verdict were shocking enough in themselves. But for many admirers of Aung San Suu Kyi and the NLD around the world, the party's reaction was even worse. Following an internal party investigation, Htin Lin Oo was sacked as its information officer, and later expelled from the party.

Amnesty International condemned his conviction and called for his immediate pardon. 'Today's verdict is another blow to freedom of expression in Myanmar and should be overturned immediately,' the organisation said. 'Htin Lin Oo did nothing but give a speech promoting religious tolerance.'[23] The United Nations Office of the High Commissioner for Human Rights (OHCHR) called the sentence 'appalling'.[24] 'Htin Lin Oo courageously spoke out against the use of Buddhism as a tool for extremism,' the spokesperson pointed out. 'His treatment and conviction are in stark contrast to the treatment of those in Myanmar who are clearly inciting violence against minority communities, particularly the Rohingya.'[25]

Why did the NLD strip this clever, wise, eloquent man of his post then kick him out of the party? Was it because it agreed with the jingoistic ranters of Ma Ba Tha? Or was it out of fear of what those people might do if the party spoke up for him? In November, after his arrest, the Patriotic Buddhist Monks Union had called on Suu to take responsibility for what he had said, 'warning', as the Irrawaddy website reported, 'that it had the potential to tarnish the opposition party's image'.[26] Was that message of quiet menace enough to persuade Suu to turn her principles upside down?

Either explanation reflects terribly on the NLD, and on Suu herself, given her essentially unlimited power within the party. Either she and her party have become as chauvinistic as

Htin Lin Oo's enemies; or they are terrified of taking a stand. It is hard to know which would be more depressing.

Twenty years ago, when Suu and other NLD leaders were detained or thrown in jail for standing up to the regime, the outside world highlighted their cause and made Suu famous as a symbol of the struggle for freedom of expression. Today when the same thing happens to a senior member of Suu's party, the message from abroad is the same one of indignation and solidarity. But the NLD doesn't want to know.

*

It was said of Tony Blair, before his triumph in the British general election of 1997, that he carried the Labour Party like a man carrying a precious Ming vase over a highly polished floor.[27] Over the past five years, Suu has carried herself and her party like that. She has preserved her dignity, kept her immense popularity, at least among the Burmans. But could she not have done much more? More to galvanise change; to throw her weight behind the reforms initiated by the president and to cement them; and then, merely by speaking up, to resist and even roll back the ugly, ethnocentric Burman and Buddhist populism that has taken the opportunity presented by the new freedoms to surge forth?

With more – dare one say courage? No: there is no doubting Aung San Suu Kyi's courage. But with more political nous, a keener instinct for the scope of what is and is not possible, she could have done much more than she did: not merely to hang on to her popularity, but to do what she has always wanted to do, to steer her nation's course into the future.

But she didn't. One explanation is that at heart she is not a political animal. It was not simply an accident that she had no political involvement of any sort until leadership was thrust upon her in August 1988: that was her temperament speaking. Had she been more conscious of her limitations, she might, since her release, have delegated, picked the winners among the young enthusiasts who clustered around her and her party, nurtured them, brought them on, then tapped them for the political wit she was deficient in. But this too has so far proved beyond her: five years after her liberation, she is almost as solitary as she had been for the previous twenty; but this time by choice.

But perhaps it is unnecessary to seek psychological explanations for her solitude. Perhaps Suu simply adapted, consciously or not, to the prevailing political culture of Burma, where power has always been concentrated in a single individual; where it is conceived as finite,[28] so that for a leader to share power is to become weaker; where loyalty is less to a party than to a leader, and a party is not a community of like thinkers but an entourage of loyal underlings. So to be a leader is inevitably to be alone.

Knowing in her blood the way things must work in her country, Suu carried that Ming vase all the way to the finishing line, leaving her doubters and opponents floundering in her wake.

15

THE LANDSLIDE

As the general election of November 2015 approached, uncertainty about the result appeared total. More than ninety parties were contesting it. Many were tiny outfits with no prospect of success; others, like the National Unity Party, avatar of Ne Win's old Burma Socialist Programme Party, were vestiges of the distant past. But others were more substantial. Burma has no opinion polls. Fighting between the army and ethnic guerrillas continued in Shan and Kachin states, making polling uncertain. Unrest in 400 villages across Kachin, Karen, Shan, and Mon states and in the Pegu region, north of Rangoon, made it 'impossible to hold elections in a free and fair manner', it was announced, so residents in those areas would not be able to vote. Elsewhere, notably in the military-dominated Coco Islands, 300 kilometres south of Rangoon, the NLD had not even been allowed to campaign.

Then in early October, to add to the nationwide jitters, the Union Election Commission floated the possibility that the whole thing might be called off. As the Irrawaddy news website reported, 'The general election slated for Nov. 8 is likely to be postponed after Burma's Union Election Commission (UEC) met with some of the nation's largest parties on Tuesday.' Seven of the ten most significant parties were invited to meet the commissioner, U Tin Aye, who according to Nay Min Kyaw, secretary of the National Democratic Front, suggested postponing the election 'because people may have difficulties in casting their votes due to natural disasters'.[1]

The 'disasters' were wide-scale flooding in Chin state and other upland areas, affecting a number of states throughout the monsoon season. But the flooding, like the monsoon, was over now. U Win Htein, a veteran member of the NLD's central executive committee, was the only party representative at the meeting to oppose the proposal. As he told the Irrawaddy, 'The excuse was lame . . . In 2008 during Cyclone Nargis, the referendum was not postponed. What happened now is not even a thousandth of the destruction we suffered at that time.'

Almost at once the Election Commission dropped the idea, but the fact that it had been floated was a reminder of the fragility of Burmese democracy. After the NLD's sweeping success in 2012's by-elections, a second round was called off, supposedly for reasons of cost.[2] These events could be seen as evidence of the military establishment's nervousness about elections. But they were also evidence of its willingness to swing events in the direction they favoured by any means that occurred to them, and of their continuing power to do so. The failure of any party other than the NLD to raise its voice in protest was a sign of the willing complicity of much of the political class in such stratagems.

The alarm passed, and campaigning, which had begun in early September, resumed. The NLD was making the running. Suu turned seventy in June, but still looked much younger, and the campaign seemed to energise her. She criss-crossed the country as she had in 1989, drawing large, enthusiastic crowds. For the first time, thanks to the end of direct censorship, she also obtained the lion's share of media attention. This was the election's biggest novelty: Suu's beaming image was everywhere. The party's head office, which had subsisted on her personality cult since her release in 2010, did a brisker trade than ever, selling party calendars, key rings, stickers, caps, T-shirts, merchandise of every sort. A selection of books about her was on sale, including my book *The Lady and the Peacock*, in an unauthorised translation. And now the images of Suu and her party's symbols were no longer confined to party HQ and people's back rooms. For the first time since 1989 the party flag of a fighting peacock on a red background flapped boldly from thousands of taxis and bicycle rickshaws.

In one respect the NLD showed itself well prepared for the struggle: it had attracted real talent for organisation. Give them an open-top double-decker lorry and a busy city street and they could turn it into a campaign meeting, an afternoon's light entertainment and a seminar on democracy for beginners rolled into one.

The street where I saw this happen was in Botathaung, near the docks in Rangoon, a tight-packed lower-middle-class area of apartment blocks, small factories and workshops with a typically mixed Rangoon community of migrants from the country and residents whose great-grandparents had come over from British India. A main road ran through it, but this didn't stop the local party branch turning the strip into an improvised campaign stop.

The lorry, painted red and covered with slogans and pictures of Suu, pulled up in front of a block of flats, occupying half the road, and locals put out plastic chairs on the other side, and while the traffic weaved between these obstacles, waved through by party wardens, a hundred people gathered to watch, ranging in age from infants to grandparents. A live rock band belted out NLD theme songs, then four young women in identical beige outfits appeared on the top deck and delivered a dynamic class, accompanied by visual aids, on how to vote, what it means, and why it is important – part of the voter education programme that was a feature of NLD campaign meetings everywhere. The afternoon concluded with yet more pro-NLD rock songs, belted out of loudspeakers. There were no campaign speeches, no discussion of the party's programmes, no effort to persuade waverers to come over to the NLD's side. Clearly the party did not feel the need to convince.

San Moe Aye had wrapped a bright red NLD bandana around her four-month-old daughter's head; the girl was called Suu, after her mother's heroine. 'I love the Lady so much,' she gushed. What did she hope would happen if she came to power? 'If the NLD wins, the poor will be freed from poverty,' she said. A retired bank employee sitting nearby said, 'I've supported the party since 1988. Everything needs to change. I have suffered, all the Burmese people have been suffering for many years in many different ways. I believe the NLD is the one organisation that can totally change our country.'

A couple of days later, on Sunday 1 November, one week before polling day, I encountered blanket endorsements of the same type, but on a very different scale. Suu's rally that day – her first and only high-profile appearance in Rangoon during the campaign – had been trailed weeks in advance. But up to the last minute the question was not whether or when it would happen, but where.

The party had applied for permission to hold the rally in the park next to the Shwedagon Pagoda where Suu had made her historic debut on 26 August 1988, speaking to a crowd thought to number a million people. During the 2015 campaign the USDP, the incumbent party, had already held three rallies in the park, which has particular significance because of its proximity to the nation's holiest shrine. But Suu was refused permission to speak there: perhaps the authorities were alarmed by its reminders of the years of insurrection and massacre. A second proposed venue was rejected, too. Finally the Election Commission ruled that she could hold the meeting in Takata, a large former parade ground in the far east of the city, beyond the Bazun Daung Creek.

The distance proved no deterrent: from early in the morning a great stream of people young and old headed towards the broad and dusty open space. Thousands of party youth members in red T-shirts and bandanas flocked to the ground in open-top lorries, waving banners and bawling out slogans. A stage was erected at the far end, decorated with giant paintings of Suu and her loyal old colleague U Tin Oo, and the party's campaign theme songs roared out from huge loudspeakers. By noon a sea of red party flags floated in the air.

The new-found organisational capacity of the NLD was amply in evidence: this was a rock festival crowd in size and enthusiasm, but the event was capably managed from start to finish. As we entered the ground, volunteers handed out cotton face masks stamped with the party logo, for use against the dust. All day long volunteers moved through the crowd with large plastic bags and tongs, collecting rubbish or handing out bottles of drinking water. No police were in evidence, and none were needed. This was less an election meeting than a working model of how Suu Kyi's Burma was supposed to be. By the time Suu Kyi came on stage at 4.22 p.m. the crowd stretched into the distance in all directions.

She had made them wait for an hour under the hot sun, but when she finally hit the stage the roar from the vast crowd was deafening. 'People power is our power,' she told them, her tone crisp and commanding despite weeks of campaigning. 'The coming election is important: this is a big opportunity to change our country, a very rare chance in our history. It's your duty to make this change. If you seize this chance you will possess your country again.'

As often before, her speech was long on moral exhortations, short on particulars. 'If a party wants to win the election, they must do it in the right way,' she insisted. 'We really want to win but only by way of people power, in a totally fair and just way . . . Our duty is to establish good relations with the losers in the election, not to marginalise them. We have no intention of taking revenge. Even if we win 100 per cent of seats, we will invite the minority parties to work hand in hand with us.' The implied reference was to the military, still the de facto power in the land and guaranteed to remain so by the constitution. 'Look at U Tin Oo,' she told the crowd, referring to the eighty-eight-year-old party chairman, who had spoken before her. 'He is a former soldier but he always supported the people. He is a good example of how a soldier ought to be . . .

'Some people are planning to use dirty means to win the election,' she said, referring to rumours that some parties had offered money and gifts or improvement to local roads in exchange for votes. 'I'm not worried because people can use their brains. Take whatever they give and vote for us anyway.' She hadn't lost her edge.

The previous day President Thein Sein was quoted as saying that Burma had no need of further change after the reforms he had enacted, and that those who insisted otherwise were communists. Suu took up the challenge. 'Some people say there is no need for change,' she told the crowd. 'But look at the people who really don't want to change. We must vote 100 per cent [to bring change]. Don't criticise our candidates, only focus on our flag. Our duty is to serve, your duty is to vote.'

There may have been more than 100,000 people at the rally – there was no practical way of counting – but after speaking for forty minutes Suu took questions. It seemed a dubious gambit, given the size of the crowd, but the questions were audible, largely sensible, there was no reason to believe they had been planted. She answered them all.

Despite the vast numbers, there was something almost cosy about this event, a sense of the coming together of friends whose bonds had survived decades of pain. Those ties of devotion between Suu and her supporters seem only to have grown stronger through her years of house arrest, and the emotion has bridged the generations, touching many who were not even born when she disappeared from sight.

'I love Mother Suu so much, that's why I'm here,' said Thi Thi San, fifty and a shop assistant. 'I've supported the party since 1988 but we could not mention our love until recently because it was dangerous to do so.' 'I love Mother Suu,' echoed Aye Chan Myint, a high school student attending the rally with her father, 'I would really like to become like her, she is our leader and well-known all over the world.' And that tide of warm emotion engulfed the rally. Speaking for nearly an hour without notes, making little jokes and homely asides, Suu Kyi's rapport with the crowd seemed as effortless as ever.

U Chit Pwe, an eighty-year-old ex-employee of the government, was one of the older members of the crowd. He had seen it all before: he was thirteen when Burma became independent and began a chaotic and ultimately disastrous ten-year experiment with democracy. But he was in no doubt that the military dictatorship that followed was much worse. 'It was so sad,' he recalled. 'Everything collapsed. You could never believe the junta – they said one thing and did another. Of course I'm worried about the political parties fighting, but I believe the NLD can bring peace, change the constitution, and implement law and order and justice.'

*

U Chit Pwe's high hopes were typical of people I spoke to in the run-up to the November 2015 polls. These were the dreams of people who had been deprived of influence over their rulers for so long that now the opportunity had arrived their expectations bordered on the ridiculous. Everything that had happened in Burma for as long as anyone could remember was wrong: one heard that from one supporter after another. Only Suu and her party were right. At last the people had, by some fluke, been given the opportunity to right all those wrongs at a stroke. And when they put their Lady, Mother Suu, in power, everything would change beyond recognition. Poverty would disappear. War would cease, peace would prevail. People's land would no longer be threatened by greedy companies. There would be no more unemployment. The millions of exiles labouring for slave wages in Thailand would come home. The Muslim troublemakers would disappear. All would be well.

Expectation this strong is a heady brew. It would have been prudent of Suu to warn her supporters of the dangers of overindulging in it, but this she did not do. In her speeches she made no mention of the lively possibility that, however well the NLD performed in the polls, in government it would not be able to do exactly as it chose, given the continuing power and preponderance of soldiers and ex-soldiers at all levels of government and administration. Likewise the party's manifesto, published in September, did little to sound a note of realism.

Suu had spoken so often since her release of the need to reform the constitution that this dry-as-dust issue had entered popular awareness. It was her insistent refrain, and ordinary voters now understood that it mattered, if only because it barred Suu from becoming president. In an extended campaign, the NLD had collected five million signatures on a petition calling for an end to the military veto on constitutional change, and in August 2014 submitted it to Parliament. It had no effect.[3] Ever since entering Parliament in 2012, Suu had been seeking a shortcut to constitutional reform, either by joint agreement of the highest office holders, by a vote in parliament, or by appealing directly to the president. Nothing worked, nor was anything likely to work, given that the army's built-in quota of seats in parliament was the military's best guarantee of retaining its privileges.

Nonetheless, amending the constitution figured prominently as a promise in Suu's manifesto.

Other things on the NLD's shopping list were less formidable, though generally vague. The party promised to cut the number of government ministries to reduce expenditure, though which ministries would be closed was not spelled out. It would develop basic infrastructure and improve tax collection. It would encourage farmers' solidarity and protect farmers from unlawful land confiscation. Primary schooling would become compulsory, though no commitment was made to raise the lamentably small budget provision for education. Health spending would be increased.

But more significant than these specific undertakings was the commitment to national reconciliation, Suu's other favourite phrase: addressing the causes of ethnic conflict by political dialogue, working towards a genuine federal union built on equal rights, self-determination and resource sharing. And bringing the armed forces under civilian control; sending the troops – in U Win Tin's formulation – back to the barracks.

Leaving aside the bread-and-butter budget commitments, this was therefore a manifesto that demanded the moon. And the scale of its unreality was apparent from the military armature within which the election was taking place. The army's strength at every level of power made this an asymmetric contest, which the NLD could win outright in the polling booths and still emerge the loser. Suu's only answer to that was to repeat her determination to change the constitution, without giving any details as to how she would go about it. Fortunately, she had one key ally in the top brass who had a practical strategy for changing the arithmetic of power.

Thura Shwe Mann had had a torrid time since I encountered him in May 2015 touring a base hospital in Shan state and offering praise and encouragement to wounded soldiers.[4] In August, three weeks before the start of the election campaign, he was on the point of cementing his grip on the ruling Union Solidarity and Development Party, the military's proxy, by registering a host of his allies within the party as election candidates while sidelining high-profile ex-soldiers loyal to his rival, President Thein Sein.

But barely a day before the deadline for registration, at 10 p.m. on Wednesday 12 August, troops surged into the party's spacious offices in the capital, Naypyidaw, to reinforce an order from the president's office: Shwe Mann was sacked as leader of the party and confined to his home. His replacement, another ex-general, U Htay Oo, was a known conservative who had been the public mouthpiece of former strongman Than Shwe since the latter's retirement in 2011. The Irrawaddy news website described the drama as a 'putsch'.[5]

Shwe Mann's crime, in the eyes of the military high command, was to have aligned himself publicly with Suu, and to have given qualified support to her attempt to amend the constitution. This broke the Burmese army's golden rule. As French political scientist Renaud Egreteau put it, 'Over the decades, Myanmar's senior officer corps have been socialised into believing that the Tatmadaw [Burma's army] shall remain the sole and uncontested embodiment of the state . . . Retired senior officers expressing discontent may only aim to adjust the trajectories of Myanmar's civil-military relations, not hurt the organisation that propelled them into the highest levels of Myanmar's polity. If they do, then as the case of Thura Shwe Mann [illustrates] . . . they fall into disgrace . . . Myanmar might have to wait a little longer for the coming of that "one brave soldier" who would drag the country away from the claws of its armed forces, as Aung San Suu Kyi once put it.'[6]

Yet the years of reform had brought some improvements. A few years earlier, Shwe Mann might have suffered the fate of General Khin Nyunt, sacked as prime minister, put on trial and sentenced to a long term of house arrest for lese-majesty when he offended his commanding officer. But now, under the milder rule of Thein Sein, he was not even expelled from the party, and according to one Rangoon insider he retained the support, tacit if not explicit, of a large majority of party members, who supported his reforming urges.[7]

Released from his brief confinement, Shwe Mann quit the Naypyidaw constituency which he had represented since 2010 – an electoral stronghold of the military from which he had become partially disaffected – and chose instead to offer himself as the USDP candidate for his hometown of Phyu, in the Pegu region, a three-hour drive on the Naypyidaw road north of Rangoon.

. . . At least it used to be a three-hour drive. But that changed as a result of the surge in car ownership since 2011. My fixer Thwin Maung Maung and I set off to catch the Brave Hero's final rally of the campaign, and it took us more than four hours, including one spent grinding through gridlocked traffic towards the outskirts of Rangoon. Looking at the solid lines of cars in both directions, Thwin Maung Maung remarked, 'Before, you could stand by this road for one hour and see only two motorbikes.'

Finally we reached the start of what is in fact the Road to Mandalay, though it's not called this, and after more than two hours on the almost empty concrete highway we took a turning marked 'Kanyunt Kwing' and drove for some distance between paddy fields turning golden in the final weeks before harvest.

At the crossroads leading to the town of Phyu was a bank of photographs of the candidates in the town's election. Shwe Mann's photo, which did not mention his party, was twice the size of all the others. Unlike the stony poses adopted by most candidates, the ex-general allowed himself the hint of a smirk.

As we approached the hall where Shwe Mann was scheduled to speak, Thwin Maung Maung gave me his thoughts about him. 'Everyone knows he is finished,' he said. 'On one side he is regarded as a traitor. On one side he is regarded as a hero. He is the only man in the military who has ever visited Suu Kyi in her home. In the former days of the regime he would be totally finished and we would never hear of him again. But now because they [the government] have to take care of international relations – public relations – he is still in play. Though everyone in Burma knows he is finished . . .'

The town meeting was held in a galvanised iron shed, open on three sides, called Great Success Hall. Next door was a handsome teak house with a steep roof, dating from colonial days, with a sign above the door that read 'Aungdawnu Free Library'. There were no books inside. We had arrived early and it took a long time for the hall to fill. Practically all who turned up were male. They had the cowed, reluctant look of people who had been required to come here under some duress. Channel NewsAsia, a Singapore broadcaster, had sent a team to film the event but apart from them and me, the media presence was small. Perhaps Thwin Maung Maung was right: only deluded outsiders held out any hope for this general. In the waste ground outside the hall a single helmeted soldier with a rifle stood guard.

Shwe Mann entered at 15.20. The contrast with Suu's rally in Rangoon could not have been more extreme: an election pop song in his support, noisy and trashy, was played repeatedly over the loudspeakers, but the stage was bare and unadorned and there was no warm-up act: just this tall former general in a collarless white tunic and a dark longyi, walking up the aisle from the back, detaching himself from a scrum of cameras and climbing onto the stage. As one, and in silence, the audience stood, then sat.

What ensued was a meditation on what was required of Burma's ruling class in the present, changed situation.

'Now that we are in a democracy,' he said in his soft, almost feline delivery, 'a different way of ruling is required, one that requires total dedication. We have to comply with the law and public opinion. It is no longer enough simply to obey orders.' It sounded like a justification of his own rebellious stance towards the president. He went on:

> Our people are living below the poverty line, so we need to change everything. Those in power must work for the people's welfare. Between 1948 and 1958 Burma had a democratic system. During this period the political parties fought against each other, so the situation was not stable. As a result democracy came to a dead halt. We need to learn the lessons of the democratic period. Every party has now drafted good policies in their manifestos, so this time every political

party must not treat the others as their enemies. We have to be friends.

In the election some people will win, some will lose . . . some people don't want to make friends, don't want to co-operate with others, but this is no good for us. If we carry on like this, the country will be in trouble. All the parties have the people's interests at heart, so co-operation is possible. If all the people co-operate, that will be good for the future of all the people of Burma.

Like much of the rhetoric in this election, the first freely fought contest for twenty-five years, it sounded like first steps in democracy. But Shwe Mann was also making a more sophisticated point. Those who must be 'friends' were his colleagues in the USDP, his ex colleagues in the army, and the NLD, which, as he like all Burmese was well aware, was much the most popular party in the country. The obligation to be 'friends' was no small object when, in recent memory, the army had locked up or driven into exile all the NLD's leaders. That long and deep bitterness had to be overcome if the country was to progress. National reconciliation – Suu's clarion call – was the first necessity. It was a basic principle distinguishing dictatorship from democracy that opposition was not treason, and that political opponents could coexist despite their differences.[8]

But Shwe Mann's most interesting ideas emerged during the question and answer session that followed his talk. A man in the audience asked him, 'If you win, what will you do for democracy and human rights?'

In reply, he described what he had learned during a recent visit to Europe. 'In Germany I studied the political system,' he said. 'Germany lost the Second World War and was reduced to poverty but they succeeded in developing the country thanks to their democratic federal system. I was surprised to learn that Germany had had a coalition government for a long time.' In Burma, by contrast, he said, 'At the time of independence, people were afraid of the federal idea, even of the word "federal".'

He revealed that he had also visited Denmark on his travels. 'In Denmark, the winning party invites the losing parties to join it in a coalition government. I learned some very good lessons from these countries.' The particular lesson he drew, he said, was that 'I will collaborate with any party and any person for our country's success. A good leader must work for the interests of the whole country.'

These answers appeared vague and abstract, but in fact they were game-changing, heady stuff. The political parties must be 'friends': the all-or-nothing approach that had characterised Burmese politics until now must be rejected. Coalition governments: no party, in a polity as diverse as Burma's, should aim to monopolise power. 'I will collaborate with any party and any person' meant simply that he was prepared to work with Daw Suu and the NLD, a revolutionary statement that no other USDP figure had ventured to utter.

Shwe Mann, in other words, looked forward to the day when Burmese politics began to resemble that of the advanced countries of the West, when the bitterness and bloodshed of the recent past would be forgiven and forgotten and former soldiers and former rebels could sit down together to work out their common destiny without rancour or exclusion. The cordial working relationship he had already established with Suu was a taste of what he hoped might lie ahead.

His stance broke new ground, but it failed to allow for the fact that the army had tyrannised the people of Burma for more than half a century: monopolising power, strangling the economy, fighting endless war on the borders and committing untold abuses in the process, all the time steadily reinforcing its position as the nation's ruling caste. As a result most ordinary Burmese regarded it with loathing, as was demonstrated in those few elections when they were allowed to register their views. How was the army and its more enlightened products, people like Shwe Mann, to overcome that legacy of hatred?

After the meeting in Great Success Hall, the candidate and his convoy drove the short distance across town to a Buddhist temple, and in the prayer hall there he settled down at a low table covered with a lace tablecloth to answer questions from the media contingent that had covered the meeting, and who now loomed over him in the dimly lit hall, standing or crouching around him in a tight semicircle. It is very unusual for a former general to open himself to interrogation in such a fashion. It was another way in which the Speaker of the Lower House put a distance between himself and the imperious fighting force he came from.

We asked about the coming election, the NLD, the prospects for a coalition government, his relationship with the president and the party from whose leadership he had been ousted. His answers broke no new ground, but the mere fact of allowing us to grill him was remarkable.

However, there was one important question we were all avoiding. I reminded him that he had been responsible for the destruction of the stronghold of the Karen rebels in Manerplaw,[9] for which he had received his decoration; and that the military was accused by many Burmese of numerous war crimes over the past sixty years, and no senior officer had ever expressed any regret. 'Are you willing to express regret for the army's actions?' I asked him. He smiled a pained smile. The gloomy hall was enveloped in silence.

'I don't want to say anything now,' he said finally. Then, in English: 'You will have to wait and see.'

*

A few days before the election, Abbot U Par Mount Kha sat on a peacock throne in the upstairs hall of his monastery outside Rangoon and laid it on the line. A leader of the Saffron Revolution in 2007, a personal friend of Aung San Suu Kyi – a crudely painted portrait of the two of them together hung in this hall – and a long-time supporter of her National League for Democracy, today he had a very different message.

'Buddhism in Burma today is in a weak condition,' he told me. 'We face pressure from the Islamic religion.' He reeled off the names of neighbourhoods in Rangoon where Muslims were a significant fraction of the population.

I pointed out that Muslims have lived in Rangoon for at least a hundred and fifty years, that the two communities coexist without apparent stress, and the city escaped the wave of attacks – mostly Buddhist-on-Muslim – that have broken out elsewhere in the past four years. Muslims in Burma constitute around 5 per cent of the population, as against the 90 per cent-plus of Buddhists. Where exactly is the threat?

'That is a superficial view,' he said. 'You don't see the inside situation. Islam's way of domination in Burma is through marrying Buddhist Burmese women. They each take four wives, each of the wives has seven children, and they are all forced to become Muslims.' This has happened before all over South East Asia, he argued. 'Malaysia and Indonesia used to be Buddhist countries, now they are Islamic states.'

The abbot's message – amplified around the country by his friend Ashin Wirathu,[10] by lesser-known monks and by the Association to Protect Race and Religion, better known by its Burmese acronym Ma Ba Tha – was perhaps the most incendiary and unpredictable element in the Burmese election.

The worst flashpoint between Buddhists and Muslims was Arakan state, where communal violence first broke out in May 2012 and flared up again later in the year, forcing more than 100,000 Rohingya Muslims to flee their homes. The great majority were still housed in squalid camps far from their homes. The government annulled their temporary identification cards. For the first time since independence, the Rohingya were barred from voting.

But Arakan – which I wrote about in Chapter 8, and which Abbot U Par Mount Kha cited early in our interview – was highly exceptional. In parts of northern Arakan bordering Bangladesh Muslims constitute more than 90 per cent of the population; in the capital Sittwe, the communities were roughly equal in number before it was ethnically cleansed. Rough demographic equivalence was at the root of the unique hostility here.

The party likely to benefit most directly from the marginalisation of the Rohingya in the election was the

Arakan National Party, the chauvinistic voice of the Buddhist community in the state. But elsewhere the calculation was different. It was the USDP government under President Thein Sein that cancelled the Rohingyas' temporary ID cards. His government chose to rush laws through parliament in the last months before the election – drafted by Ma Ba Tha – imposing strict rules on Buddhist women who want to marry outside their faith, on conversion from one religion to another, and on the right of women to bear as many children as they want.

The president's embracing of these divisive, repressive measures, which he described as among his greatest achievements, was puzzling. As we have seen, he began his term as an improbable liberal reformer. When that process ran out of steam – after he lost the trust of Aung San Suu Kyi over his failure to do anything to amend the constitution – he tried another tack, aiming to make a name for himself as Burma's great peacemaker. His cherished nationwide ceasefire agreement, described in Chapter 14, was finally concluded in October 2015, but in the end it was not an inspiring deal: only half the insurgent groups involved actually signed it, and the ones that stayed away included all those who were still fighting. It was a damp squib, and his hopes of cruising back into power on the strengths of this were poor indeed.

So to improve his chances of being elected to a second term as president, he set about reinventing himself as a Buddhist firebrand. As an intelligent man he was well aware that a party packed with old soldiers was likely to be trounced at the election, as it had been before. How to avoid that fate? The Saffron Revolution of 2007, during which he had served as Than Shwe's prime minister, gave him the clue he needed.

Back then, the mobilisation of hundreds of thousands of monks had led to the humiliation of the military government, and its replacement by his own pseudo-democratic regime four years later. Pious Burmese greatly value their monks; when the monks or the religion they represent are seen to be under threat, as in 2007, the Burmese masses quickly become a force to be reckoned with in their defence.

So Thein Sein set about turning this fact on its head. Arakan gave him the opportunity. By adopting the Arakanese Buddhists' claim that their faith was under threat from the historic enemy, and encouraging chauvinistic Buddhist preachers to spread it throughout the country, he clearly hoped to benefit by depicting the ruling party as the religion's protectors, and hence deserving of the popular vote. Ramming through the laws drafted by Ma Ba Tha underlined the point.

And if the umbilical link of the USDP to the military made the party unelectable no matter how loudly it banged the Buddhist drum, in the final months before the election one of his former advisers, a businessman called Nay Zin Latt, founded a new party, the National Development Party (NDP), which rapidly grew in size to become (or so it claimed) the third biggest in the country after the NLD and the USDP.

The NDP put the protection of Buddhism at the heart of its programme. 'Our country is the last stronghold of Theravada Buddhism,' the party's vice-chairman, Aung Htwe, told the Irrawaddy news website, 'so we are responsible [for] the protection of our religion and nationality. But we reject the accusation that we are using religion for political influence.'[11] Though founded only in March and registered in July, the party found the means to field more than 350 candidates at the election, and Aung Htwe claimed it had 'hundreds of thousands of members across the country'.[12]

These were the contrasting strategies that ex-members of the military adopted to try to win the electorate's favours: on the one hand the Shwe Mann approach, embracing national reconciliation, coalition government and perhaps, in the fullness of time ('you will have to wait and see'), remorse and repentance for the army's sins past; and on the other that of Thein Sein, whipping up ancient hostility and paranoia towards Muslims in the hope of herding voters into the nationalist camp. It remained to be seen if either strategy would bear electoral fruit. But in the meantime the nationalistic approach weighed heavily on both the Muslim community and the NLD.

*

In Mingala Taungnyunt township in central Rangoon, where Muslims account for 70 per cent of the local population, a homeopathic doctor called San Tin Kyaw, a forty-nine-year-old Muslim, was running for election. He decided to stand when Aung San Suu Kyi's NLD – an avowedly non-sectarian party, with Muslims among its founders and prominent members – announced in September that it would field no Muslim candidates. 'We have qualified Muslim candidates,' U Win Htein, an NLD founder member admitted candidly, 'but we can't select them for political reasons.'

Ma Ba Tha and its political allies had sounded the nationalist trumpet and the NLD, forgetting its decades of struggle against intolerance, had gone weak at the knees and crumpled. The expulsion of Htin Lin Oo, described in the last chapter,[13] was one such sign; the purging of highly qualified Muslim NLD candidates was another, and arguably far more serious. It revealed the NLD as a party which, despite its national popularity, was deeply insecure about its basic principles.

The intended NLD candidate for Mingala Taungnyunt was Ko Mya Aye, a Muslim and a leading member of Generation 88, the activists in the uprising of 1988 who had also played important roles in the so-called Saffron Revolution of 2007. He was the man who'd told me, 'I'm not interested in the Rohingya as such. I'm doing politics . . . for human beings.'[14] Now he was the candidate no more, replaced by a Buddhist.

So in order to give his fellow Muslims a Muslim candidate to vote for, San Tin Kyaw decided to run. In Burma's worsening climate of intolerance, his co-religionists needed someone to defend their interests. In his rudimentary election office above a tea shop, he described to me how since independence his community had seen its rights and status shrivel.

'A long time ago there were no divisions,' he said. 'Buddhists and Muslims lived together and together they struggled for independence from Britain under one flag.' But the paranoid nationalism of successive Burmese rulers, starting with General Ne Win, had slowly eroded the position of Muslims: schoolchildren learned only about Buddhism, not other religions, and increasingly Muslims found it harder to move around the country and get decent jobs.

'During the independence struggle, Aung San included Muslims in his coalition, and Buddhists and Muslims lived together without divisions,' he said. 'Discrimination began under General Ne Win in 1974 when our ID cards were taken away and replaced by a slip of paper which prevented us from travelling. Muslim graduates were increasingly prevented from getting jobs. Not only Muslims but all religious and ethnic minorities were marginalised.

'But the situation has got much worse since the reforms started four years ago. The anti-Muslim violence that spread around the country in 2013 was a political plot, masterminded by the authorities. That's clear from the way they were able to bring it to a halt before it arrived in Rangoon.'

If the NLD won, would the situation improve? 'In the past I would have said "yes". But now the party is scared: if it forms the government it may face pressure from Buddhist extremists and other nationalists. All the minority communities must understand that they can't depend on the NLD: they must struggle by themselves for their rights.'

*

Muslims weren't the only ones who were falling out of love with the NLD. As the election approached, disaffection could be found even among the former party faithful.

Born and raised in one of Rangoon's poorest slums, U Myo Khin, aged fifty-seven, has been a political activist all his adult life. When Aung San Suu Kyi and her colleagues launched the National League for Democracy in September 1988, he was a volunteer worker from day one. He paid for his activism with a total of twelve years in jail.

But on the threshold of Burma's most important general elections in half a century he was an ex-member: contesting his constituency of Yankin, the slum where he still lived, as an independent, fighting the NLD candidate. After more than twenty-three years of struggle in and for the party, he had quit in deep disillusionment.

'Activists like me sacrificed our blood, sweat and tears for the party over many years,' he told me. 'But we've been marginalised.'

He explained that, in preparation for the elections, the NLD's central committee had set strict criteria for selecting candidates: they should have experience in the party, enjoy local support and have political gifts. Younger candidates were preferred over older ones, women over men, and people from the ethnic minorities over Burmans. But in practice, he said, these benchmarks were frequently ignored: what counted was cosy relations with the party's grandees, or willingness to obey orders, or both.

'I satisfy four of the benchmarks,' he said. 'My rival has no experience in the party, and he's ten years older than me. But he is very close to people on the central committee. That's why they picked him.' On 1 August he resigned from the party.

And he is far from being the only one. Other potential candidates, some with long years in the party and high local profiles, were also rejected and responded by running as independents.

Daw Khin Phone Wai, a married woman from a poor quarter next to Yankin, also left the party when she was turned down as a candidate. Interviewed in August by the *New York Times*, she said that Suu Kyi was out of touch. 'She cannot relate to ordinary people,' she said. 'People are facing hardship every day, and she can't feel their needs. She's not in touch with the people at the bottom.'[15] Another woman activist passed over was Daw Nyo Nyo Thin, who as a local politician had gained a reputation for exposing and fighting corruption in big Rangoon construction projects. Dropped from the NLD's candidate list in August, like Myo Khin she was fighting the election as an independent.

'This is a general problem in the party,' Myo Khin said. 'The great majority of people who fought for the party's survival during its years of crisis have been marginalised. Twenty per cent of them survive because they are yes men, willing to toe the party line. Nearly all the strong candidates have been rejected.'

His claim feeds the suspicion which recent remarks by Suu Kyi have raised: that she considers loyalty and docility more desirable in her party's candidates than political vigour or independent thought. At the party's rally in Rangoon, she told the crowd, 'Don't criticise our candidates, only focus on our flag. Our duty is to serve, your duty is to vote.'[16] In August she made a similar point in an interview with Radio Free Asia. 'The responsibility of the people is simply to vote for the party, not the name of the candidate,' she said. 'The NLD is a political party and we have rules. If you can't follow these rules you can't work for the NLD.' That impression of imperiousness was starting to drive people away.

'Suu Kyi is authoritarian,' Myo Khin said bluntly. 'The goal is democracy, but their way of trying to achieve it is authoritarian.' He related how more than a hundred party members in towns north of Rangoon complained about the candidates the party had selected for their constituencies. 'The following day they were all expelled.'

Suu Kyi's refusal to reveal who she had chosen as the party's presidential candidate also rankled. 'We are close to a historic election,' he pointed out. 'Everyone wants democracy, which means transparency. But the leader of our democratic party has no transparency – she and her central committee have never announced who is the presidential candidate.'

Myo Khin lives with his family in a small, ramshackle clapboard house deep within the labyrinthine lanes of Yankin. The neighbourhood is only a mile from the villas and broad streets of Bahan township where Suu lives, but this is the Rangoon the tourists never see: startlingly poor and congested, with alleys too narrow for anything wider than a bicycle rickshaw, where children play under the stilts of their homes among the neighbourhood cats and chickens. Myo Khin has done no paid work since throwing himself into political work twenty-seven years ago: instead his heroic wife Daw Khin Khin Win became the breadwinner in between bearing his five children, and supported him through his spells in six different jails around the country. 'We talk about politics together,' she said, sitting in their microscopic front room with her husband, while a grandson watched Cartoon Network in the background. She supported all his political activity, she said. 'When he went to jail for the first time, I joined the NLD. We left the party on the same day.'

She went on, 'When my husband was first in jail, the children were very young. We struggled to survive as a family, it was a very tough for us, but that is normal for people who are committed to a political struggle. Now I look back and I am very proud of our family. We made every effort for the benefit of the people. And we got a lot of support from our neighbours. I have no particular hopes for my family but I hope things will improve for the township, and that they will get better education and health care.'

Life in these lanes improved in the five years after President Thein Sein came to power. Outside the township a new road was built, and the previously erratic electricity supply became more reliable. But life was still a struggle: the government announced with a flourish that primary schooling would be free – but then the teachers, who are very poorly paid, demanded informal payments from parents, ranging from 8,000 kyats (£4) per month in primary school to 100,000 kyats (£50) per month in high school. The family's only breadwinner was their second daughter, who had a job in a company and brought home 300,000 kyats (£150) per month. Life remained very tight.

But Myo Khin's political passion was undiminished. 'I love truth and justice,' he said. 'I totally trusted my leader and my party. Now the decisions they are taking are not fair. I don't want to see injustice succeed. That's why I am standing for Parliament. There should be people in Parliament who love justice.'

*

Journalists covering Burma had long grumbled about the near-impossibility of securing an interview with Aung San Suu Kyi. With the great litmus test of the general election fast approaching, her elusiveness became absolute, the rejections of her aide-de-camp Dr Tin Mar Aung more peremptory, and the moans louder. But three days before polling the Lady silenced all such complaints when she invited the world's media to the garden of her family home for a press conference.

The event was scheduled to start at 9 a.m.; when I arrived shortly after 7 a.m. there was already a queue stretching fifty metres down the street. More than 300 journalists from around the world had registered to attend. Most of us writers had spilled much ink about 54 University Avenue, the house where Suu had grown up then spent fifteen years in detention, over the past few years, but few had ever been invited inside its gates. So simple curiosity was one factor. But we were also aware that history was being made here: that Suu had this opportunity to redeem her years of suffering and sacrifice with an electoral triumph that would change Burma's destiny. The stakes were that high.

As at her rally the previous Sunday, we were made aware that this was a party which, in organisational terms, had grown up. As requested by courteous emails in correct English, we had registered to attend the event at NLD headquarters earlier in the week, where we were issued with laminated passes. Inside the gates our names were checked on lists. A red plastic roof had been erected over the lawn to keep the sun off, hung with theatrical lights to make it easy for the television cameras, and at the back of the garden there were tables piled with finger food and fridges stacked with bottles of water. On the stage, large sparkling letters made of polystyrene attached to a crimson backdrop spelled out 'National League for Democracy Press Conference' and the date. The long table was draped in white. More than twenty microphones clustered before the Lady's chair reminded us that the whole world was watching.

Suu appeared on the stage at precisely 9 a.m., told the photographers to sit down, made a short introductory speech, then took questions. She wore a pale mauve top, and her face, too, looked mauve in the harsh theatrical lighting. Her eyebrows had never looked bushier; lines under her sunken eyes emphasised the strain of the many weeks of campaigning. But the tension in her expression, which hardly changed throughout the whole event, was also to do with the occasion. Only days before, at the rally in Takata, she had appeared relaxed, funny, informal, spontaneous. Here, before the judge and jury of the fourth estate, her performance prickled with stress and antagonism. For an hour and a half she stared out at us, her expression unchanging, her eyes barely blinking. In all that time she neither took a sip of water, nor consulted notes or colleagues, and never paused or hesitated in her replies. It was a steely, bravura performance.

Suu faced a conundrum. She was much the most popular politician in Burma. Likewise her party was in many parts of the country the runaway favourite to win, always supposing the Union Election Commission – headed by a former general – played fair. But even if she were to win every seat in the country, she would still have no chance of going on to fulfil her long-standing ambition to become Burma's ruler. Due to clause 59(f), a clause no one doubts was inserted deliberately to thwart her, she could not become president because her sons held foreign passports.

But before the world's press she revealed that she had a solution to this problem. In a recent interview with an Indian television channel she had said that, if her party won, she intended to rule, no matter what. But how would she do that? If she were not the president, a French journalist suggested, wouldn't it be unconstitutional to rule? She retorted, 'The constitution says nothing about someone being *above* the president.' When someone suggested she might be the prime minister – though under Burma's constitution there is no such role – she shot back, 'Who said I'm going to be prime minister? I've already said I'm going to be above the president – I've already made plans.'

And in a final blow at those pettifoggers maundering on about the constitution she added, 'I don't see why we shouldn't be able to overcome minor obstacles like the constitution . . . I don't know if you can call a constitution "silly", but this is a very silly constitution.'

Was that some kind of joke? Had she – one Burmese colleague suggested – perhaps gone mad?

Her plan was as follows: if the NLD were to win an overwhelming majority – and it needed at least 67 per cent of seats for a simple majority, as one-quarter of seats in both houses of Parliament were reserved for serving soldiers, who would oppose the NLD – they would have a fighting chance of getting their candidate into the job of executive president, the person who picks the cabinet and runs the country. That could not be Suu Kyi – but she could choose a willing puppet to occupy the top chair, and she would be the puppeteer. A Burmese editor told me she had already picked the person, though the identity was being kept secret: he was male, aged about sixty, a former senior diplomat and a near-neighbour of hers in leafy Bahan township; not yet a member of the NLD, but willing to become one when required.

This would be a uniquely anomalous arrangement. The analogy with Manmohan Singh and Sonia Gandhi, the widow of Rajiv Gandhi and the head of the Congress Party in India, had been suggested, but that was a case of power-sharing: not what Suu Kyi has in mind at all. And as ultimate power would continue to be held by the head of the army, whatever happened on election day, one fundamental question – impossible to answer – was whether the army would stand for it. The rumour mill said that General Min Aung Hlaing, the army chief, who was believed to have high political ambitions of his own, was most unhappy about the idea.

Of course all this was hypothetical: first the NLD had to win. 'To begin with,' she said, 'at the start of the campaign, people seemed not to be too interested in the election, but as we proceeded with our voter education we found that people were taking an increasing interest . . . we have been very encouraged by the enthusiasm of people about being part of the electoral process.'

She went on, 'We have however been very concerned about the lack of enthusiasm on the part of the UEC [Union Election Commission] to ensure free and fair elections.' Complaints included voter lists padded with phantom voters, to allow for last-minute ballot box-stuffing, and the sort of mass advance voting which gave the USDP a fraudulent landslide majority in 2010's election.

But in 2010 Burma was a very different country. Suu Kyi was rude about President Thein Sein's government – asked if the NLD would govern well she replied, 'I always say it can't be worse than what we've had already,' and she dismissed his reforms as a 'veneer'. That was unfair: five years before, she was still under house arrest, the media were shackled by draconian censorship, the jails were full of political prisoners. None of that was true today. But the underlying reality, she argued, had not improved. 'The great majority of people have not become better off,' she said, 'and some especially in rural areas have become poorer since the lifting of sanctions.'

For the Rohingyas of Arakan state, whose sufferings and recent disenfranchisement had been one of the dominant themes in international coverage of the election, she had few words of comfort. Asked whether she considered the treatment of the community to be genocide, she said, 'I think it's very important that we should not exaggerate the problems in this country . . . Remember the Burmese saying: you have to make big problems small, and small problems disappear.' And she was unrepentant about the elimination of all Muslims from the ranks of NLD candidates in Muslim-majority areas, as well as members of Generation 88, the group of leading democracy activists. The choices had been hard, she said. 'We rejected 3,000 NLD stalwarts as candidates.'

But the tone of her replies suggested that she viewed these and many other matters as secondary. Even the challenge of winning the election seemed dwarfed in her mind by what lay beyond it: a sullen, stubborn military establishment, jealous of its power, and of the cast-iron constitution in which they had wrapped themselves.

We all knew her thoughts about the constitution but we also knew how difficult it was to amend it, how all-consuming such a task might become. I wanted to know if there were other things she could do before tackling that, things that would be easier to achieve. 'If you got into government,' I asked her, 'would it be possible to do anything to change things in the country without changing the constitution first?'

'It's not just a matter of getting into government,' she said, repeating my formulation in a sardonic tone. 'It's a matter of forming an NLD government that will have the requisite strength within the legislature to initiate amendments to the constitution. If we win enough of a majority, it will show that we have public opinion behind us and that will be the beginning of the process of amending the constitution.' So no, in other words: those other things in the manifesto – ethnic peace, a federal state, educational reform, a better health system, the end of arbitrary land confiscation for farmers, etcetera, etcetera – these would have to wait until the constitution had been fixed and Suu could become president. First of all, David must defeat Goliath.

*

I had joked with Thwin Maung Maung, my assistant, that another coup like those of 1962 and 1988 was out of the question today because the tanks wouldn't be able to get through Rangoon's traffic. One shouldn't joke about such matters. As polling day approached the city went into hibernation. The broad, winding, tree-lined boulevards leading north from the city centre, which make this Asia's most handsome postcolonial city, could once again be enjoyed rather than endured. Traffic all but vanished from the streets. The raucous lanes of downtown Rangoon were strangely quiet. Many people had gone back to their hometowns to vote;

those who remained preferred not to make too much noise. This was prudence or trepidation or at any rate anticipation of a day of special importance. On Friday 6 November the red-emblazoned lorries of the NLD and the green-adorned lorries of the USDP made their final noisy rounds, blaring out the campaign songs and pre-recorded rants by their candidates; that was the final day of campaigning, and after that the city fell into an uneasy sleep.

*

Sunday 8 November, polling day, 7.40 a.m. Very little traffic. Outside my hotel on Nawaday Street small groups of people strolling along, coming from the local primary school – all polling stations in the country are schools I was informed (unreliably as it turned out; at least one, in Muslim-majority Mingala Taungnyunt township, was in a mosque). Shops were shuttered.

Maung Maung and I hired a taxi for the day and set off to Yankin, the poor quarter where former NLD activist Myo Khin – one of the 3,000 'NLD stalwarts' Suu had referred to at her press conference who had been rejected as candidates – was standing as an independent. We breakfasted at a large modern tea shop on the main road where waiters and waitresses in orange T-shirts with the logo 'A.K's', few of them looking more than ten years old, scurried between the tables, all of which were occupied by families. All the time new families arrived, scoured the hall for an empty table then gave up and went away, disappointed. Sleepy Sunday breakfast was never like this. Everyone had come from voting.

8.15 a.m.: two minutes' walk away was the neighbourhood primary school, its cement walls painted pale green. The courtyard, behind breeze-block walls, was crowded with people waiting to vote. The classrooms were divided into separate polling rooms for women and men, and there were separate long queues. Our friend Myo Khin turns up in a dazzling white shirt and maroon longyi with small white dots. 'I got up and came here at 4.30 a.m.,' he said. 'Already there were crowds waiting for the polling station to open.' Maung Maung reported the same phenomenon in his local polling station near the airport: 500 voters waiting in the dark, as if they feared that if they didn't vote at dawn they might not get another chance (polling stations were due to close at 4 p.m. but due to the press of would-be voters many stayed open for hours longer).

We spoke to some of the people waiting in line. 'No, I'm not worried about rigging,' Daw San Te, a woman who sold vegetables in the local market, told us. 'Buddha cannot ignore the truth.' 'I came to support the organisation that is really working for the country,' a housewife called Daw Suu Suu Than told us. 'I voted in 2010 but this is quite different. Now we are expecting change.' Phyo Thazin Min, a teenager, who turned eighteen – the minimum voting age – two days before, who was in her second year studying business administration at Yangon University of Economics, and who (like many younger voters) spoke to us in serviceable English, said, 'I'm voting because I hope the whole country will develop.'

Naing Naing Yee, a volunteer monitor in the polling station, commented, 'I was really surprised by the numbers waiting to vote. I volunteered during the election of 2010, too, but that was a silent election: people knew the system would not change whether they voted or not. Today they know things will change.'

What party were people voting for? There was scarcely any need to ask. Floating voters do not rise at 4 a.m. to queue for two hours in order to dither inside the polling booth. They were practically all voting one way, as the results soon revealed. Our friend Myo Khin was not to get much satisfaction – nor were the other non-NLD candidates.

*

In order to witness Suu voting we had been advised by NLD sources to present ourselves at her local polling station in Bahan township at 6 a.m., as it opened. I thought about this for a while and decided that, while it was not impossible that she might blurt out the name of her presidential nominee, it was unlikely, and that this was just a photo opportunity. When Maung Maung and I arrived at the place shortly after 9 a.m. it was still pullulating with international media who had been waiting since 6 a.m. – for Suu had arrived nearly three hours later than expected, departing soon afterwards and saying nothing to anybody. The journalists hung around in large numbers after she left, taking photographs of each other. We decided to move on.

In Muslim-majority Mingala Taungnyunt township, as in Yankin, the polling station was crowded and the queues were long. Again, the overwhelming majority were voting NLD. 'I'm so happy this morning because I am free to vote,' said Aung Thein, a dark-skinned thirty-one-year-old in a sky-blue T-shirt emblazoned with the letters of the alphabet. 'Freedom will start now.' What did he hope would change? 'I hope everything will improve, especially the economy, and I hope all we Muslims will be given registration cards and permitted to travel.' Was he unhappy about the lack of Muslim candidates selected by the NLD? 'I don't want to divide people by religion – it's no problem if the NLD has no Muslim candidates – whoever the candidates are they will do their best.' Daw Hla, a middle-aged woman with a sequin-studded purple velour cap covering her hair and a blouse to match, told us, beaming broadly: 'I'm so happy today, I've kept hope in my heart for many years, waiting to vote. I am so happy to express my desire. I woke at six and took care to put on a nice outfit . . . I strongly believe that everything must change, the economy, education for children, and above all the system of government. Please pray to God to fulfil the hopes of everyone . . .'

*

When we arrived at NLD headquarters at 5.20 p.m. that afternoon, party volunteers were handing out long red balloons to the rapidly growing crowd that packed both sides of the road outside the office. As the crowd grew, the traffic on the road was reduced to a trickle, and soon after that it stopped completely. Nobody in the cars seemed to mind.

The weather had been mild and dry all day but now as darkness fell lightning crackled in the sky, thunder rumbled above and the tropical rain came pelting down. The party supporters didn't care. Some raised umbrellas. The rest just got wet.

The NLD's campaign songs blasted out of the loudspeakers at high volume. Most of them were newly minted and horrible. But one of them was a plangent ballad about General Aung San that dated from 1947, narrating the events of his life and mourning his death – reminding us of Suu's great father, the heroic example he set, his martyrdom; and the famous phrase of Suu's which so shocked and alarmed the ruling junta when she first used it back in 1989 – 'This is the second struggle for independence.' The sopping wet fans joined in with all the songs, including the old one, roaring along with the choruses.

At this moment in its history the NLD headquarters consisted of two buildings: the unprepossessing two-storey 'cowshed', essentially unchanged from 1989, and a very narrow multistorey concrete building under construction next door. Large video screens had been erected on the facades of both structures, carrying live coverage of the election count from around the country – Burma's first ever experience of the electronic thrills and spills of a modern election. And now they were watching the results come in, vote by vote. To disprove charges of fraud, a teller at a polling station in Mandalay was pulling out one voting slip at a time, showing it to the camera and intoning the party selected before marking the result in the appropriate column. Every time she showed another NLD vote to the camera, which was most of the time, a wild cheer went up and the crowd smacked their balloons together. The rain poured down, the songs blasted out of the speakers, the votes mounted up one by one, cheered to the echo, the rain-soaked revellers danced and sang. I wrote in my notebook, 'If the NLD is half as good at governing as it is at throwing a party, this will be a great five years.'

At 6.05 p.m. U Tin Oo, the NLD's co-founder and Suu's oldest comrade, astonishingly spry throughout the campaign despite his eighty-eight years, came out on a balcony on the half-built concrete tower to tell the crowd that Suu would not be coming to the headquarters tonight. 'She asked me to tell you that the NLD is in a very good position but it will take a while for the results to be announced, and that she is sorry but she won't come here today because she is very tired,' he said. 'She asks you to please go home to wait for the results.' Not a single result had come in so far. It was tantalising. But the rumours of success – fabulous success – were gaining momentum. Tired, wet, happy, the crowd did as they were told and drifted away.

*

Twenty-four hours later – on deadline for the *Independent* – enough results had been logged for me to file the following story:

Monday 9 November, Rangoon

Twenty-five years ago, the National League for Democracy triumphed over the proxies of the Burmese military dictatorship in a free and fair election, but the generals brushed the result aside.

Yesterday – after a wait of twenty-five years, with untold suffering in between – the NLD triumphed again. And this time the generals will let it stand.

Outside NLD headquarters under Shwedagon Pagoda last night, hundreds of supporters waved red flags and danced to the party's repertoire of rock songs, while a red and green drone floated overhead. 'We're going to take the whole night for the NLD,' a reveller screamed in my ear. 'We've waited a long time for this.'

The party had already been going on for more than twenty-four hours since polls closed on Monday, and the fatigue was beginning to show: close to the headquarters, many were sitting on the tarmac. But when the night's final tranche of results came through from the Election Commission, indicating that the party had won 178 out of 188 seats in four vital areas, the crowd leapt to their feet, thrust their fists in the air and roared their approval.

. . . In 1990 a junta shocked by the discovery of its own deep unpopularity was caught in the headlights of popular disdain. This time around the military saw it coming, and have conceded defeat with good grace. And the NLD is relishing its long-overdue triumph. Outside the NLD office last night as the latest tranche of victories was announced, those celebrating represented the party in all its variety: babies and grandmothers, Buddhists and Muslims, students and professionals and market traders. With its warmly inclusive message, its secular vision and its optimism for the future, Suu Kyi's party has brought Burma together like nothing before or since.

*

During the following days it emerged that that the NLD's success was even more dramatic than had first appeared. It won nearly 78.9 per cent of elected seats in the Lower House, with 255 out of 323 elected seats, and 80.4 per cent, or 135 out of 168, elected seats in the Upper House. It thus obtained nearly 10 percentage points more than the minimum it needed to have the decisive say in choosing the next president.[17]

The USDP, despite spending huge sums on the election, was thoroughly humiliated, winning only 42 seats in the national parliament's two houses, 6.4 per cent of the total. Thura Shwe Mann's courageous and thoughtful attempt to re-cast himself as a real democrat had failed – he too was defeated by the NLD, though as the charismatic voice of a large number of USDP candidates disillusioned with Thein Sein's leadership, it would be premature to write his political obituary. More encouragingly, the president's craven attempts to inflame the Buddhist population against Muslims gained no traction whatsoever. The chauvinistic National Development Party splashed money around and attempted to capitalise on Buddhist prejudice, but of its 350 candidates not one gained a seat. Burma's Buddhists, it seemed, were far more level-headed and compassionate than their politicians gave them credit for. The moral weakness of Suu and her party in failing to hold the line against such bigotry now appeared even worse than before – because so unnecessary.

In this regard, the darkest spot in the election results was the sweeping success in Arakan state of the Arakan National Party. With that triumph, achieved precisely because the Rohingya were barred from voting, the prospect for any improvement in the living conditions of the dispossessed Muslims was even worse than before polling day.

None of this, however, took away the excitement, the elation, the euphoria of seeing democracy vindicated in Burma, after fifty-three years of tyranny, and vindicated with such clarity and emphasis. Outside NLD headquarters on the night after polling day, as the results came in, a young man called Mitt Aung roared into my ear above the jubilant noise, 'My mother took part in the 1988 protests. In 2010 I waited outside Daw Suu's house to greet her when she came out of house arrest. We trust her completely. We stand with the NLD. I hope she can change the constitution. She will be our Abraham Lincoln.' For the first time since the British flag was hauled down in 1948, the Burmese people felt the future was theirs.

NOTES

INTRODUCTION

1 Peter Popham, *The Lady and the Peacock* (UK hardback ed., 2011), p.58.
2 ibid., p.54.
3 Discussed in *Beyond the Last Village*, Alan Rabinowitz, p.136.
4 Quoted in *The Art of Not Being Governed*, James C. Scott, 2009, p.239.

1. SUU KYI FREE

1 '. . . there were rumours of dissension from the precedent-mad people at Westminster': http://www.telegraph.co.uk/news/politics/9307900/How-David-Cameron-won-battle-over-Aung-San-Suu-Kyi.html
2 Peter Popham, *The Lady and the Peacock*, p.245.
3 http://www.networkmyanmar.org/images/stories/PDF6/132newsn.pdf
4 Peter Popham, *The Lady and the Peacock*, p.103.
5 On 30 June 2002, Germany played Brazil in the final in Yokohama, Japan. Brazil won 2–0, both goals scored by Ronaldinho.
6 Win Tin obituary, *Guardian*, Larry Jagan, 1 May 2014.
7 Rosalind Russell on Win Tin: *Burma's Spring: Real Lives in Turbulent Times*, p.75 et seq.
8 ibid., p.75.
9 http://www.irrawaddy.org/from-the-irrawaddy-archive-burma/prison-life-u-win-tin.html
10 Win Tin on his jail sentence, and the attempt to bring him over to the junta's side: http://www.irrawaddy.org/from-the-irrawaddy-archive-burma/prison-life-u-win-tin.html
11 ibid.
12 ibid.
13 U Win Tin obituary, *Independent*, Peter Popham, 23 April 2014.

14 Burman: the ethnic majority in Burma, which occupies most of the central part of the country and amounts to about 68 per cent of the total population.

15 Win Tin with Wirathu: DVB video, https://www.youtube.com/watch?v=MjIceTf5_o0

16 Suu in Oslo giving Nobel Prize acceptance speech: http://www.nobelprize.org/nobel_prizes/peace/laureates/1991/kyi-lecture_en.html

17 'Ethnic Cleansing in Myanmar', Moshahida Sultana Ritu, *New York Times*, 13 July 2012.

18 Bertil Lintner, quoted in 'Is Burma regime inciting Rakhine conflict to discredit Aung San Suu Kyi?', by Edward Loxton, *The Week*, 12 June 2012.

19 University of Oxford News & Events, Transcript of Aung San Suu Kyi Speech, 20 Jun 2012: http://www.ox.ac.uk/news/2012-06-20-transcript-aung-san-suu-kyi-speech

20 Suu Kyi speech to both houses of UK Parliament in Westminster Hall, 22 June 2012: 'Suu Kyi recalls . . .' Rediff.com, http://www.rediff.com/news/column/suu-kyi-recalls-nehru-in-historic-speech-at-uk-parliament/20120622.htm

21 Aung San Suu Kyi at Westminster Hall: https://www.youtube.com/watch?v=Uo1MHK1FBic

22 Aung San Suu Kyi's speech when collecting her Honorary Doctorate in Civil Law at Oxford, Peter Popham, *Independent*, 20 June 2012.

2. MAN OUT OF TROUSERS

1 Aung San Suu Kyi, *Letters from Burma*, pp.8–9.

2 Interview with President Thein Sein by Gwen Robinson, *Financial Times*, 12 July 2012: http://www.ft.com/cms/s/0/98722032-cba8-11e1-911e-00144feabdc0.html#axzz3rxWahcx8

3 Evan Osnos in The Burmese Spring, *New Yorker*, 6 August 2012.

4 'I was in Mong Ton and Mong Hsat for two weeks. U Wei Xuegang and U Bao Youri from the Wa groups are real friends.' Thein Sein speaking

of friendship with Golden Triangle drug barons, quoted in *Merchants of Madness*, Bertil Lintner & Michael Black, 2009.

5 *Myanmar Internet, E-Commerce Investment and Business Guide – Regulations and Opportunities*, by Ibpus.com

6 Bertil Lintner, email to author.

7 US Embassy cable, 20 October 2004, published by Wikileaks, republished by Burma Campaign UK in Burma Briefing – Thein Sein – President of Burma: http://burmacampaign.org.uk/media/Thein-Sein-President-of-Burma.pdf

8 President Thein Sein inaugural speech, 31 March 2011, reproduced in Burma Net News from *New Light of Myanmar* newspaper: http://www.burmanet.org/news/2011/03/31/the-new-light-of-myanmar-president-u-thein-sein-delivers-inaugural-address-to-pyidaungsu-hluttaw/

9 Bertil Lintner, *Land of Jade: A Journey from India through Northern Burma to China*, p.279 et seq.

10 ibid., p.286.

11 ibid., p.296.

12 President Thein Sein inaugural speech, 31 March 2011, reproduced in Burma Net News from *New Light of Myanmar* newspaper: http://www.burmanet.org/news/2011/03/31/the-new-light-of-myanmar-president-u-thein-sein-delivers-inaugural-address-to-pyidaungsu-hluttaw/

13 'License to Rape: The Burmese military regime's use of sexual violence in the ongoing war in Shan State', by the Shan Human Rights Federation and the Shan Women's Action Network, May 2002.

14 Burma Briefing – Thein Sein – President of Burma, http://burmacampaign.org.uk/media/Thein-Sein-President-of-Burma.pdf, p.5.

15 Peter Popham, *The Lady and the Peacock*, p.302.

16 ibid., p.345.

17 ibid., p.363 et seq.

18 EBO Analysis Paper no. 2, 2011.

19 President Thein Sein inaugural speech, 31 March 2011, reproduced in Burma Net News from *New Light of Myanmar* newspaper: http://

www.burmanet.org/news/2011/03/31/the-new-light-of-myanmar-president-u-thein-sein-delivers-inaugural-address-to-pyidaungsu-hluttaw/

20 President Thein Sein's inaugural speech, European Business Organisations Analysis Paper 2/2011: http://www.europarl.europa.eu/meetdocs/2009_2014/documents/droi/dv/601_ebopaper2_/601_ebopaper2_en.pdf

21 President Thein Sein inaugural speech, 31 March 2011, reproduced in Burma Net News from *New Light of Myanmar* newspaper: http://www.burmanet.org/news/2011/03/31/the-new-light-of-myanmar-president-u-thein-sein-delivers-inaugural-address-to-pyidaungsu-hluttaw/

22 President Thein Sein inaugural speech, 31 March 2011, op. cit.

23 ibid.

24 ibid.

25 ibid.

26 Peter Popham, The Road to Manerplaw, *Independent* Magazine, 25 May 1991.

27 President Thein Sein inaugural speech, 31 March 2011, op. cit.

28 ibid.

29 http://www.burmalibrary.org/docs5/Myanmar_Constitution-2008-en.pdf: Burma 2008 constitution

30 http://www.biicl.org/documents/469_symposium_paper_-_naina_patel_et_al_constitutional_reform_in_myanmar_-_priorities_and_prospects_for_amendment_jan_2014_english.pdf: Bingham Centre for the Rule of Law

31 ibid.

32 ibid.

3. SNAPSHOTS OF FREEDOM

1 http://foreignpolicy.com/2012/11/26/the-lady-and-the-general/

2 Aung San Suu Kyi's opposition to Myitsone dam revealed on 13 Sept 2011 when the NLD announced it would publish a book

on the project: http://burmariversnetwork.org/index.php/news/news-archives/2014?view=archive&month=9

3 BBC news website, 30 September 2011: http://www.bbc.co.uk/news/world-asia-pacific-15121801

4. THE CLINTON CLINCH

1 http://archive-2.mizzima.com/news/inside-burma/3922-us-envoy-meets-suu-kyi-ends-visit-upset-at-junta-pre-poll-conduct-.html

2 Hillary Clinton, *Hard Choices*, Kindle location 1835.

3 ibid., Kindle location 2142.

4 ibid., Kindle location 2142.

5 Admin official quoted by Evan Osnos, 'The Burma Spring' in the *New Yorker*, 6 August 2012, p.6.

6 Hillary Clinton, *Hard Choices*, Kindle location 2142.

7 Admin official quoted by Evan Osnos, op. cit.

8 http://iipdigital.usembassy.gov/st/english/texttrans/2012/03/201203101945.html#axzz3WvUwSAUt

9 Reith Lecture One, June 2011, answers to questions.

10 Hillary Clinton, *Hard Choices*, Kindle location 2158.

11 ibid., Kindle location 802.

12 ibid., Kindle location 878.

13 Quoted in Indonesia Diplomatic Handbook, 2007, p.68, USA International Business Publications.

14 *Sydney Morning Herald*, 6 October 2007.

15 David Steinberg lecture, St Hugh's College, Oxford, 28 April 2015.

16 *Straits Times*, 20 December 2007. *Straits Times* cited is source for all quoted matter here.

17 https://www.youtube.com/watch?v=wXfxOiMwwtU/The Election Channel Breaking News/Metro TV Indonesia

18 http://www.reuters.com/article/2009/02/18/us-indonesia-clinton-idUSTRE51H15A20090218#8QrZgeKXx7WsqFEo.97

19 Beginning of a New Era of Diplomacy in Asia, 18 February 2009: http://www.state.gov/secretary/20092013clinton/rm/2009a/02/119422.htm

20 Agence France-Presse, 10 November 2011.

21 Hillary Clinton, *Hard Choices*, Kindle location 995.

22 Quoted in The Joke's on the Junta, Irrawaddy news website, by Wai Moe, 12 August 2009: http://www2.irrawaddy.org/article.php?art_id=16544

23 'Clinton Says Iran Process on "Dual Tracks"', *Wall Street Journal* Washington Wire, 22 April 2009, by Timothy J. Alberta, http://blogs.wsj.com/washwire/2009/04/22/clinton-says-iran-process-on-dual-tracks/

24 https://www.whitehouse.gov/the-press-office/2011/11/18/statement-president-obama-burma

5. INTO PARLIAMENT

1 Peter Popham, *The Lady and the Peacock*, pp.101–2.

2 *Straits Times*, 31 March 2012, by Teo Cheng Wee, dateline Rangoon.

3 Peter Popham, *Independent*, 5 May 2013.

4 http://www.ibtimes.co.uk/aung-san-suu-kyi-wins-myanmar-elections-322547

5 'Burma celebrates Aung San Suu Kyi's apparent election victory', Esmer Golluoglu, *Guardian*, 1 April 2012, http://www.theguardian.com/world/2012/apr/01/burma-election-suu-kyi-victory

6 *Guardian*, Nicholas Watt, 11 April 2012.

7 *Guardian*, Nicholas Watt, 14 April 2012.

8 *Economist*, 13 April 2012.

9 *Independent*, Patrick Bodenham and Andrew Buncombe, 14 April 2012.

10 *Guardian*, Nicholas Watt, 14 April 2012.

11 'Aung San Suu Kyi could visit Britain as early as June' by Oliver Wright, *Independent*, 18 April 2012: http://www.independent.co.uk/news/world/asia/aung-san-suu-kyi-could-visit-britain-as-early-as-june-7657250.html

12 'NLD to boycott parliament?', Mizzima News, 20 April 2012.

13 Weekend *Australian*, 21 April 2012.

14 AP story headlined 'Dissident Suu Kyi drops oath objection, joins Myanmar's parliament', dateline Naypyidaw, http://www.cleveland.com/world/index.ssf/2012/05/dissident_aung_san_suu_kyi_dro.html

6. OPEN FOR BUSINESS

1 Private information.
2 Press Association story, 14 April 2012.
3 http://www.boultbeeflightacademy.co.uk/#!spitfire-flights/c1exu
4 'Burma's buried Spitfires', *Daily Telegraph*, Adam Lusher, 23 January 2013.
5 *Daily Telegraph*, op. cit.
6 *Daily Telegraph*, op. cit.
7 *Independent on Sunday*, Peter Popham, 20 January 2013.
8 Unpublished interview with author.
9 *Daily Telegraph*, op. cit.
10 ibid.
11 *Daily Mail*, Ian Drury, 28 November 2012.
12 Letter to Keith Win, 11 December 2012.
13 *Independent on Sunday*, op. cit.
14 *Independent on Sunday*, op. cit.
15 Patrick Bodenham in the *Independent*, 28 April 2012.
16 Mark Magnier in the *Los Angeles Times*, 22 February 2013.
17 ibid.
18 *Independent on Sunday*, op. cit.

7. THE WEST POURS IN

1 Joshua Hammer, The Race for Rangoon, Bloomberg, 20 July 2012, http://www.bloomberg.com/bw/articles/2012-07-03/the-race-for-rangoon
2 Quotes from Prospect House conference all from author's notes.
3 *Dancing with Dictators*, ABC (Australia) documentary: http://www.abc.net.au/tv/programs/dancingwithdictators.htm

4 *The Lady and the Peacock*, p.340.

5 ibid.

6 http://www.mekongpress.com/subregion/cambodia/dunkleys-chance/ by Luke Hunt, 13 September 2009.

7 *The Lady and the Peacock*, p.340.

8 *Dancing with Dictators*, op. cit.

9 ibid.

10 ibid.

11 ibid.

12 ibid.

13 ibid.

14 *Myanmar Times*, 4 February 2013.

15 *Dancing with Dictators*, op. cit.

16 http://www.irrawaddy.org/burma/amid-burma-tourism-boom-calls-govt-aid-development.html

17 Investvine, South-East Asian business news website, http://investvine.com/tourist-income-surges-70-in-myanmar/

18 *Independent*, 5 March 2014, headline Inside Burma Part 1.

19 ibid.

8. ALIENATION

1 Human Rights Watch, 'Burma: Government Forces Targeting Rohingya Muslims', 31 July 2012: https://www.hrw.org/news/2012/07/31/burma-government-forces-targeting-rohingya-muslims

2 ibid.

3 ibid.

4 ibid.

5 Dr Aye Chan, The Development of a Muslim Enclave in Arakan (Rakhine) State of Burma (Myanmar), SOAS Bulletin of Burma Research, Autumn 2005, p.9.

6 *Akyab Gazetteer*, p.89, edited by Deputy Commissioner R. B. Smart, quoted by Derek Tonkin, Network Myanmar bulletin, 9 April 2014.

7 See Derek Tonkin, Network Myanmar bulletin, 11 November 2012.

8 'A Comparative Vocabulary of Some of the Languages Spoken in the Burma Empire', Francis Buchanan, 1799, reproduced in SOAS Bulletin of Burma Research, Vol. 1, No. 1, Spring 2003, ISSN 1479-8484.

9 Dr Aye Chan, op. cit., p.17.

10 ibid., p.11.

11 ibid., p.11.

12 ibid., p.12.

13 ibid., p.12.

14 Anthony Irwin, *Burmese Outpost*, 1946, p.21.

15 Dr Aye Chan, op. cit., p.13.

16 ibid., p.16.

17 Dr Aye Chan, op. cit., p.17.

18 ibid.

19 Prof. Robert H. Taylor on Ethnicity in Myanmar Politics, interviewed by Geoffrey Goddard, Mizzima.com, 13 June 2015.

20 World View, *Independent*, Peter Popham, 27 February 2014.

9. THE ROAD TO NIRVANA

1 All quotes from Ingrid Jordt come from the essay by Ingrid Jordt: 'Breaking bad in Burma' in *Religion in the News*, Fall 2014, Vol. 15, no. 2, a Publication of the Leonard E. Greenberg Center for the Study of Religion in Public Life at Trinity College, http://religioninthenews.org/author/ingridjordt/

2 Jason Szep, 'Buddhist monks incite Muslim killings in Myanmar', Reuters, 8 April 2013.

3 *Independent*, 10 April 2013.

4 Kyaw Zwa Moe, Irrawaddy Daily Newsletter, 30 March 2013.

5 http://www.mmtimes.com/index.php/opinion/6422-a-plea-for-peace-from-a-religious-leader.html: *Myanmar Times*, 8 April 2013.

6 Adapted from piece by Peter Popham in the *Independent*, 26 May 2013.

7 'Killing with Kindness', *Independent on Sunday*'s New Review, Peter Popham, 26 May 2013.

8 'Genocidal Buddhists': An Interview with Burmese Dissident Maung

Zarni, Alex Caring-Lobel in Tricycle, 28 March 2013, http://www.tricycle.com/blog/genocidal-buddhists

9 Ingrid Jordt, op. cit.

10 'Genocidal Buddhists', Maung Zarni interview in Tricycle, op. cit.

11 Ingrid Jordt, op. cit.

12 Ingrid Jordt, op. cit.

13 Ingrid Jordt, op. cit.

14 Ingrid Jordt, op. cit.

15 Burma's Mass Lay Meditation Movement, Ohio University Research in International Studies, 2007.

16 Ingrid Jordt, op. cit.

17 *The Lady and the Peacock*, p.56.

18 Private information.

19 Aung San Suu Kyi, 'Intellectual Life in Burma and India under Colonialism', in *Freedom from Fear*, Penguin paperback edition, pp.88–9.

20 ibid., p.91.

21 ibid., p.92.

22 ibid., p.120.

23 ibid.

24 ibid., p.180.

25 ibid., p.183.

26 ibid., pp.184–5.

27 ibid., p.183, p.185.

28 Ingrid Jordt, op. cit.

29 'A Suu Kyi Presidency Would Bring "Chaos" . . .', Sanay Lin and Simon Roughneen, Irrawaddy, 28 November 2013, http://www.irrawaddy.org/election/news/a-suu-kyi-presidency-would-bring-chaos-says-firebrand-monk

10. THE ENIGMA OF SUU

1 Daw Aung San Suu Kyi's lecture, Tokyo University, 17 April 2013 https://www.youtube.com/watch?v=311BI-5PPyo plus author's own notes.

2 ibid.

3 ibid.

4 ibid.

5 ibid.

6 *The Lady and the Peacock*, p.193.

7 Private information.

8 *Freedom from Fear*, Aung San Suu Kyi, pp.56–7.

9 *The Lady and the Peacock*, pp.240–1.

10 ibid. p.239.

11 ibid. p.234.

12 Aung San Suu Kyi: 'The Halo Slips', *Economist*, 15 June 2013: http://www.economist.com/news/asia/21579512-running-president-comes-risks-halo-slips

13 Private information.

14 Dalai Lama hints successor won't have political role: Press Trust of India report, 12 September 2012.

11. IN THE LINE OF FIRE

1 Private information.

2 *New York Times*, Thomas Fuller, http://www.nytimes.com/2012/05/30/world/asia/uncertainty-hangs-over-aung-san-suu-kyis-visit-to-thailand.html?_r=0 – 'Amid disorganisation, ASSK visits Thailand'

3 ibid.

4 ibid.

5 'National League for Democracy will soon have its first policy', Burma Tha Din Network, 25 November 2014.

6 Aung San Suu Kyi faces anger over Myanmar mine project – No Comment TV, 15 March 2013: https://www.youtube.com/watch?v=qLeFiuVzV6w

7 *The Lady and the Peacock*, pp.354–5.

8 *Los Angeles Times*, Mark Magnier, 15 December 2012, p.8.

9 ibid.

10 Associated Press, 31 December 2012.

11 Private information.

12 AP News, 14 March 2013, dateline Monywa. http://asiancorrespondent. com/2013/03/burma-villagers-unhappy-that-suu-kyi-backs-mine/

13 ibid.

14 ibid.

15 Toru Takahashi, *Nikkei Weekly* (Japan), 24 December 2012.

16 Private information.

17 Private information.

18 Aung San Suu Kyi, *Freedom from Fear*, pp.180, 183.

19 Maung Zarni, quoted in Associated Press piece 'Suu Kyi's silence on Rohingya draws rare criticism', by Jocelyn Gecker, 16 August 2012.

20 Daw Aung San Suu Kyi's lecture, Tokyo University, 17 April 2013: https://www.youtube.com/watch?v=311BI-5PPyo

12. THE LADY AND THE GENERALS

1 *The Lady and the Peacock*, p.172

2 *The Voice of Hope*, Aung San Suu Kyi, p.62.

3 *Desert Island Discs*, 27 January 2013.

4 *Financial Times* magazine, David Pilling, 28 January 2011.

5 *Independent*, 13 May 2002.

6 Prime Minister U Nu first handed power to General Ne Win in 1958, four years before the decisive army coup.

7 International Human Rights Clinic at Harvard Law School/Legal Memorandum: War Crimes and Crimes against Humanity in Eastern Myanmar, November 2014.

8 Simon Tisdall, 'UK backs move to refer Burma's leaders to war crimes tribunal', *Guardian*, 25 March 2010.

9 'UK government supports Burma regime referral to International Criminal Court', 25 March 2010, Burma Campaign website: http:// burmacampaign.org.uk/uk-government-supports-burma-regime-referral-to-international-criminal-court/

10 e.g., Sappho Dias, 4–5 Gray's Inn Square Barrister Chambers.

11 One view of Than Shwe's achievement in dodging an ICC indictment appeared (without a byline) in the *Asian Tribune*: 'With the coming

of two prominent Burmese to America' – a reference to the simultaneous journeys to the United States of Suu and President Thein Sein in September 2012 – 'the crafty Senior General Than Shwe will be laughing up his sleeve as he relaxes and enjoys his Asian-style elderly dictator retirement . . . There is no fear of being overthrown, or tried at the ICC. His family is protected. All is well. Tatmadaw commanders and soldiers are now off the hook. The generals and officers, whether they retain their uniforms or not, will . . . cement their positions as the new upper-class elite of Burma, a nouveau riche, as they become part-owners and signatories to the new development deals. Not only will they not be charged for their crimes, they are being given preferred positions as the Gold Rush, otherwise known as the initial stage of astronomical corruption for the country, commences. To them we can also add all the regime cronies and fixers, such as Tayza, Myanmar Egress, etc., Burmese and international consultants, and corrupt ethnic leaders and "pro-democracy" politicians, who are also well positioned for the start of the nation's new road to people's degradation', from 'The Evil Genius, Than Shwe and the Current Reforms', *Asian Tribune*, 15 September 2012, dateline Sweden.

12 Conversation with U Win Thein, veteran NLD official.

13 Gwen Robinson, *Financial Times*, 'Suu Kyi's role under scrutiny as parliament reopens', 5 July 2012.

14 Quoted in Burma: Resignation of Constitutional Court Justices, Law Library of Congress/News and Events/Global Legal Monitor, 12 September 2012.

15 Agence-France Presse story dated 7 May 2015 and posted on the Channel NewsAsia website, http://www.channelnewsasia.com/news/asiapacific/myanmar-s-suu-kyi-praises/1832132.html

16 *The Lady and the Peacock*, p.268.

17 ibid., p.275 et seq.

18 ibid., p.392.

19 Wikileaks cable: https://wikileaks.org/cable/2007/03/07RANGOON283.html

20 Burma Alert January 1995, Vol. 6, No. 1, Karens Give Up Manerplaw: http://www.burmalibrary.org/docsBA/BA1995-V06-N01.pdf
21 Wikileaks, op. cit.

13. IN ARCADIA

1 Background information from Western diplomats, May 2015.
2 23.2 per cent in 2014. Often more than 30 per cent in earlier years. http://www.globalsecurity.org/military/world/myanmar/budget.htm
3 George Orwell, *Nineteen Eighty-Four*, Chapter 9, https://ebooks. adelaide.edu.au/o/orwell/george/o79n/chapter2.9.html
4 https://wikileaks.org/cable/2007/03/07RANGOON283.html
5 Hla Oo's Blog, 4 May 2014: http://hlaoo1980.blogspot.co.uk/2014/05/shwe-mann-parliament-speaker-and-secret.html
6 ibid.
7 ibid.
8 James C. Scott, *The Art of Not Being Governed: An Anarchist History of Upland Southeast Asia*, p.41.
9 ibid., p.42.
10 This section is based on my article 'Journey into Unseen Burma', published in the *Independent* Magazine, 3 May 2014.
11 Mentioned in 'Re-fighting Old Battles . . .: the Politics of Ethnicity in Myanmar Today' by Robert H. Taylor, Institute of Southeast Asian Studies, Singapore, March 2015.
12 Taken here and elsewhere from: Laura Hardin Carson, *Pioneer Trails, Trials and Triumphs: Personal Memoirs of Life and Work as a Pioneer Missionary among the Chin tribes of Burma*, Baptist Board of Education, New York, 1927. The full text can be found here: https://archive.org/stream/MN41707ucmf_3/MN41707ucmf_3_djvu.txt
13 Published by CreateSpace Independent Publishing Platform, 2013.
14 The title of James C. Scott's book, cited above.
15 Not only the Chin but also large numbers of Kachin, Karen and many smaller tribes were converted to Christianity, mostly by American missionaries. In the plains, by contrast, their success among the Buddhists was negligible.

16 Quoted in *Burma: Insurgency and the Politics of Ethnicity* by Martin Smith, 1999, p.62.

17 https://en.wikipedia.org/wiki/Panglong_Agreement

18 From 'Eloisa to Abelard' by Alexander Pope.

14. PEACE IN OUR TIME

1 'Burmese activist in exile: Aung Naing Oo', ABC online, 30 September 2007: http://www.abc.net.au/sundayprofile/stories/s2046431.htm

2 *Straits Times*, Aung Naing Oo, 12 August 2013.

3 'Homecoming at last for a Myanmar son', ibid.

4 ibid.

5 'Burmese activist in exile: Aung Naing Oo', ABC online, op. cit.

6 ibid.

7 ibid.

8 'The Core Issues Not Addressed', Irrawaddy magazine, May 2015, pp.20–3.

9 Interview with author, May 2015.

10 Interview with author in Rangoon, May 2015.

11 Interview with author, May 2015.

12 Interview with author, May 2015.

13 Inaugural address 1948, published in Irrawaddy website, 25 July 2010.

14 Quoted in Irrawaddy website, 6 May 2015.

15 Irrawaddy website, 5 May 2015.

16 Aung San Suu Kyi's speech when collecting her Honorary Doctorate in Civil Law at Oxford, Peter Popham, *Independent*, 20 June 2012.

17 Adapted from 'Einstein MC King Skunk . . .' by Peter Popham in the *Independent on Sunday New Review*, 16 March 2014.

18 Based on the article 'Exploding Media: Inside Burma Part 2', *Independent*, Peter Popham, 5 March 2014.

19 Original source Myanmar State Radio, first quoted by Radio Free Asia News and Information, 'Thein Sein Warns Myanmar Media Against Instigating Violence', 8 July 2014.

20 Irrawaddy website, 10 July 2014, http://www.irrawaddy.org/editorial/back-square-one-press-freedom-burma.html

21 Reported in '2 Years Hard Labour for Htin Lin Oo in Religious Offence Case' by Zarni Mann, Irrawaddy, 2 June 2015, http://www.irrawaddy.org/burma/2-years-hard-labor-for-htin-lin-oo-in-religious-offense-case.html; video of speech at https://www.youtube.com/watch?v=aDwNX_8RdAA

22 Reported in '2 Years Hard Labour for Htin Lin Oo in Religious Offence Case', op. cit.

23 ibid.

24 ibid.

25 ibid.

26 ibid.

27 '. . . it was said of Tony Blair . . .': by Roy Jenkins: http://labourlist.org/2015/03/milibands-carefully-calibrated-balancing-act/

28 cf. David I. Steinberg, *Burma/Myanmar: What Everyone Needs to Know*, p.150: 'Power is unconsciously conceived as finite' . . . there is an unwillingness to share power because it is finite; to do so would diminish the authority of the leader. Power thus tends to be a zero-sum game.'

15. THE LANDSLIDE

1 http://www.irrawaddy.org/election/news/election-commission-may-postpone-november-poll

2 See Chapter 12: 'The reform process got stuck. A second round of by-elections was scheduled, then cancelled, reportedly because they would have been too expensive – a disastrous explanation in a democracy as new and fragile as Burma's . . .' See also note 12 for Chapter 12.

3 For a discussion of the constitution. See Chapter 2.

4 'touring a base hospital . . .' See Chapter 12.

5 Ministerial Resignations Linked to Shwe Mann Purge, Yen Snaing, Irrawaddy, 13 August 2015: http://www.irrawaddy.org/election/news/ministerial-resignations-linked-to-shwe-mann-purge

6 'A Generals' Election in Myanmar', in the *Diplomat*, 4 November 2015.

7 Private information.

8 cf. *The Lady and the Peacock*, p.91: 'Burma had not digested the concept of a loyal opposition . . . As in many other traditional societies, writes [David] Steinberg, "power was conceived as finite". To share power, "from centre to periphery, between leaders, etc", was to lose power: it was a zero-sum game. "Loyalty becomes the prime necessity, resulting in entourages and a series of patron–client relationships . . . a 'loyal opposition' thus becomes an oxymoron."'

9 See Chapter 12.

10 See Chapter 9.

11 Burma's New Nationalist Party Surges into Election Race, Irrawaddy, 29 October 2015: http://www.irrawaddy.org/election/feature/burmas-new-nationalist-party-surges-into-election-race

12 ibid.

13 See Chapter 14: 'Htin Lin Oo was sacked as its [the party's] information officer, and later expelled from the party.'

14 Quoted in Chapter 8.

15 'Myanmar icon of democracy loses supporters' by Thomas Fuller, *New York Times*, 29 August 2015.

16 Author's notebook.

17 Tallying the Triumph, by San Yamin Aung, Irrawaddy, 23 November 2015.

TIMELINE

1947: Suu's father, Aung San, founder of Burma's army and prime minister-in-waiting, is assassinated by a political rival.

1948: Burma gains independence from Britain; U Nu becomes prime minister.

1958: When his party splits, PM U Nu invites army chief General Ne Win to become prime minister.

1960: Power returns to U Nu after his party wins a clear election victory.

1962: Ne Win seizes power in a largely bloodless coup d'état. His revolutionary council abolishes Parliament and pronounces 'the Burmese Way to Socialism'. Foreign organisations and companies and tens of thousands of ethnic Indians are expelled.

1974: After a new constitution is affirmed in a referendum, Ne Win transfers nominal power to the Burma Socialist Programme Party (BSPP) while retaining ultimate control. Official discrimination against Burmese Muslims instituted.

1987: Burma granted special assistance, having gained 'least developed country' status at the United Nations. Ne Win orders the demonetisation of large-denomination banknotes on the advice of his soothsayer.

1988: Students protest against demonetisation; after the army kills a number of people the protests become a general and prolonged insurrection, forcing Ne Win's resignation, dissolution of the BSPP and imposition of direct army rule through SLORC, the State Law and Order Restoration Council. Suu emerges as leader of the democracy movement and co-founder of the National League for Democracy (NLD).

1989: Suu and colleagues defy SLORC and campaign countrywide, gaining millions of new party members. In July Suu's party colleagues are arrested and jailed, while she is put under indefinite house arrest. In the same year, the regime announces the replacement of 'Burma' with 'Myanmar' and other name changes for use internationally.

1990: SLORC stages general elections, despite nearly all NLD leaders being in jail or detention. The National Unity Party, successor to BSPP, is crushed by NLD, which wins a landslide victory. Regime refuses to convene Parliament, claiming the vote was not for a government but a constitutional convention. NLD MPs-elect are jailed or flee into exile. Suu, still in detention, awarded the Nobel Peace Prize.

1993: Convention meets to draw up a new constitution under strict army control.

1994: Under pressure from Japan, top generals hold two meetings with Suu but these produce no concessions and she remains in detention.

1995: Suu released after 2,180 days under house arrest. Impeded from travelling, she begins speaking to crowds gathered outside her home. NLD joins the constitutional convention but is expelled after demanding the convention's reform.

1999: Michael Aris, barred from returning to Burma to be with his wife, dies of cancer in England.

2000: Suu is placed under house arrest for a third time after being barred from leaving Rangoon.

2002: With a political thaw in the air, Suu is freed again and quickly resumes travelling to meet party supporters.

2003: Suu narrowly avoids being assassinated by a regime-sponsored mob outside Depayin, near Mandalay. She is taken to Rangoon's Insein Jail, then returned to house arrest. As the West tightens sanctions, reform-minded Lieutenant General Khin Nyunt appointed prime minister.

2004: Khin Nyunt's attempt to bring the NLD back into the stalled constitutional convention is rejected by Senior General Than Shwe. Khin Nyunt is put on trial and sentenced to house arrest.

2005: Overnight and without prior notice the new city of Naypyidaw becomes Burma's capital.

2007: Cuts in fuel subsidies trigger cost-of-living protests and escalate into another nationwide rebellion against the regime, in which monks take a leading role – the 'Saffron Revolution'. This is suppressed by force of arms, with many monks killed.

2008: Cyclone Nargis kills more than 130,000, and seen by many as karmic retribution for the regime's killing of monks the previous year. The regime, now known as the State Peace and Development Council, presses on with a constitutional referendum despite the disaster. Popular endorsement of the new, military-dominated constitution seen as flawed by the West.

2010: New-minted regime proxy party the Union Solidarity and Development Party (USDP) wins a rigged general election. Suu released one week later to ecstatic welcome.

2011: Former General Thein Sein is elected president by Parliament and promises reforms. Meets Suu in August and reform process begins, with political prisoners released. US Secretary of State Hillary Clinton visits.

2012: Suu elected MP as her party triumphs in by-elections, and travels abroad for first time in twenty-four years. Addresses joint session of UK Parliament and travels to Washington DC to meet President Obama. Communal violence between Buddhists and Muslims in Arakan state kills hundreds and leads to ethnic cleansing.

2013: Anti-Muslim pogroms occur in several central Burma towns, notably Meiktila. Suu's refusal to condemn one side or the other draws international criticism. Abolition of dual exchange rates for Burmese currency paves the way for international investment.

2014: NLD campaign for constitutional reform fails to produce change. Suu forges tactical alliance with speaker of Lower House of Parliament, former General Shwe Mann. President Thein Sein pushes for nationwide ceasefire with ethnic armies, but fighting resumes in Kachin state.

2015: The plight of Rohingya and Bangladeshi boat people again focuses a spotlight on Burma's most deprived minority. Nationwide push for a ceasefire produces a limited agreement. A closely monitored general election in November yields another landslide victory for Suu and the NLD, twenty-five years after the first. This time President Thein Sein and army chief Min Aung Hlaing promise Burma's first ever smooth transfer of power.

GLOSSARY

ABSDF: All-Burma Students' Democratic Front; umbrella student group dedicated to armed struggle against regime from 1988

ASEAN: Association of Southeast Asian Nations

baung-bi-chut: 'men out of trousers', i.e. military men who formerly wore military uniform but now, as civilian politicians, wear longyi, the traditional skirt-like garment.

Bogyoke: army general; term for Aung San, Suu's late father.

BSPP: Burma Socialist Programme Party

Daw: honorific prefix for mature woman

Dharma: the teachings of the Buddha; *dhamma* in Pali

dukkha – suffering

DVB: Democratic Voice of Burma

gaung baung: formal Burmese turban

hpoun: spiritual potency

htamein – ankle-length woman's longyi

ICC: the International Criminal Court

ikhwan: brethren

kalar: hate word for ethnic Indian or Muslim

KNLA: Karen National Liberation Front

KNU: Karen National Union

kyat: unit of currency; 100 kyats was roughly equivalent to seventy-seven cents (US) and fifty pence (UK) in December 2015.

longyi: traditional skirt-like garment for men and women

Ma Ba Tha: Burmese acronym for the Association to Protect Race and Religion

majime: devoted to duty (Japanese)

MI: Miliary Intelligence, now defunct agency headed by Lieutenant General Khin Nyunt until its dissolution.

mohinya: fish noodle soup, with a claim to be Burma's national dish

mujahideen: warriors for Islam

nat: spirit requiring to be propitiated in Burma's pre-Buddhist religion

nat kadaw: medium capable of being possessed by a *nat*

nat pwe: traditional ghost ceremony at which possession by *nats* is said to occur

NCGUB: National Coalition Government of the Union of Burma; rebel government formed on the border after the NLD's 1990 victory was discounted by junta

NDP: National Development Party, founded 2015

NDSC: National Defence and Security Council, successor to SPDC, since 31 March 2011, the supreme power in Burma

ngapi: pungent paste made from fish or shrimp

nirvana: state of release from the cycle of birth and death, seen by some schools as the final goal of Buddhism; *nibbana* in ancient Pali language used in Burmese Buddhism.

NLD: National League for Democracy

NUP: National Unity Party, successor to BSPP

OHCHR: United Nations Office of the High Commissioner for Human Rights

patta: monk's alms bowl

Pyidaungsu Hluttaw: Burma's bi-cameral Parliament

Pyithu Hluttaw: lower house of parliament, house of representatives *sangha*: the community of monks; more broadly, the larger community of Buddhist practitioners

saopha: prince

SBY: Susilo Bambang Yudhoyono, former president of Indonesia

Sepoy: Indian soldier in British imperial army

SLORC: State Law and Order Restoration Council

SNLD: Shan Nationalities League for Democracy

SPDC: State Peace and Development Council, successor to SLORC

Tatmadaw: Burmese term for Burma's national army

Thingyan: annual Burmese water festival

Thura: military decoration, meaning 'brave hero'

TTO: Dr Tin Tun Oo, one-time co-owner of *Myanmar Times*

U: honorific prefix for mature men

UEC: Union Election Commission

USDP: Union Solidarity and Development Party, ruling party 2011–2016

zamindar: hereditary aristocratic landlord in Indian subcontinent

zedi: stupa

FURTHER READING

The Burma bookshelf is short compared with that of other nations of South and South East Asia. The fact that books by or about Aung San Suu Kyi form such a large proportion of the total reflects not only her fame and popularity abroad, but also the reclusive nature of the state under military rule and the extreme difficulty of working there as a journalist or academic researcher. However, this has begun to change since the re-opening of the country, and the range of published material is slowly expanding.

The first biography of Suu to appear was *Aung San Suu Kyi: Toraware no Kujaku*, by Yoshikazu Mikami (1991), which is particularly strong on the Japanese connections of Aung San and his daughter. Several other biographies have been published subsequently. *The Lady: Burma's Aung San Suu Kyi* by Barbara Victor (1998) and *Aung San Suu Kyi: Towards a New Freedom* by Ang Chin Geok (1998) are slim volumes, and both now very dated. *Le Jasmin ou la Lune* (2007) by the Bangkok-based Belgian journalist Thierry Falise is a fast-paced and fascinatingly detailed account of Suu's career, in French. *Perfect Hostage: A Life of Aung San Suu Kyi* by Justin Wintle (2007) devotes much space to the pre-modern history of Burma and is often sceptical about Suu's career, blaming her 'intransigence' as the reason she has spent so many years in detention. *Aung San Suu Kyi and Burma's Struggle for Democracy* by Bertil Lintner, published in the same year (2007), commands respect as Lintner can claim to be the best-informed Western commentator on the country. The latest edition to the biography shelf, excluding the present volume, is *The Burma Spring: Aung San Suu Kyi and the New Struggle for the Soul of a Nation*, by Rena Pederson (2015), which has a foreword by Laura Bush.

Of Suu's own written work, the most important essays are collected in *Freedom from Fear* (1995), which contains her short biography of her father, her seminal long essay 'Intellectual Life in Burma and India under Colonialism', and other political landmarks such as her first speech at the Shwedagon Pagoda in August 1988. It also contains the tributes of friends, including Ann Pasternak Slater's moving and intimate memoir, *Suu Burmese. Letters from Burma* (1997) is a collection of the pieces Suu wrote regularly for the *Mainichi Daily News* in Tokyo after her release from house arrest in 1995.

One of the most revealing works about Suu's life and beliefs is *The Voice of Hope* (2008), a series of interviews conducted over a period of months by Alan Clements, a former Buddhist monk, in which Suu speaks more candidly about herself than ever before or since.

Mental Culture in Burmese Crisis Politics by Gustaaf Houtman (1999) is a fascinating scholarly account of the role Suu plays in Burmese politics, informed by the author's excellent knowledge of Burma and Burmese. Though out of print, it can be downloaded from Google Books.

For more on other aspects of Burma, the following can be recommended:

INSURGENCY AND DEMOCRACY STRUGGLE

Outrage by Bertil Lintner (1990): a blow-by-blow history by the Swedish journalist, a veteran Burma-watcher, of the great Burmese uprising and its bloody suppression, enriched by numerous interviews and depositions by Burmese in the front line.

Land of Jade: a Journey through Insurgent Burma (1990) by Bertil Lintner: the story of Lintner's unique journey with his young and heavily pregnant wife – she gave birth en route – through the war-torn badlands of the Burmese frontier. A gem that deserves to be much better known.

Burma: Insurgency & the Politics of Ethnicity by Martin Smith (1991): a detailed history of the insurgencies that have bedevilled Burma since independence and their causes.

Little Daughter by Zoya Phan (2009): the moving autobiography of a Karen girl born and raised in the thick of Burma's ethnic wars.

Than Shwe: Unmasking Burma's Tyrant by Benedict Rogers (2010): the only detailed biography of the man who bent Burma to his will from 1993 to 2011.

The Lizard Cage by Karen Connelly (2008), an ambitious novel set in a Rangoon prison which tells of the sufferings and redemption of a young political prisoner with great insight and detail.

Burmese Lessons: A True Love Story, also by Karen Connolly (2010) recounts the author's lengthy and intimate involvement with the country and its political struggle.

The Rebel of Rangoon: a Tale of Defiance and Deliverance in Burma by Delphine Schrank (2015): a harrowingly vivid account of what regime opponents experienced as they fought their non-violent war against one of Asia's most brutal regimes – all true, but reads like a novel.

Burma at the Crossroads by Benedict Rogers: a frequent visitor to Burma and a tireless campaigner for civil rights, Than Shwe's biographer brings the story of the travails of the nation's minorities up to date (new edition 2016).

HISTORY

The most readable general introduction to Burmese history is *The River of Lost Footsteps: A Personal History of Burma* by Thant Myint-U (2007), grandson of the late UN secretary-general U Thant, which contrives to bring the region's endless dynastic wars and reversals of fortune to life.

Thant Myint-U's second book *Where China Meets India: Burma and the New Crossroads of Asia* (2011), places Burma in its challenging regional context.

Bertil Lintner's latest book, *Great Game East: India, China, and the Struggle for Asia's Most Volatile Frontier* (2015), tackles similar themes, deploying his vast knowledge of the region's numerous insurgency movements.

Forgotten Land/A Rediscovery of Burma by Harriet O'Brien (1991) blends personal reminiscence – the author spent years in the country when her father was the British ambassador – with a pithy yet vivid account of Burmese history.

Defeat into Victory by Field Marshal Viscount Slim (1956) describes how the Second World War unfolded in Burma and includes a memorable account of the British commander's meeting with Aung San.

Two concise and authoritative works on contemporary Burma are: *A History of Modern Burma* by Michael W. Charney (2009), and *Burma/ Myanmar: What Everyone Needs to Know* by David I. Steinberg (2010).

RELIGION

In This Very Life: The Liberation Teachings of the Buddha by Sayadaw U Pandita (1989) is the book that Michael Aris gave Suu at the start of her first spell of detention: a bracingly straightforward manual of how to attain wisdom and peace through meditation, hugely influential in Burma and beyond, by a living master.

Burma's Mass Lay Meditation Movement: Buddhism and the Cultural Construction of Power by Ingrid Jordt (2007) is the only scholarly account of this important movement.

Religion and Politics in Burma by Donald Eugene Smith (1965): a scholarly description of the political role played in Burma by Buddhism, before, during and after annexation by Britain.

SOCIETY

The Burman: His Life and Notions by Shway Yoe (first published 1882, reissued in 1989): a beautifully written and frequently hilarious exploration of Burmese life from birth to death and beyond, a cornucopia for anyone intrigued by the country. Shway Yoe was the pen name of J. G. (later Sir George) Scott, a colonial administrator who spent many years in the Shan states.

Karaoke Fascism: Burma and the Politics of Fear by Monique Skidmore (2004) and *Burma at the Turn of the 20th Century* edited by Monique Skidmore (2005): two brave efforts by intrepid anthropologists and social scientists to get to grips with Burma, despite great discouragement by the authorities.

Burma's Spring: Real Lives in Turbulent Times by Rosalind Russell (2014): the most charming and personal attempt to describe what actually living in the country is like, for both native and foreigner, by an English journalist who spent years in the country as wife, mother, and undercover reporter.

Blood, Dreams and Gold: the Changing Face of Burma (2015): former *Economist* correspondent Richard Cockett tackles Burma in transition.

MISCELLANEOUS

Beyond the Last Village: A Journey of Discovery in Asia's Forbidden Wilderness by Alan Rabinowitz (2001): the fascinating account of an American zoologist's intrepid journey to Burma's far north, his discovery of a dying tribe of Asian pygmies and his encounter with Burma's own community of Tibetans.

Bones Will Crow: Fifteen Contemporary Burmese Poets, edited and translated by ko ko thett [sic] and James Byrne (2012):

very few works of contemporary Burmese literature have yet been translated. This pioneering book introduces some of the nation's best living poets.

The Road to Wanting by Wendy Law-Yone (2011): a fast-paced novel about the life and hard times of a young woman struggling for freedom and fulfilment in one of Burma's wild borderlands.

Golden Parasol: A Daughter's Memoir of Burma (2014): Ms Law-Yone's father was a Rangoon newspaper editor and her memoir of this mercurial character brings the post-independence 'parliamentary era' to life.

Burmese Days by George Orwell (1944) and *Finding George Orwell in Burma* by Emma Larkin (2006): Burma, where Orwell served as a colonial policeman, played an important role in the formation of his political ideas, confirming his hatred of colonialism. His first novel is a deeply unflattering portrait of Burma under the British – and Burma under the generals bears a striking resemblance to the world of *Nineteen Eighty-Four*. Larkin, an American journalist and Burmese speaker, travelled through Burma in Orwell's footsteps, teasing out the parallels.

From the Land of Green Ghosts by Pascal Khoo Thwe (2002), the vivid memoir of the up-country boy from the Padaung tribe, famous for their 'giraffe-necked' women, who fled into exile in 1989 and went on to study English at Cambridge.

The Trouser People: A Story of Burma in the Shadow of the Empire by Andrew Marshall (2002): a witty travelogue

411

entwined with a re-telling of the life story of Sir George Scott (see *The Burman*, above).

The Native Tourist: A Holiday Pilgrimage in Burma by Ma Thanegi (2005): what Suu's former friend did next; a whimsical but informative journey through the country.

CURRENT AFFAIRS

The lifting of censorship and other reforms have dramatically improved media coverage of Burma. The international news agencies all now have bureaux in Rangoon, and the outfits run by dissident expatriates who formerly reported the country from Thailand and India now have offices in Rangoon: Irrawaddy, which has distinct print (monthly) and web (daily) versions, and Mizzima, which produces a *Time*-like weekly magazine. Democratic Voice of Burma (DVB) beams radio and television news programmes into Burma in Burmese and English from Chiangmai in Thailand. The *Myanmar Times*, whose problems with the authorities are described in this book, now has a daily English language edition, while its former co-owner, Sonny Swe, has launched *Frontier Myanmar*, a weekly news magazine in English. The *New Light of Myanmar*, now re-branded as the *Global New Light of Myanmar*, has continued to function as the regime's mouthpiece, though after 2015's election result some changes may be in store.

ACKNOWLEDGEMENTS

No foreigner can hope to understand Burma without capable help, and I owe a great debt of gratitude to Han Thar, my assistant during several visits, who set up meetings all over the country with panache. During the 2015 election period, when he became very busy, he introduced me to Thwin Maung Maung who not only arranged a series of fascinating encounters but also took a number of the photographs that appear in the book. Both of them work for Kamayut Media, a Rangoon-based digital news company, whose founder, Nathan Maung, allowed them to take time off to help me and was himself a great source of insight and gossip. A warm 'thank you' to all three.

My friends and colleagues at the *Independent* have encouraged my obsession with Burma, commissioning numerous on-the-spot reports and comment pieces and covering expenses. Thank you to Amol Rajan, Dan Gledhill, David Wastell and Sean O'Grady. Other colleagues at the paper to whom I am indebted include Rachael Pells, Emma Gatten, Sam Masters, Chris Stevenson and Jen Stebbing.

My old friend Chris Steele-Perkins, the great Magnum photographer, accompanied me into the wilds of Chin state and has kindly allowed me to use photographs he took on the trip. Daniele Tamagni, the prize-winning Italian photographer, opened a door for me onto the world of Burmese punks and lent me photographs of the most picturesque of them.

Others I would like to thank include:

Mark Farmaner and Anna Roberts of Burma Campaign UK; Benedict Rogers of Christian Solidarity Worldwide; Maureen Aung-Thwin, Director of the Burma Programme at the Open Society Foundation; Andrew and Jane Heyn; Robert and Pam Gordon; Robert Cooper; Rosalind Russell; Jason Cowley and his colleagues at the *New Statesman*; Ingrid Jordt; Guy Dinmore at the *Myanmar Times*; Derek Mitchell and colleagues at the US Embassy in Rangoon; Andrew Patrick at the British Embassy in Rangoon; Keith Win; Aung Zaw, founder editor of Irrawaddy; Bertil Lintner; Adam Burke; Joe Fisher; Gwen Robinson; Joe Woods; U Ko Ni; Lucinda and Adrian Phillips; and the staff of the Alfa Hotel in Rangoon.

This is the second book on which I have worked with Judith Kendra, Sue Lascelles and Martin Bryant at Rider, and their warmth and professionalism have again made the process a pleasure. My agent Gillon Aitken and his colleagues, including Andrew Kidd and Imogen Pelham, at Aitken Alexander, provided advice and support whenever I needed it.

Liz Nash, my companion in just about everything, has never set foot in Burma, being an expert in other parts of the world, and this made her my ideal first reader: the book benefited greatly from her perceptive comments. As she is also a world-class copy-editor, the text I submitted was much cleaner and more readable than it would otherwise have been. Thank you.

INDEX